PASSION & PROFIT SERIES

BOOKS 1-4

- HOW TO FIND YOUR PASSION
- QUIT YOUR JOB AND FOLLOW YOUR DREAMS
- WORK FROM HOME AND MAKE SIX FIGURES
- MAKE MONEY WHILE YOU SLEEP

MICHELLE KULP

Table of Contents

How to Find Your Passion

23 Questions That Can
Change Your Entire Life
Michelle Kulp

Introduction

One question has the power to completely transform your entire life.

Einstein once said,

"If I had an hour to solve a problem and my life depended on the solution. I would spend the first 55 minutes determining the proper question to ask; for once I know the proper question, I could solve the problem in less than five minutes."

Einstein was a brilliant man.

In his #1 Wall Street Journal bestselling book, "The One Thing," Gary Keller, founder of Keller Williams Realty, Inc., wrote:

"Life is a question. You may be asking, 'Why focus on a question when what we really crave is an answer?' It's simple. Answers come from questions, and the quality of any answer is directly determined by the quality of the question. Ask the wrong question, get the wrong answer. Ask the right question, get the right answer. Ask the most powerful question possible, and the answer can be life altering."

Over the years, I too have learned the power of asking the right questions.

This is a story of a powerful question that changed the trajectory of my life...

On October 23, 1992, I serendipitously met country music singer and actor Billy Ray Cyrus after a concert he performed at and had the pleasure of spending a few hours chatting with him. During our time together, Billy Ray asked me, "What are your dreams?"

At the time, my marriage had recently ended. I was struggling to financially support my three children, living paycheck-to-paycheck in a high-stress job in the legal field, I was having severe panic attacks that led me to the emergency room where I thought I was having a heart attack, and my older brother and best friend, Michael, was diagnosed with AIDS and was dying. I was 29 years old.

Needless to say, it was a dark time in my life, and I was living in survival mode. I didn't have the time or energy to think about "dreams."

When you are struggling and in survival mode, you simply don't have the capacity to reflect on higher level things like *dreams*.

Abraham Maslow spoke about this in his hierarchy of needs which are:

- **Basic Needs** – Physiological Needs: food, water, warmth, rest

- **Safety Needs** – security, safety

- **Belongingness and Love Needs** – intimate relationships, friends

- **Esteem Needs** – prestige and feelings of accomplishment

- **Self-Actualization** – achieving one's full potential, including creative activities

Anyone struggling to get their basic physical or psychological needs met is not in a frame of mind to focus on self-actualization.

Billy Ray's question struck a chord deep inside of me. During our conversation, Billy Ray said, "We all have a dream buried inside of us and it's our job to go out and find that dream and once we do, we must never ever give up on our dream."

I took Billy Ray's advice and went out searching for this elusive dream; the one that would bring me a deep feeling of purpose, passion and fulfillment; the things that were severely lacking in my life at the time.

It took about a year of soul-searching before I figured it out. Once again, it was because of a question I read in a tiny book that fell into my hands at the bookstore. That book was "How to Find Your Mission in Life" by Richard Bolles.

When I read the question, I immediately knew the answer and what my dream was. I suddenly felt renewed and alive with purpose, passion and direction in my life.

The life-changing question in Richard Bolles book was "What do you love to do where you lose all sense of time?"

Pause and think about that question for a few moments before reading on.

When I read that question and reflected on it, I suddenly drifted back to my childhood remembering how I loved to write; how five hours of writing seemed like five minutes to me. I loved writing poetry, essays, short stories and even reports for school. Writing is where I lost all sense of time.

Unfortunately, as we "grow up" and become adults, we leave behind our childhood interests and passions and take the more practical path of getting a job that pays the bills. We often choose salaries over our soul's aspirations.

The unfortunate part is that when you're stuck in a job you hate, it can feel like a prison.

I worked in the legal field as a paralegal in a high-stress environment for 17 years until I couldn't breathe any longer. It was literally sucking the life out of me.

I wrote about how I freed myself from job prison in my book, "Quit Your Job and Follow Your Dreams: A 12-Month Guide to Being Joyfully Jobless." Now, I teach others how to do the same.

Rumi reminds us, "What you are seeking is seeking you."

When Billy Ray Cyrus asked me that question about what my dreams were, it started me down a path which eventually led me to the answer I was looking for.

This book contains 23 life-altering questions. Before we begin, my first question for you is:

Do you listen to your head more than your heart?

Too often, we make decisions solely from our logical minds, and that might be okay for a while, but when we are experiencing deep feelings of unhappiness, unfulfillment and purposelessness, it's time for a change and a new direction.

If we make decisions solely from our logical minds, we leave our heart and soul out of the equation. When we do that, we often feel depleted, drained as well as mentally, physically, spiritually and emotionally worn out.

The 23 questions in this book are designed to help you find your passion.

Do not rush through the book. Read each question and the short chapter, then contemplate your answer and write it out in long-hand. Search your heart and soul, and not your logical mind.

Before we dive into the questions, I have some tools that I've been using for over 25 years that I believe can help connect your head to your heart during this journey so you can hear the answers deep inside.

Tuning In Tools

I was sitting in my therapist's office when suddenly she announced, "I know your problem Michelle; your heart and head aren't connected."

She was right. I spent my entire life listening to my "head" and completely ignoring my heart.

The decisions I made up to that point were practical and based on obligation and responsibility and left my heart out of the equation.

It's been a long arduous journey connecting my heart and my head, and thankfully I discovered some tools that have helped me along the way. I want to share those tools with you now so you can receive the same benefit as I have using them.

Two of the tools (*The Morning Pages* and the *Artist Date*) are from Julia Cameron, a recovered blocked artist and author of the bestselling book, "The Artist's Way: A Spiritual Path to Higher Creativity."

I'm adding one more tool of my own which will help quiet down your egoic mind and help tune you into the whispers of your heart and soul: *meditation*.

It's not required that you use these tools, but if you are overly practical, responsible, conscientious and deeply connected to your logical mind like I am, I truly believe it will help you tremendously.

Let's begin…

Morning Pages

In her book, "The Artist's Way," Julia Cameron introduces two pivotal tools in 'creative recovery' which are the *morning pages* and the *artist date*.

In order to retrieve your creativity and your passion, you need to find them. The morning pages are a vehicle that will help you do that.

Morning pages are simply three pages of longhand writing, strictly stream-of-consciousness writing. You might think of them as *brain drain*.

There is no wrong way to do the morning pages. They are a primary tool of creative recovery and finding your passion which is part of that creative recovery.

Unfortunately, we are all victims of our inner critic, inner perfectionist and our inner troublemaker.

This is not the truth of who we are or what we are capable of doing. These collective inner voices are a blocking device that keep you from your creativity and your passions.

By writing three pages in a notebook or journal every morning, you will get to the other side of your inner censor, troublemaker and critic.

It doesn't matter what you write about. Just write without thinking about what you're writing. No one is going to see your morning pages so you can vent, complain, cuss, fuss, nag, protest, process, imagine, dream and invent.

The morning pages will feed your inner artist and you will begin hearing that quiet voice within and eventually you will connect with your own quiet center.

Logic brain is our survival brain, and it fears the unknown. Logic brain tells us to be responsible and sensible always.

Artist brain is our creative and holistic brain that wants to come out and play!

Don't underestimate the power of the morning pages as they are a spiritual practice, and they will lead you to your inner power and your own source of wisdom.

The only rules are that you write your morning pages as soon as you wake up (stream of consciousness writing) and that you write three pages in longhand in a notebook or journal that you do not share with others. That's it.

Morning pages help chart our own inner interior and without them our dreams and passions will remain buried.

After you are consistent with them, morning pages will point out the need for a *course adjustment*.

Here's what Julia Cameron says about morning pages:

- Your morning pages are your boat. They will both lead you forward and give you a place to recuperate from in your forward motion.

- …writing pages can open an inner door through which our creator helps and guides us. Our willingness swings this inner door open. The morning pages symbolize our willingness to speak to and hear God…it is very powerful.

- The snowflake pattern of your soul is emerging. Each of us is a unique, creative individual. But we often blur that uniqueness with sugar, alcohol, drugs, overwork, underplay bad relations, toxic sex, under-exercise, over-TV, under-sleep— many and varied forms of junk food for the soul. The pages help us to see these smears on our consciousness.

I love what May Sarton, author of dozens of inspirational books including "Journal of a Solitude," says, "It always comes back to the same necessity: go deep enough and there is a bedrock of truth, however hard."

ACTION STEP: Purchase a notebook or journal,
label it and start your morning pages tomorrow.

The next tool up is the artist date…

Artist Date

On the surface, this may seem like a distraction or a diversion, but the artist date is very powerful and is designed to bring you more insight, inspiration and guidance.

An artist date is just a block of time – two hours per week – where you set aside time to nurture your creative consciousness; your inner artist.

Your artist needs to be taken out, listened to, indulged and pampered. Think of your inner artist like a child and the artist date is self-nurturing to your child artist.

I find when I set aside this time for my artist date that all kinds of emergencies and crises oddly happen that block my artist date from happening.

When we are following our passions and purpose, we have to fight off a force called "the *resistance*" that does not want us to grow, evolve or succeed.

Steven Pressfield, the author of several bestselling books like "The War of Art" and "Turning Pro: Tap Your Inner Power and Create Your Life's Work" explains this resistance we all have to face like this:

> *"Resistance stops us from committing to the important work of our lives – not just committing to it but fighting like hell to get it done."*

He goes on to explain that *the resistance* hates two qualities above all others: Concentration and Depth. *Why*? Because when we work with focus and we work deep, we succeed.

This *resistance* wants us to stay unfocused and shallow – in other words checking social media 50 times a day, getting caught up in other people's drama, watching endless amounts of television and binging on Netflix instead of doing deep work and activities that are meaningful to our heart and soul that we are *called* to do.

In her book, "Big Magic," Elizabeth Gilbert, says:

> *"The universe buries strange jewels deep within us all, and then stands back to see if we can find them. The hunt to uncover those jewels – that's creative living. The course to go on that hunt in the first place – that's what separates a mundane existence from a more enchanted one."*

Just know that when you set aside time for your morning pages and artist dates (your creative work), everything that can block you from using these powerful tools will happen. Don't let it.

Creative living is a path for the brave. It takes courage, persistence, having a daily practice and moving past your fears.

So plan your artist date and watch all kinds of blocks happen. Rise above them.

Keep your artist date sacred and treat it like an appointment with a Very Important Person, and that VIP is your inner artist child! If you have to reschedule, make sure you put it on the calendar or you will completely forget about it.

Artist Dates don't have to be expensive outings. If you are low on cash here are some ideas:

- Go to a local park, lake or beach.
- Go to a pottery place and create art or just observe others.
- Go to a museum.
- Attend an artist event.
- Go to a cooking store and explore.
- Take a hike with beautiful scenery.
- Attend a paint night.

Any activity that makes your inner artist happy!

ACTION STEP: Go ahead and schedule your first two artist dates on your calendar and watch the resistance show up and try to block them. Don't let it!

Next up is the final tool – *meditation*.

Meditation

Michael Singer, author of the bestselling book "The Untethered Soul says, "When you contemplate the nature of Self, you are meditating, that is why meditation is the highest state. It is the return to the root of your being, the simple awareness of being aware."

Meditation stops the incessant chatter going on in your mind and allows you to connect to your true self. We all have this "monkey mind" that never stops. We wake up in the morning and these thoughts take over our minds like little monkeys jumping from tree to tree. Meditation helps the monkey become still and listen.

Meditation is a very powerful tool. You can start with a few minutes a day and gradually increase the time. I started with two minutes a day and I now do 20 minutes a day.

Spiritual teacher Pema Chodron, says this about meditation:

"Meditation is a process of lightening up, of trusting the basic goodness of what we have and who we are, and of realizing that any wisdom that exists, exists in what we already have. We can lead our life so as to become more awake to who we are and what we're doing rather than trying to improve or change or get rid of who we are or what we're doing. The key is to wake up, to become more alert, more inquisitive and curious about ourselves."
– Pema Chodron

Meditation has changed my life, taken away my anxiety and helped me to connect to my heart and soul.

Meditation is a tool I recommend as you do this deep work.

ACTION STEP: Download a meditation app and start with 2-5 minutes of meditation today. I use the app called "Chime".

Now it's time to get started on the 23 questions that can change your entire life...

Chapter 1: Hate

Question: What do I absolutely hate about or hate doing in my job or in my life? (Be specific)

Sometimes when we're lost and confused, we don't know what we're looking for or what exactly it is that we want.

I've found we can get clues by starting with what we *hate* or what isn't working.

These clues can lead you to what you do want.

For example, let's say you have a job as a paralegal (as I once did) and you are spending 80% of your time at the computer. You hate spending time at the computer, so you write "I hate sitting at a computer for 8 hours a day."

This insight gives you the ability to change things in your life that are draining you and also prevents you from repeating them down the road. I know a lot of people who change jobs without taking the time to figure out why they hated their jobs, only to end up repeating the pattern and hating the next job.

You can also write about things you hate in your personal life.

- I hate going to the grocery store.
- I hate cleaning the house.
- I hate volunteering on specific committees.

Don't be afraid to be radically honest with yourself. You can't get to the truth if you aren't being honest; the words you are writing are for your eyes only.

For example, when I was raising three kids as a single mom, it was highly stressful. I was a working mom and I looked forward to going to my job at the law firm. I respect stay-at-home moms, but there is no way I could have been one full-time. I think it would have driven me mad. I loved my career for many years when I was in it and it also supported my family.

So be completely honest about what you *hate* in your life right now. It doesn't mean you have to quit your job or divorce your spouse or live like a slob or eat out at restaurants all the time.

We're looking for clues here that will lead to your passion. Think of these questions as a means to an end. The questions will help you get more clarity in your life.

Hate is a strong emotion so pay attention to it.

When I started my online business becomea6figurewoman.com in 2005, I had a fairly large house and I "hated" cleaning it. I remember saying to my best friend that I would rather figure out how to make more money and pay for a cleaning company than to clean it myself. And that's exactly what I did.

I got creative and started selling online courses from my website and then I was able to pay for a cleaning company to take care of the house.

What do you *hate* in your life right now?

Chapter 2: Youth

Question: When I was a youngster, I always wanted to...?

What kind of things did you like as a child?

Did you love being outdoors?

Were you a bookworm?

Did you love writing? Drawing?

Did you love pretending to be a firefighter or a police officer?

Did you play dress up?

Did you love makeup?

Did you love cooking?

Did you love swimming, hiking or fishing?

What kind of kid were you?

Your childhood often holds clues to your passions. When I started reflecting back to my childhood, I remembered how much I loved writing. I also loved being outdoors, riding my bike, putting on neighborhood skits, going to the beach and I loved reading books.

This is the time to remember things you loved about your childhood and that you found a lot of happiness and joy doing. Again, these are little clues we are looking for to help us remember.

The reason you're reading this book is because you're having a bit of amnesia about your passions and you're probably making most of your choices based on safety and security instead of your imagination, joy and fun!

So play a little and go back to your youth and see what you can remember.

As a child, I loved putting on neighborhood skits and entertaining people. I involved my three brothers and my best friend who lived next door and we had so much fun. We actually made money selling tickets to our events.

As a teenager and adult, however, I was very shy and self-conscious. Eventually, I realized my shyness was holding me back in life. I wanted to be that fun, outgoing person again like I was when I was a child.

So, I enrolled in Toastmasters and was a member for many years. I even became President of my local club and eventually I was Area Governor.

Then, I found *Speaking Circles*® which was about learning to speak from the heart and connect with people through relational presence.

Speaking Circles changed my life and I eventually became a facilitator helping others who were struggling with speaking and connecting.

Without Speaking Circles, I would probably still be a very shy introvert. Now, I happily do speaking engagements, teach workshops and I love working with people.

Go back to your childhood and remember what you loved doing and what came so natural to you.

Chapter 3: Guidance

***Question: What do people come
to me for advice or guidance about?***

People always come to me for:

- Legal advice because I was a paralegal for 17 years (even though I've been out of the legal field for almost 20 years now).

- Advice about writing and/or publishing books since I have my online business www.bestsellingauthorprogram.com

- Details on how to start an online business, make six figures and find their passion.

I am asked for guidance on these topics because I have done all those things myself.

So what do people come to you for advice? Not just in business, but on a personal level too?

I am also often asked for cooking and decorating advice because I love cooking and decorating, they come natural to me and I truly enjoy them.

Think about what questions people ask you about when they need help or guidance. This can be a clue to what others see you as skilled at and that you might just take for granted.

I used to think everyone was a great writer until I taught business writing at the community college and quickly realized a lot of people struggle with writing and don't like it.

The reason we take our gifts for granted is because when something comes natural to us, we don't see it as something special, but instead we see it as an ordinary part of who we are.

*Write down at least three things
people come to you for advice on.*

Chapter 4: Time

Question: What do I love to do where I lose all sense of time while doing it?

I'm very fond of this question because it changed my whole life. I found the question in Richard Bolle's extraordinary book "How to Find Your Mission In Life," and as soon as I read it, I knew the answer: Writing!

I loved to write as a child, as an adolescent and as an adult. The only difference was that the writing I did as an adult was legal writing in my job as a paralegal, but I still *loved* that part of the job.

Writing came natural to me and I never thought about it at all until I read this question; I remembered when I was younger that feeling like time was flying by when I was involved in this activity.

When does time stand still for you when you're involved in something you love? This could be a huge clue to what your passion is.

We can have more than one passion too. I love research almost as much as I love writing. I love teaching as well. There is no rule that you can only have one passion.

I think it's miraculous when you can turn your passions into a profitable business because then you can get paid to play and earn "Play-checks" instead of "Pay-checks."

When you get paid to do what you love, then it doesn't seem like work.

In my online business, I do a lot of writing, research and teaching so I am very happy getting paid to do what I love.

You might have to go back to your childhood and try to remember that feeling when time flew by.

Answer the question from your childhood years and also as an adult.

Is there anything you do in your current life where time flies by?

I love watching the HGTV shows; especially the ones where people relocate to new homes and new states or countries. Often these people had successful corporate careers, but that joy, purpose and fulfillment was missing. So, they took a leap and changed everything including what they did for a living.

I've noticed that most of the time people who were leaving corporate careers were choosing brand new creative careers or starting their own business in a creative field.

What do you love to do where you lose all sense of time? Maybe it's something as simple as baking cupcakes.

Chapter 5: Guess

If I had to guess what my passion is, I would say it is...?

When Billy Ray Cyrus asked me what my dreams were, my answer at the time was "I don't have any dreams. My life is about survival."

Sometimes, we simply have amnesia when it comes to our dreams and passions.

In my book, "Quit Your Job and Follow Your Dreams," I talk about the four distinctions of a job, a career, your calling and hobbies that I read in a blog post by Elizabeth Gilbert. These distinctions are detailed below:

Job – You undeniably need a job to pay your bills and you don't have to be in love with your job. It is a means to an end. Money is how we all survive in this world and a job pays the bills. If you despise your job, by all means get a new one, but a job is vital. Just don't make it your whole life.

Career – A career is different from a job and is something you build over time with passion, energy and commitment. Careers are huge investments and require strategy, hustle and ambition. Not everyone has a career or will have a career and that's okay. A career is a choice.

Calling (vocation) – Vocation comes from the Latin verb "vocare" which means "to call." Your vocation is literally *your calling*. It is an invitation from the Universe, and it shows up as your soul calling to you. You do not need to make money from your calling although some people do.

Hobby – Something you do in your spare time for pleasure, relaxation, distraction or curiosity. Hobbies change and your attitude towards them is relaxed and playful. Hobbies are a wonderful reminder that we are not just slaves to the capitalist machine or our own ambitions. You don't need a hobby, but it's sure nice to have one. You do not need to make money from your hobby although some people do.

I hope reading these four distinctions helps you think about your passions in a different context. I see people mixing these up all the time. Making hobbies into jobbies or quitting jobs they aren't in love with but that pays the bills or feeling bad because they don't have a career.

We are all unique and these four distinctions are unique to each of us.

As you reflect on what you think your passions are, think about what brings your soul to life. Your passions are hinted at through your talents, tastes, excitement and curiosities.

Chapter 6: Truth

What do I truly want, but don't believe I can ever have?

Is there something you really, really want to have in your life but don't believe you can have it?

I truly want a house on the water. Right now I don't have a house on the water, but I do have a beautiful house across the street from the water with lovely water views. In fact, I can see the water from my bedroom window while sitting at my desk as I am writing this chapter.

The reason I don't have my house on the water is because the price difference between these two houses is substantial. Sometimes I wonder if I will ever have my dream house on the water.

Is there something you truly desire in your life — a relationship, a material possession, a job, starting your own business or maybe it's something emotional — like less anxiety and more peace.

Write down whatever comes to your mind. No one is judging you. These answers are for your eyes only.

Be honest with yourself about what you want.

For example, I know a lot of independent women who don't want to admit they would love to be in an intimate and committed relationship with a man but seem conflicted because of their freedom and independence; they feel like they might have to give up some of that freedom to be in a relationship.

Maybe you want more free time in your life to daydream, travel or write. Whatever it is, you're entitled to want those things.

You must be radically honest about your desires if you ever want to achieve them.

I've found another block to wanting things is we don't want to surpass where our family and friends are. We feel bad about doing better than people close to us.

It's time to turn that misguided thinking around and view being successful (however we define it) as a way to help our families and friends. We can also be a role model and an inspiration to others too.

Yes, some people might be jealous, but jealousy usually stems from envy. These people actually envy what you have because they want it for themselves, so it comes out negatively as being jealous.

Don't take it personally and don't let it stop you from going after what you truly want in life.

Chapter 7: Freedom

What gives me a sense of freedom when I do it?

Freedom is everything to me. When I was trapped in my corporate job what I craved most was freedom – time and money freedom.

I wanted control of my time, especially since I was a single mom with three young children. It was awful having to miss out on special events and activities with them as well as struggling with the choice of staying home with a sick child or going to work so I didn't get fired.

I think deep down we all have a desire for freedom; however, many of us fall into the trap of trading in our time for material things and then get stuck in that high-priced lifestyle with a lot of debt.

When I left my corporate job, I made the decision that I would never trade in my freedom for money again. I'm happy to say I've been out of the corporate world for almost 20 years now and *freedom* is the driving factor in my life.

I don't have 100% freedom because I run an online business and I have responsibilities and accountability in my business, but I am free to choose what I do in my business, what hours I work, who I work with and how much money I make…and that is priceless!

So when do you feel freedom in your life? Is it when you are involved in a certain activity or maybe when you are on vacation or when you're not glued to technology?

Take some time to reflect on what *freedom* means to you and look back and see at what times in your life you've felt free.

Looking back at my life, I've had two types of jobs:

1. Energy-draining jobs
2. Freedom jobs

An energy-draining job is one that consumes your time and energy so that at the end of the day you have none left to pursue your passions and curiosities.

If you are going to have a job that pays the bills and gives you freedom to pursue your passions, you want a freedom job.

Going from an energy draining job to a freedom job is a step in the right direction as long as you can figure out the financial part.

I went from a full-time paralegal job to a part-time job at the law firm (working three nights a week from 5:30 p.m. to 12:30 a.m.) and that gave me the *freedom* to pursue my passions. I did that for five years. Then, I found another freedom job which was an outside sales job working 20-25 hours a week and making six figures!

Every step you take in your life should be towards more freedom, not less.

Chapter 8: Failure

If I knew I couldn't fail, I would be doing ...?

Failure is how we learn. If we're afraid to fail, then we're afraid to learn.

If you knew you couldn't fail, what would you be doing?

Be completely honest with yourself.

We can't let this fear of failure prevent us from following our passions and dreams. We have to do it in spite of those fears.

Every successful person has these fears, they just don't allow these fears to prevent them from achieving their dreams and goals.

You make a choice every single day when you decide not to take action towards your goals and dreams.

I can't tell you how many years I struggled with the imposter syndrome around starting and running an online business because I didn't have any "credentials." I finally got over it, but I wasted a lot of time looking for approval, validation and praise instead of just doing what I loved and learning from my failures.

That's what we are all doing. There are no exceptions. Don't let the filtered world of social media taint your view of successful people. They all have fears and are dealing with them in their own way so they can achieve their goals and dreams.

If you have an intense fear of failure, you will waste a lot of time and money looking for external validation and approval instead of doing *the work*.

Years ago, I read a great book by Susan Jeffers called "Feel the Fear and Do it Anyways." I think the older I get, the less I care about these fears of failure. I know failure is inevitable and it teaches us what works and what doesn't.

Many people want to start an online business, but until you actually put yourself out there and try, you have no idea about the process. It's like writing a book, you can have a great idea and test titles and covers, but until you actually write it and put it out in the marketplace, you won't know if people want it or not.

I tell my clients in my bestselling author program, that we will put out a high quality book with a strong foundation, but at the end of the day, the market decides what it likes.

And guess what?

The market is fickle and constantly changing. So, if you are going to write a book, start a business, I suggest you do it fast.

Another great book I recommend is the "7-Day Start Up: You Don't Learn Until You Launch" by Dan Norris. It will change your entire perspective from inaction to fast action.

So, if you knew you couldn't fail, what would you be doing

Chapter 9: Success

If it was guaranteed I would be massively successful, I would be ...?

First, what does massive success look like to you?

One person might say, "Massive success would mean my house is paid off, I have no debt, and I can live fully on my retirement money."

Another person might say, "I am living in my mansion on the water with my beautiful boat and three jet skis. I also have lots of passive income from my books and courses that pay all of my living expenses."

Write down what massive success looks like to you because if it is guaranteed then you can dream bigger than you ever have before. Sometimes our fear of not achieving our dreams makes us shrink them or not be real with ourselves about what we truly desire.

I have always wanted a house on the water. I currently live across the street from the water, so I am getting closer. It's not my whole dream, but it is a part of my dream. As a writer, the water brings out my creativity and I feel very peaceful being near the water.

Years ago, I saw an interview on a morning talk show with William Haley, the son of Alex Haley, the famous writer and creator of the blockbuster book and miniseries, "Roots."

Alex Haley's book, "Roots," sold over one million copies in the first year, and the miniseries was watched by an astonishing 130 million people. It also won both the Pulitzer Prize and the National Book Award.

William was explaining to the reporter that his father said he did his best writing when he was near the water. He would often hop on board a freight or cargo ship and take long trips to do his writing.

Alex Haley said,

"I find that's why I just love to get out in the ocean.
And I find that you are really out there, find yourself
thinking in ways you haven't thought before."

Seeing that interview made me realize how important being near the water is to me; it is magical, miraculous, mysterious and brings out a level of creativity that I just can't find sitting at my computer under artificial lights. I find that being near the ocean also helps me discover answers to my deepest questions.

So, dream big and write down all the details to what massive success looks like to you when you know it's guaranteed!

Chapter 10: Future

What would the 'future me'
— 10 years from now - tell the 'current me' to do?

First, think about what the 'current you' would tell the 'past you' 10 years ago. You've learned a lot in the past 10 years. What words of wisdom can you share with her or him?

I would tell the past me:

- You don't need external approval from others, just follow your heart and trust your intuition.

- Stop trying to do everything in your business by yourself; hire contractors who specialize in what you need for your business and let go of the reins.

- Don't be afraid to hire a business coach as it can change your entire business and will grow your profits exponentially.

- Have a morning routine to start the day off in a conscious, peaceful and intentional way.

- Learn to say 'no' and set boundaries and you will have less drama and miscommunications in your life.

- Create more passive income.

Think about all the areas of your life. Where are you struggling? What do you want your life to look like in ten years?

One of my goals was to generate six figures in "passive" income from the royalties of my books. In January of 2020, I made a life-changing decision to write a book a month. In 12 months, I created $3,150 in passive monthly income. By the end of 2021, I should be earning six figures from book royalties.

The key to my success was creating a written plan for writing a book a month. I also have a written plan to create one new product or publish a book each month until I am earning six figures in passive income.

There is research that says a written down goal is 33% more likely to be completed. There is power in the written word.

We think thousands of thoughts every day, but when we consciously and intentionally choose to focus on a few, then our lives change.

Think about the past you 10 years ago, the current you, and now the future you 10 years from now.

What age will you be? Where do you want to be living? What daily activities do you want to be involved in? Who do you want to be spending time with? How do you want to earn money?

Of course, we want some spontaneity in our lives, but we also want to set intentions or else we end up living a default life and before you know it – your life has flown by.

They say the days are long, but the years pass by fast.

Chapter 11: Anger

What makes me so angry and heated I get all charged up?

There is wisdom in our anger. It's here to tell us something about ourselves. It contains hidden messages.

If we're angry at bouncing a check, then the anger is there to tell you that maybe living paycheck-to-paycheck isn't working and something needs to change.

If we're angry at a client who is being disrespectful or taking advantage of us, then maybe the message is you need to have clearer boundaries or have a signed contract with clients to set the expectations.

If we're angry about domestic violence, maybe we need to get involved in being part of the solution and become an advocate or volunteer.

Usually when I get angry, I've let things go far too long and they've started to fester until finally I have to release some of that steam I've been repressing.

Harriet Lerner, author of "The Dance of Anger," says, "Anger is a signal and one worth listening to."

Anger has a hidden message for you. Listen to it.

What are you angry about? Be honest? Even if it's something you can't change right now, write it down.

David R. Hawkins, M.D., Ph.D., in his book "Power vs Force," says that anger stems from "frustrated want."

He also says that "Anger can lead to either constructive or destructive action."

So, anger can lead to constructive action, but if you let it, anger can also lead to belligerence, arguments, irritability, explosiveness, and even rage.

Listen to your anger and see what changes you need to make because of it.

When I was angry at having to go to my 9-5 job at the law firm and leave my kids, my anger was telling me there was another path for me.

Anger can be your friend if you listen to it.

Chapter 12: Contribution

What would I like to change or contribute to the world?

We all have the ability to contribute something to the world to make it better.

It doesn't have to be large scale or grand, just some way you want to contribute your time, energy, knowledge and expertise to improving the world.

For me, writing books is the way I contribute to the world. The most powerful shifts have happened in my life as a result of books so I know the power of a great book; one sentence in a book can change someone's life.

In the book, "Who Do We Choose to Be: Facing Reality, Claiming Leadership, Restoring Sanity" written by Margaret J. Wheatley, she asks the question:

> *"If it's not creating change at the large scale...*
> *then what does it mean to make a difference?*

Her answer...

> *"Focus on serving others. Serve individuals, serve small*
> *groups; serve an entire community or organization. No*
> *matter what is going on around us, we can attend to the*
> *people in front of us, to the issues confronting us and there,*

we offer what we can. We can offer insight and compassion. We can be present. We can stay focused and not flee. We can be exemplars of the best human qualities. That is a life well lived, even if we didn't save the world."

Humans cannot live without meaning.

Making a contribution by being of service gives us meaning and purpose.

Think about the people in your life who have been there for you as ground and support; we all stand on the shoulders of others.

At some point, we must be those shoulders for others and that's where service and contribution come in.

Chapter 13: Practice

If I had time to practice more, I'd be really good at?

In my senior year of high school (circa 1981), I took a typing class. At first, I hated typing and didn't really see the value of learning this skill, but I'm glad I stuck with it.

We had to memorize the location of the keys and be able to type with a piece of copy paper taped above our hands that blocked us from seeing the keys.

It took a lot of practice and I went from pecking at the keys to memorizing all the keys to then typing about 40 words per minute when I graduated from that class.

After graduation, I typed papers when I was in college and then I typed a lot when I worked as a paralegal and legal secretary for many years. The more I used this skill, the better and faster I got. At one point, I was typing 100 wpm.

What could you excel at if you practiced?

People think great writers or great artists are just born; what they don't see are the copious number of hours of *practice* they spend developing their skills.

Many famous writers are really bad writers at first. They become great writers because they continued to write, and they gradually got better. That's the art of practice.

I remember reading a story about a writer who was working on a manuscript for over a year. The writer got to page 200 and realized that was where the story began; so those first 200 pages ended up in the trash.

Can you imagine throwing away 200 pages of a manuscript? As a writer, I know how painful that would be, but those 200 pages essentially were his *practice*.

Practice requires focus and attention.

In Cal Newport's book, "Deep Work: Rules for Focused Success in a Distracted World," he says:

"To learn hard things quickly, you must focus intensely without distraction. To learn, in other words, is an act of deep work."

We live in a high-distraction world and the ability to focus intensely is getting harder and harder with so many demands on our time.

Imagine for a moment that you can take a break from all distractions – television, social media, text messages, your phone, your job – and you could *practice* one thing…what would that be?

There is no wrong or right answer.

Chapter 14: Flow

When I am in a state of flow, I am…?

Mihaly Csikszenthihalyi, a well-known psychologist, once said:

"The best moments usually occur when a person's body or mind is stretched to its limits in a voluntary effort to accomplish something difficult and worthwhile."

Csikszenthihalyi calls this mental state *flow* (which was also a book he wrote in 1990 by the same title).

Sometimes we think of *flow* as complete relaxation as in sitting in a hammock, but Csikszenthihalyi's research revealed that human beings are at their best when they are *immersed deeply in something challenging.*

So, think about a time when you were immersed deeply in something challenging and felt you were in that *flow* state.

What were you doing?

For me, the *flow* state happens when I am working on a book. It is challenging and it is something I care deeply about. I also lose my sense of time when I'm doing it.

Bono once said,

"Good things come to those who work their asses off and never give up."

I believe that's true. We aren't born to sit around sipping daiquiris at the beach all day. Although having downtime is very important to a creative life, our minds require and also thrive on deep challenging work.

Flow is about stretching your mind to its limits, concentrating and losing yourself in an activity.

Can you think about a time when you felt all three of those? What were you doing? How long were you doing it? What were the results?

Chapter 15: Interests

***I have a lot of interests and things I enjoy,
but if I had to pick only one of those things to
spend time on now, I would choose...?***

In his #1 Wall Street Journal bestselling book, "The One Thing," Gary Keller, founder of Keller Williams Realty, Inc., wrote:

> *"Going small is ignoring all the things you could do and doing what you should do. It's recognizing that not all things matter equally and finding the things that matter most. It's a tighter way to connect what you do, with what you want. It's realizing that extraordinary results are directly determined by how narrow you make your focus."*

> *We have no shortage of options of how we can spend our valuable time. In fact, having too many options can lead to decision fatigue or making no decision at all because you're feeling overwhelmed with too many choices.*

So, how do we decide on *one thing* when we have so many options to choose from?

Instead of asking yourself, "What do I have to give up?" instead ask yourself, "What do I want to go big on?"

This small change in your thinking can have a profound affect in your life.

Another way to make decisions is to explore and evaluate a **broad set of options** *before* committing to any. This way, you are giving yourself time to play, think, question, listen, try out and debate, and the pressure is minimized. Once you've given yourself the gift of exploring, then you can decide what you want to "go big on."

Think about some of the interests you have right now or in the past that you've explored. If you could only pick one "for right now" (not forever), which one would you go big on?

One of the core premises in "The One Thing" is: **I can do anything, but not everything.**

As poet Mary Oliver wrote,

> *"Tell me what it is you plan to do*
> *with your one wild and precious life?"*

Chapter 16: Fears

My biggest fear about being successful and living a passionate life is...?

Years ago, I attended a 3-day event with author T. Harv Eker who wrote the bestselling book "Secrets of the Millionaire Mind."

During that workshop, we did an exercise to see what fears were stopping us from living our dream life and it turned out my biggest fear was not a fear of failure, but a fear of success.

Sounds crazy, right?

Why would I be afraid of success?

Fears aren't always logical and stem mostly from our emotions.

Since I was a big people pleaser, I thought people wouldn't like me if I was super successful and made more money than they did.

Of course, I turned my thinking around and now I look at all the ways I can inspire others to live their dreams, and also how I am in a position to help my family and friends because I have financial freedom. I am no longer living paycheck-to-paycheck (which was how I was living at the time of the workshop).

So, what is your biggest fear about being successful and living a passionate life?

When I started www.becomea6figurewoman.com in 2005, I had just started making six figures in 2004. I went from working in a 9-5 corporate job in the legal field to selling hot tubs in-house. I literally doubled my income and my time off! Life was good.

When I was doing research for my website, I noticed that a lot of women said they only wanted to make "enough to pay the bills" and they didn't want to make six figures because they didn't want to work 60+ hours a week and give up time with their family and friends. They assumed you could only make six figures if you worked long hours... which isn't true as I am living proof of that. I still only work about four hours a day, four days a week and make six figures.

It's all about designing a life you want. However, we also have subconscious fears that are blocking us and causing us to sabotage ourselves in the process of going after our dreams.

Pia Mellody, author of many books on co-dependency once said,

"If you don't face your fears, they will bite you in the ass!"

It's true. Your fears will block your success, so you need to identify them and face them head on and then take action anyway.

Most fears aren't real and just knowing what they are puts you in a position of power.

So, be radically honest and list your fears out. Then feel the fear and do it anyway!

Chapter 17: Less

What do you want to have less of in your life?

Cheryl Richardson, Life Coach and Author of "Stand Up For Your Life," said,

> *"A high quality life has more to do with what you remove from it than what you add to it."*

That sentence has always stuck with me.

Many of us get caught up in the hamster wheel of chasing more, more, more. But there's a price to pay for having more, more, more.

Years ago, I owned a million-dollar house with a million-dollar mortgage. Of course, I had a nice 6-figure income to pay for it all and a fiancé that paid for half at the time, but when the housing market crashed, the value of my million dollar house went to almost half.

My sales income at the time (2008) also decreased as the product I was selling was a luxury product (hot tubs) that people really didn't need.

So, in an instant, my life changed, and I had to make some big changes as a result. I sold the million-dollar house and downsized to a smaller home. I am so much happier now because the less I have to pay, the more I can play!

So, what do you want less of in your life? Be specific.

If you say you want less stress, that's very general. Be more specific like, "I want less stress at my job" or "I want less stress in my relationship with _____."

Often, what we want less of can give us clues to changes we need to make in our lives.

Maybe you are always saying yes to others and consequently are overbooked in your schedule. Therefore, you need fewer time commitments and the action you need to take is learning to say no.

In this moment, if I was answering this question, I would say I would want less back and neck issues. I also know that when I consistently do my 20-minute back care yoga DVD and my 3-mile walks, that I reduce my back and neck issues. So, that is a clue letting me know I need to be more consistent with my routine and also less sitting at the computer.

I did purchase a standup desk a couple of years ago so that has helped as well.

This is a great question to ask yourself regularly because sometimes we are just living our lives on autopilot.

Keep removing things you don't want, and you'll have a high-quality life.

Chapter 18: Millions

If I had $10 million dollars in the bank, I would...?

This is a great question. At first you might think, "I'd quit my job, travel to a tropical island and sip margaritas on the beach and chill all day."

Sounds great but I can promise that within a short time you would be bored with that.

As I mentioned in the chapter about *flow*, our minds were created to be stretched and challenged.

I'm not saying you wouldn't quit your job, but you would want to be involved in something you truly care about, even if you didn't get paid for it.

This is an exercise in using your imagination. Money can and does change everything.

Because of my online business, I am able to save a percentage of what I make each year (which happens to be the equivalent of my entire annual salary when I worked as a paralegal in the corporate world). Having this money in the bank gives me more freedom and options. It also helped me with one of my goals – which was to write more books and take on less done-for-you clients for my best-selling author program.

The money I save isn't close to $10 million dollars but having six figures in the bank gives me a lot more options about my business, my life and where I choose to spend my time.

Besides buying material things like a house, a new car, new furniture and taking some trips, once that was all out of the way, what would you do with your time?

This is a clue to your passions. There are some things we do in life for a paycheck and others are just solely for pleasure or fulfillment. For example, let's say you would like to get involved in a non-profit organization and volunteer. That is something you might be able to do right now that would bring you a great deal of fulfillment and satisfaction in your life.

We're here to be of service to others. Of course, when we're living in survival mode, it's hard to do that, but once we are able to get our finances working for us, then we can look at how we can be of service to others.

After I left the legal field, I wanted to get involved in helping women who were struggling with domestic violence issues and I was able to volunteer for a non-profit organization called the House of Ruth that provided legal services for people dealing with domestic violence. This gave me a high level of fulfillment because I was using my legal knowledge to help others.

Maybe you want to start your own business. So many people have that dream, but the obstacles are usually lack of time and/or money.

Dream big.

What type of business would you want to start? Give details about what you would do with $10 million.

Chapter 19: Others

*If I didn't care what other people thought or
how it might affect them, I would be ...?*

Is there something you are not doing because of what others
might think? Or maybe you're doing a lot of things out of obligation
and therefore if you stop doing them, it will negatively impact others.

I have a high level of the "disease to please" and I tend to do for
others what they can do for themselves. I've done it with my children and in relationships, but at the end of the day, it leaves me
exhausted, resentful and unhappy. My "overdoing" means I'm putting other people's happiness and needs above my own.

Some people say you need to be more selfish. I even saw a woman
on a talk show wearing a necklace that read "Selfish."

It's not so much about being "selfish," but it is about caring
enough about your "self" to put your needs, desires, energy, time,
money, and dreams at the top of the list.

A book I read that helped me do this was "Boundaries: When to
say Yes, How to Say No to Take Control of Your Life" by Dr. Henry
Cloud and Dr. John Townsend. In that book the authors said:

*"People with boundary problems usually have distorted
attitudes about responsibility. They feel that to hold people
responsible for their feelings, choices and behaviors is mean."*

I know I felt that way. I didn't want to let people down and I wanted to help, but my actions resulted in enabling others.

They also say that a boundary shows you where you end and someone else begins.

So, do you have clear boundaries with others?

If not, you may not be taking the path to your dreams because of distorted responsibilities and the disease to please.

It's hard to imagine not caring about what others think, but the older I get the less I seem to care. I do what makes me happy as long as it does no harm to others.

Imagine doing what you truly want to do and not wondering what others think or how it might affect them.

What would you be doing right now?

Chapter 20: Obstacles

What are three ways you create obstacles in your life and why?

There is an ancient saying: "The road is smooth. Why do you throw rocks before you?"

I'm sure you can relate to this as I know I can.

Why do we throw rocks on the road before us?

Self-sabotage is a real thing that we do when we are afraid or don't feel deserving of something or are stuck and unable to take action.

We all have sabotaged ourselves so don't feel bad about it. Observation without condemnation is a great viewpoint to follow.

Think about three ways you have created obstacles in your life and then write down why you think you have done that.

For many years, I lived paycheck-to-paycheck and I blamed everyone else for my money problems. Then one day, I heard one of my mentors say, "Take 100% responsibility for everything in your life." And when I did take 100% responsibility, I realized I had the power to change my financial situation.

Now I save 25-50% of my income every year and don't live on the financial edge any longer.

Life Coach, Author, Speaker and Talk Show host, Mel Robbins, said,

> *"If you have a problem that can be fixed by action,*
> *then you really don't have a problem."*

Sometimes we create problems by our inaction and procrastination. Think about a time perhaps when a bill came due and you procrastinated about paying it and then you had terrible consequences. If you would have just paid it when you received it (taken action), you wouldn't have had those consequences.

Living a life of passion requires action. You can't get other people to do your push-ups for you. Only you can do them. We can try to blame our parents, our spouse, our children, our family, our geography, or our life situation, but at the end of the day, we have the power to take action and make changes.

Start noticing when you are procrastinating and journal about why you aren't taking action. Usually, it's an emotional block and you can journal through it.

The problem is most of the time, we don't bring it to our awareness and our unconscious minds are running the show.

What are these areas of your life and the three ways you have created obstacles? Are they all in finance, relationships, business, etc.? Take notice and examine the feelings underneath your inaction.

Chapter 21: Principle

What principle, cause, value or purpose would you be willing to defend to the death or devote your life to?

Billy Sunday once said,

> *"More men fail through lack of purpose than through lack of talent."*

I have a few things that motivate me:

1. Family

2. Freedom

3. Finances

When I was stuck in my 9-5 corporate job, I had no freedom and now that I'm out of that life, I value my freedom more than anything.

My family means everything to me and so that motivates me to be successful and to be a great example.

Having my finances in order gives me *freedom* and options. As I mentioned earlier, I'm now able to save 25-50% of my income every year. There was a time when I was making six figures and had very little in my savings account. My goal now is to save 50%

of my income and this year I'm focusing more on leveraging my time and creating additional passive income streams.

What motivates you? It could be a value like freedom or justice; or a cause like helping feed the homeless; or a purpose like changing lives through speaking or writing.

Books are part of my life purpose and are very important to me personally because books have changed my life and saved my life in many ways. I know the power of a book and that's why I'm so passionate about them. It is part of my purpose to spread powerful messages to the world with my own books and with my clients' books.

Think about things that have changed your life or saved your life. Have you ever heard the saying "Make your mess your message?" What messes have you been in? What obstacles have you overcome?

Many times, our purpose involves helping other people overcome those same messes we've been in.

Chapter 22: Inner Voice

What has your inner voice been saying to you that you have been ignoring?

One of my favorite authors is Richard Bode who wrote, "First You Have to Row a Little Boat and Beachcombing at Miramar." In his book, he said,

> *"I believe we are born with a power to heal our wounds, not through miracles, but through a silent voice that speaks to us from within ourselves and won't be stilled; a voice that tells us where to go and what to do, which is a miracle of another kind. It is the refusal to heed that inner voice that causes the incurable sickness of the soul which makes us wither before our time."*

Are you ignoring your inner voice? Ghosting it?

After I left the legal field, I started practicing meditation every morning. Soon, my inner voice repeatedly said, "It's time to get over your fear of public speaking. If you don't get over it, it will hold you back from becoming a successful writer."

Now this made no sense to my logical mind, so I ignored it for a long time. But the voice was relentless. It wouldn't go away.

My logical mind kept trying to figure out what in the world public speaking had to do with writing?

Eventually, I surrendered and listened to my inner voice. I joined Toastmasters and within a short time and against all odds, I became President and Area Governor. That led me to Speaking Circles®, which I spoke about in an earlier chapter and believe it or not, all of this helped me become a better writer because it improved my communication skills, allowed me to connect with others and gave me the confidence I needed to stop hiding from the world.

I don't want you to misunderstand, I am still a huge introvert who loves sitting at home by myself and writing books. But I know deep down that was not the sole (soul) purpose of my life. My inner voice told me I had to get out into the world and connect with others through networking, speaking and teaching.

As a result of listening to my inner voice, I now have a very successful business where I get to do things I love like writing books, teaching, hosting writer's retreats like www.oceanwriting.com, and helping clients with their books.

Public speaking made me a better writer and gave me more things to write about.

Listen to your inner voice, even if it makes no logical sense. Pay close attention; especially if it is relentless and keeps saying the same thing.

Chapter 23: Suffering

What has your suffering taught you?

"Some people once brought a blind man to Jesus and asked him, 'Rabbi, who sinned, this man or his parents, that he was born blind?' They all wanted to know why this terrible curse had fallen on this man. And Jesus answered, 'It was not that this man sinned or his parents, but that the words of God might be manifest in him'. He told them not to look for why the suffering came, but to listen for what the suffering could teach them." –Wayne Miller

---

Suffering is our greatest teacher and is also a necessary step to evolving and transforming our lives. Of course, we have the choice to be a victim of our suffering or to learn from our suffering.

My suffering has taught me to pay attention to my inner voice, my heart and my soul. It reminds me that when I don't listen to that still voice within, then my life gets painful and difficult.

We can't escape suffering. No one is exempt from it. We can have a pity party for ourselves, but if we stay in that state of mind we become victims.

David R. Hawkins, M.D., Ph.D., in his bestselling book, "Power vs. Force: The Hidden Determinants of Human Behavior" says,

"It isn't life's events, but how one reacts to them and the attitude that one has about that, that determines whether such events have a positive or negative effect on one's life, whether they're experienced as opportunity or as stress."

He goes on to say that nothing has the power to create stress. A divorce may be traumatic if it's unwanted or a release into freedom if it's desired.

When we feel powerless, we feel like we are at the mercy of life and that the source of our happiness, or unhappiness, is "out there."

When we take back our power, we realize the source of our happiness is within ourselves.

Victor Frankl, Austrian psychiatrist and Holocaust survivor is well known for his book, "Man's Search for Meaning" — a meditation on what the gruesome experience of Auschwitz taught him about the primary purpose of life: the quest for meaning, which sustained those who survived.

For Frankl, meaning came from three possible sources: purposeful work, love, and courage in the face of difficulty.

Frankl reminds us,

"Everything can be taken from a man but one thing: the last of the human freedoms — to choose one's attitude in any given set of circumstances, to choose one's own way."

Learn from your suffering and choose not to be a victim.

What has your suffering taught you?

Bonus Question: Waiting

In what ways are you "waiting" to start living?

Eckhart Tolle, a prolific spiritual author of transformational books like "A New Earth and The Power of Now," says:

> *"Large scale waiting is waiting for the next vacation,*
> *for a better job, for the children to grow up,*
> *for a truly meaningful relationship, for success, to make money,*
> *to be important, to become enlightened. It is not uncommon for*
> *people to spend their whole life waiting to start living."*

Seems sad, but it's true. We all have played the waiting game. Waiting for a promotion, waiting for our perfect house, perfect job, or perfect relationship in order to be "happy".

When we choose external things in order to be happy, then what happens if those things don't come to fruition?

It means we are wasting precious time, not allowing ourselves to be happy in the present.

It doesn't mean that we can't *desire* a better job, relationship, house or situation, it's just that if we are waiting for that event to happen in order to be happy, then the waiting time is time wasted by not living in the present moment.

What activities or non-activities bring you back to the present moment?

For me, it's being out in nature and near the water. Also feeling sick or having an injury brings me to the present because it makes everything else seem less important. Meditation helps me be more present. When we are truly present, we aren't worrying about the future or spending time regretting the past.

The World Health Organization has named depression as the greatest cause of suffering worldwide. In the U.S., 1 out of 5 people deal with depression or anxiety. For youth, that number increases to 1 in 3.

The good news is that 40% of our happiness can be influenced by intentional thoughts and actions, leading to life changing habits.

We do choose our thoughts; however, we don't have to be a victim of them. When we are not living in the present moment, we can easily become a victim of our negative thoughts.

In the #1 New York Times bestselling book by Michael Singer, "The Untethered Soul," he says that we have two voices inside of us – one is our habitual voice (narrating voice) or what he refers to as our inner roommate and the other is the observer.

He goes on to say:

"Problems are generally not what they appear to be. When you get clear enough, you will realize that the real problem is that there is something inside of you that can have a problem with almost anything. The first step is to deal with that part of you... You have to break the habit of thinking that the solution to your problems is to rearrange things outside. The only permanent solution to your problems is to go inside and let go of the part of you that seems to have so many problems with reality."

Here is an excerpt from Oprah.com about author Bryon Katie and her view on suffering:

"All the suffering that goes on inside our minds is not reality, says Byron Katie, it's just a story we torture ourselves with." She has a simple, completely replicable system for freeing ourselves of

the thoughts that make us suffer. "All war begins on paper," she explains. You write down your stressful thoughts, and then ask yourself the following four questions:

Question 1: Is it true?

This question can change your life. Be still and ask yourself if the thought you wrote down is true.

Question 2: Can you absolutely know it's true?

This is another opportunity to open your mind and to go deeper into the unknown to find the answers that live beneath what we think we know.

Question 3: How do you react—what happens—when you believe that thought?

With this question, you begin to notice internal cause and effect. You can see that when you believe the thought, there is a disturbance that can range from mild discomfort to fear or panic. What do you feel? How do you treat the person (or the situation) you've written about, how do you treat yourself, when you believe that thought? Make a list and be specific.

Question 4: Who would you be without the thought?

Imagine yourself in the presence of that person (or in that situation), without believing the thought. How would your life be different if you didn't have the ability to even think the stressful thought? How would you feel? Which do you prefer—life with or without the thought? Which feels kinder, more peaceful?

Turn the thought around: The "turnaround" gives you an opportunity to experience the opposite of what you believe. Once you have found one or more turnarounds to your original statement, you are invited to find at least three specific, genuine examples of how each turnaround is true in your life.

****

We need to stop waiting for some future event to happen before we can be happy. Happiness is a choice.

It's important to observe what you are "waiting for" so that you don't let life pass you by.

List three things you are waiting for right now to be happy.

Years ago, I hired a career coach because I was so miserable in my legal job. While I was building my online business part time on the side, she encouraged me to transform my thoughts about my law firm job and to start seeing it as a means to an end. My legal job paid the bills, took care of my family and allowed me to build my online business part time. It also gave me many of the skills I needed to build my online business.

So instead of thinking I couldn't be happy until I was free from my legal job, I turned my thinking around to enjoying the present moment more and knowing that while I was working toward something greater, I could be happy with where I was too.

Where are you playing the waiting game in your life? How can you appreciate what you have now and be happy in this moment?

Like Mel Robbins, Life Coach and author of the bestselling book, "The 5 Second Rule" says,

> *"If a problem can be solved by action,*
> *then you really don't have a problem."*

So, if you're in a bad relationship that is sucking the energy out of you, you can leave that relationship. Same with a bad job or a stressful situation.

If you can't leave it, then you can transform your thoughts about the current situation, so you are at peace about it.

Closing Thoughts

Finding your passion isn't a one and done event.

I think our passions change and constantly evolve during our lives, and if we pay attention to our heart and soul, we can live our passions every day.

We don't have to think "large scale" or "change the world" passions, but we do need to think about the simple everyday things that make us happy and bring us joy.

A few additional questions to ponder:

- What gives you energy and what depletes your energy?

- What do you want more of in your life and less of in your life?

For anything you want in your life, answer the question:

In order to have _____, this must die _____.

In nature, there is a natural life-death-life cycle.

In her book, "Women Who Run With the Wolves," author Clarissa Pinkola Estes, says:

"The only trust required is to know that when there is one ending there will be another beginning."

We are always creating. We are born to create.

Live your life more by your curiosities than by your fears and you will find yourself happier, more joyful and more energetic.

Go forth and create a passion-filled life.

The treasures are hidden inside of you waiting for you to say "Yes"!

Notes

About Michelle Kulp

Michelle Kulp is passionate about teaching women to find their purpose, passion and calling and creating their Dream Life!

Website/Blog: www.Becomea6FigureWoman.com

Motto: "Build a Life that Nourishes Your Soul!"

Advice: "Do What You Love! Love What You Do!"

*   *   *   *   *   *   *   *

In 2000, after a 17 year career in the legal field, Michelle was "let go" from her job at the law firm. At the time, she felt extremely unfulfilled, drained and confused. After she left her legal job, she decided to follow her passions and her intuition and stop making the "safe" choices. She pursued her writing passion and became a reporter for a few years. She also pursued her love of teaching and writing and started her online business in 2005:

www.becomea6figurewoman.com

Michelle helps women transform their intellectual knowledge into PLAY-CHECKS, not PAY-CHECKS!

"Freedom is what motivates me as I was trapped in a cubicle for 17 years and I'm never going back to that corporate prison!"

Michelle also helps her clients write, publish and profit from bestselling books through her *"Bestselling Author Program."* Getting a book published and on the Bestsellers list, not only helps with lead generation, but also helps boost her client's credibility so they are seen as the "go-to" expert in their field. And of course, the added benefit of creating another stream of online income!

Michelle teaches, *"Do the work once and get paid over and over so you can leverage your time.* When you have multiple streams of income and you are selling your knowledge and expertise, then you will have more freedom in your life.

Many of Michelle's clients are #1 bestselling authors and have gone on to create successful coaching, consulting, speaking and online businesses.

Michelle is the bestselling author of several books on Amazon, including:

- *28 Books to $100K: A Guide for Ambitious Authors Who Want to Skyrocket Their Passive Income by Writing a Book a Month*

- *Digital Retirement: Replace Your Social Security Income in the Next 12 Months & Retire Early (Wealth With Words)*

- *How NOT to Write a Book: 12 Things You Should Never Do If You Want to Become an Author & Make a Living With Your Writing*

- *Self-Publishing Secret Sauce: Write High-Profit Books Readers Want, Using Data to Verify Your Ideas*

- *Wealthy Writers Series: 4 Books in 1 Box Set*

- *Backwards Book Launch*

Quit Your Job & Follow Your Dreams

A 12-Month Guide to Being Joyfully Jobless

Michelle Kulp

Two Weeks in the Sun?
Why Not 52 Weeks?

We devote not only the best years of our life, but also most of our waking hours to work. And for what? Counting the days until Friday? An employee of the month certificate? A couple of week's holiday a year? The hope that when retirement comes, we will be able to heat our homes in the winter?

There are people who are very happy in their job, who enjoy going to work every day, and who are well rewarded for their time and effort. It may even be one of their dreams to land the job they have. Good luck to them, but they aren't likely to be the one's reading this book.

Some of us seek to escape from wage slavery, and the debt, insecurity and unhappiness that comes with it, by living for the weekends. Some pretend that everything is hunky dory and have multiple credit cards and mounting debts to prove it. Others seek comfort in drink, drugs and other vices.

For decades now, we have been force fed a system that gives us bread and water when we could be dining out on milk and honey. Every day that you do a job that you hate, that neither pays you enough to fully enjoy life nor allows you to pursue the dreams that lie at the soul of your very being, you are a prisoner of that system. A Prisoner of Work.

~ Excerpt from "Get Out While You Can"
by George Marshall

"Follow your bliss and doors will open where there were no doors before." *~Joseph Campbell, author of "The Power of Myth"*

"There is a great hunger in our culture right now for meaning, for things that connect us with the world and with other people, things that really nurture the soul...." *~Bernadette Murphy, author of "Zen and the Art of Knitting"*

"Most people live in survival, not in fulfillment." *~Tony Robbins, "The Power to Shape Your Destiny!"*

"To find the best job in the world, sometimes you have to create it yourself." *~Jeff Taylor, founder and CEO of Monster.com*

"The best way to learn is from someone else's experience, as long as it feels real enough to be your own." *~Esther Dyson, Editor-at-Large, CNET Networks, Chairman, PC Forum*

Dedication

This book is dedicated to my three amazing children whom I love and adore, Jason, Christine, and Brittany. You all truly inspire and motivate me every day to be the best I can be! I love you all to the moon and back!

To my beautiful granddaughter, Callie Rae who brings endless joy, love, laughter and unconditional love to our family! Glamma loves you!

And to my father, William J. Bachteler, an ex-Marine, who has taught me so many life lessons. Most importantly that the example you set for others speaks volumes and is more important than the words you say. He taught me to be humble, to be grateful, to love myself, to love others and to believe in my dreams! I love you!

This book is for all the seekers out there looking for more purpose, passion and fulfillment in their lives and in their careers. Just know that what you are seeking is also seeking you!

Cubicle Prison

Summer of 1999

It's 6:30 a.m.

The alarm clock jolts me awake pestering me to get out of my warm, comfy bed to prepare for my job as a Paralegal at a law firm with 600+ employees in Washington, D.C. I hit the snooze button multiple times wishing I could stay in my favorite place of all – my bed! The truth is, I wish I had a permanent snooze button so I could go back to sleep and skip work forever. Unfortunately, that's not the case.

Most mornings, I feel like a sloth. Ever so slowly I move out of my bed to begin my morning routine so I can get to the office by 9:00. I trick my body with heaps of caffeine that take me from barely alive to high functioning in a matter of minutes. I need to make breakfast, pack the lunches, feed the dog, and drop my three children at school.

Then, I've got to put on the oppressive business attire. I fantasize about staying home in my favorite pajamas and skipping the whole business suit routine; especially wearing those dreaded high heels that restrict the much-needed blood flow to my aching feet. I make the mad rush out the front door by 7:00 to get on the train for my 1½ hour commute into the city.

I'm not a morning person. Never have been, never will be. As a teenager, I loved to sleep in on the weekends until noon or so. My pops, an ex-Marine, would come into my bedroom early in the morning banging pots and pans around while screaming "Michelle, the day is half over! Rise and Shine! You're sleeping your life away. Time to poop the poop decks. You can sleep when you're dead!"

Not sure what "poop the poop decks" had to do with anything, but what I did know was my father was interrupting my much-needed beauty rest.

Getting up before noon as a teenager was painful because I was going against my internal clock which said I needed more sleep. As an adult with loads of responsibilities, I was once again forcing myself to do something my body, mind, and soul despised doing–getting out of bed at a designated time to be at a place I didn't want to be, to do work I no longer enjoyed doing, while stuck in a cubicle for 8+ hours a day.

I was on the intolerable hamster wheel, and I didn't know how to get off.

Don't get me wrong. For many years, I loved my job at the law firm; it was a career path I had chosen during a Business Law class in my senior year of high school. I was certain I would one day become an attorney.

I went down the path to becoming an attorney but ended up taking a few detours (I married young and had three children), so I ended up with a paralegal degree and never made it to law school.

In 1983, I got my first job at a law firm performing tasks I loved doing like legal writing, legal research, interviewing clients, attending court cases, and negotiating out-of-court settlements. It was all so much fun to me! I was truly passionate about the law.

Although I hated the morning hours, I loved the work I was doing at the law firm, until one day (about a decade later) something radically changed.

The alarm clock went off at the usual time, but on this particular day, I couldn't seem to get myself out of bed no matter how hard I tried. An overwhelming sense of anxiety consumed me. Thoughts raced through my mind like "What excuse can I make to get out of work today?" "How can I stay home?" "Why do I hate my job so much?"

I called the Human Resources Department and left a voicemail while holding my nose pretending to be too sick to come to work that day. The reality was – I was sick; not physically, but mentally and spiritually. I was sick and tired of a job and career that was sucking the life out of me. I hated this job so much; all I could think of was how NOT to go to cubicle prison. I played hooky that day, stayed in my warm comfy bed and tried to figure out why I wasn't in love with my job anymore and why I couldn't force myself to get out of bed as I had done so many times before.

Too young to fully grasp that nothing lasts forever, and people fall in and out of love all the time; not just in relationships, but with careers too; I was completely baffled as to how a career I once loved was now a job I detested.

How did I go from LOVING my job to LOATHING my job and my chosen career?

The answer was TIME; time changed me, and time also changed the tasks I was performing at my job. I call this phenomena *Career Creep* which we will talk about in an upcoming chapter.

I believed whole-heartedly that this was my forever job. That nagging feeling, however, wouldn't go away. From that day forward, it required more and more of my energy just to get out of bed and go to work until one day, I couldn't force myself to do it any longer.

Unable to be my True Self in a Fake Environment

The cubicle I was assigned to at the 600+ person law firm had no natural light, no fresh air, and was the size of a walk-in closet. I spent a lot of time in "war rooms" which were designated office spaces where thousands of documents and files were stored during massive litigation cases.

I worked 8-12 hour days under artificial lights, forced air, in a cubicle with no windows, all the while pretending to be happy; until one day I couldn't breathe any longer.

I started to feel like the goldfish I had when I was a kid. Bubbles was her name, and she lived in a tiny glass bowl filled with water, fake plants, and was adorned with plastic shells and rocks. No matter how many artificial accoutrements I added to the tank, it was never going to be the real thing.

Going to the law firm every day made me feel like my little goldfish Bubbles– like a fish swimming in an artificial, too-small environment going against who I was deep inside my soul. No matter how hard I tried, I just didn't want to be there anymore. I simply couldn't fake it!

To counteract my increasing unhappiness and feelings of exhaustion, I started taking extended lunches at the nearby National Mall in DC. I found a spot under a weeping willow tree that spoke to my soul. I ditched my high heels so I could walk barefoot in the cool grass; the fresh grass breathed life into my aching feet. I fantasized about throwing my high heels into the water and ditching my law firm job forever.

Some days I imagined being five years old again and living in our little red house on Casco Street in Milford, Connecticut; climbing the apple tree in our front yard and feeling free again. My older brother Michael and I would spend our days playing outside in the yard, making tree forts, running through the sprinkler, breathing in the fresh air until it was dark outside and then catching fireflies in jars at night until our parents forced us to come inside. I loved being in nature where I always felt happy and carefree.

Suddenly, the cubicle on the 17th floor at the law firm felt like a prison that I desperately needed to escape from.

During these extended lunches to the National Mall, I basked in the warmth of the sun which seemed to breathe new life into me, even if it was just for an hour or so. I was chronically late returning to work after my stretched-out lunches. I figured sooner or later they just might fire me. The crazy part was, I really didn't care.

THE HIDDEN BLESSING

As fate would have it, I was called into a meeting one day and told, "The department you work in has been restructured and your job no longer exists."

Code for: "You're fired!"

I didn't have the courage or the cash to quit my job, so the universe helped me out.

Looking back, getting fired from my job was a blessing in disguise. At the time, however, it was terrifying to unexpectedly leave a 17-year career in the legal field with very little money in the bank (by very little, I mean none) and three young children to support as a single, divorced mom. I needed cash to pay the bills, and I needed it fast.

The three questions that consumed me were:

1. How was I going to pay the bills?

2. What could I do to make a living that was comparable to the salary I was making at the law firm?

3. Was there a way to find something I LOVED to do and that PAID the bills?

Reality set in. I had NO answers. I had NO plans. I had NO funds.

What I did have though was a massive opportunity to create a new life...and that was priceless.

A Serendipitous Meeting With Billy Ray Cyrus

Yes, that' me with Billy Ray Cyrus after a concert in 1992. Billy Ray Cyrus completely changed the trajectory of my life, so I want to share this transformational (and crazy) story with you…

My Pivotal Moment

On October 23, 1992, I met a man by the name of Billy Ray Cyrus (Country Music Singer and Actor), who changed the entire direction of my life. Some might say it was merely a coincidence, but I strongly believe it was my spiritual destiny. In 1992, I was at a very dark and desperate place in my life. My marriage had recently ended, and I was raising three children (then ages 1, 3 and 5) on my own with no financial or emotional support from my ex-husband; I was let go from the law firm where I had worked for 17 years; I was living cut-off notice to cut-off notice; and my older brother and best friend, Michael, was diagnosed with AIDS and was dying. At the time, I was also having chest pains I thought were from heart issues only to learn they were panic attacks from the chronic and severe stress I was experiencing.

Music that Spoke to my Soul

Late one evening in the summer of 1992, a neighbor stopped by and asked me if I had ever heard of Billy Ray Cyrus. Up until that point in my life, I had only listened to rock-n-roll. Growing up on 80's rock music, I was not interested or familiar with country music. My neighbor gave me a tape of Billy Ray's music and encouraged me to listen to it, especially the song, "Achy Breaky Heart." I quickly got hooked on this very addictive tune. Many nights, I blasted that song and danced around my townhouse with my three young children who also loved the song. It was a wonderful escape from my very stressed out life!

A couple of weeks later, the same neighbor reappeared to tell me that Billy Ray was playing at a concert on October 23, 1992 at the Patriot Center in Fairfax, Virginia and that I should attend. If it had been October 22nd or October 24th, I wouldn't have even thought twice about attending, but because it was October 23rd — my birthday — I felt it had a special meaning. In fact, the thought instantly popped into my head, "Billy Ray is playing on my birthday for a reason...I am going to meet Billy Ray and he has something very important to tell me." Perhaps all the stress was causing me to be delusional, but I honestly believed with every fiber of my being that I was going to meet Billy Ray Cyrus and that he had something important to tell me.

No Doubts, But Lots of Obstacles

Because I was 100% certain about this meeting with Billy Ray (absolutely no doubts were lingering in my mind), I purchased two tickets to the concert and recruited one of my adventurous friends to attend. The plan was simple: I would dress to stand out from the crowd (I wore a bright red spandex dress with very high red pumps), and after the concert, we would get one of the roadies to give us a backstage pass. It had worked during my teenage years to get backstage to meet the bands, so I figured it would work again.

After four failed attempts to get backstage, my friend and I were kicked out of the Patriot Center in Fairfax, Virginia and told we would be arrested if we returned. We immediately went to Plan B…which again was very simple. We would wait for Billy Ray to come out of the Patriot Center and follow his limo to the hotel where he was staying.

An hour or so later, Billy Ray finally came out; he was signing autographs and videotaping his fans…he adored his fans! We stayed in our car, ready to follow the limo. Unfortunately, we weren't the only ones with this bright idea. There were hundreds of women ready to follow the limo for a chance to meet the very handsome and very talented Billy Ray Cyrus. This did not discourage me in the least. I drove like a maniac so I wouldn't lose sight of the limo! I cut off other drivers, ran red lights, and sped down the highway blindly following Billy Ray's limo!

I would NOT give up

We followed the limo to the Hilton Hotel where Billy Ray's bodyguard, Steve, was taking Billy Ray up to his hotel room through a side door. Luckily for me, all the other women who were following the limo jumped out of their cars and ran towards the side door of the hotel. My friend jumped out of our moving car and went inside to tell Billy Ray to wait for me because it was my birthday. I illegally parked the car in a handicapped space and ran to the elevator where

Billy Ray was standing inside. Billy Ray saw me (I guess the red dress stood out!) and he took my hand and pulled me inside the elevator. I told him it was my birthday, the bodyguard snapped a picture of us, and Billy Ray autographed a tee-shirt as well as a book I had with me ("Creative Visualization" by Shakti Gawain). Maybe all the adrenaline in my body was making me have crazy thoughts, but I felt a special chemistry with Billy Ray, but before I could do or say anything, bodyguard Steve abruptly pushed me out of the elevator and told us, "Billy Ray is going up stairs now. Good night!"

In that moment, the elevator doors closed not only on me, but on my dreams! I looked at my friend and told her that whatever we did, the other women would do as well, so we need to "FAKE" leaving the hotel premises to get rid of our competition. About 10 minutes later after all the others had cleared out, my friend and I came back in; I wasn't about to give up on my dream of meeting Billy Ray Cyrus; after all, he had something important to tell me. So, we got in the elevator and pushed all the buttons. I thought that the hotel would block out the floor that Billy Ray was staying on, but they didn't – all the lights lit up!

We started at the top floor and went down

We got off the elevator on each floor and looked for clues to find Billy Ray. It didn't take us very long. On the 12th floor, I looked down the hall and saw the bodyguard, Steve, go into the last room. I was so excited! Finally, my dream was coming true. As I got near the room, bodyguard Steve heard me and came out to inform me that if I didn't leave, he was calling hotel security to have me re-moved. I thought I could sweet talk him into letting me see Billy Ray, but the more I talked, the more irritated and aggravated he became. I argued with him for a while until my friend told me she didn't want to get arrested and she thought we better listen to him and leave. I hesitantly left and headed back towards the elevator.

I couldn't give up at that point

I was so close. I told my friend the only thing standing between me and Billy Ray was the hallway and that I was not going to let a hallway come in between me and my dreams. Come hell or high water, I was going to figure out some way to meet Billy Ray Cyrus. So, I stood at the elevator and searched my mind for anything that would get me closer to Billy Ray. I looked up and noticed a small sign that had the room numbers printed on it, which read something like "Rooms 1200-1223" with an arrow pointing towards the direction I saw the bodyguard go. I looked across the hall and noticed a house phone on a table. I picked up the phone and dialed the last number on the sign and Voila! Billy Ray answered the phone (apparently the bodyguard was staying in a separate room). When Billy Ray answered the phone and asked who was calling, I told him it was the "Birthday Girl," to which he replied, *"You mean the girl in the red dress?"* Wow! I couldn't believe it! Billy Ray remembered who I was. He told me that he had something to tell me that I wasn't going to believe." Curiously, I waited for his explanation. He said that if there hadn't been all those women in the elevator and lobby, he would have invited me to his hotel room for some Chinese food. I told him, *"I'm here now!"*

Better Late Than Never

Billy Ray explained that he had hurt his back on stage, and that a masseuse was coming, but I could come to his room when the masseuse was done. My friend did not want to wait, so I gave Billy Ray my phone number (this was before cell phones) at the hotel where we were staying and told him to call me when he was done.

A couple of hours went by and no call from Billy Ray. Finally, I changed out of my red dress and into my pajamas, but I left my hair and make-up intact just in case he called. At about 2:00 am, I was listening to Billy Ray's music, still on an adrenaline rush, when the phone in my hotel room finally rang and it was Billy Ray! He asked me what my birthday wish was. I quickly told him, "To meet and talk to you in person." He said if it wasn't too late, he would love it if I would come over to his hotel and visit. I hung up the phone and I put that red dress back on and was speeding down the highway to the Hilton Hotel within minutes.

3-5 am

I arrived back at the Hilton Hotel and was heading down the hall toward Billy Ray's room when bodyguard Steve heard me and came out to investigate; he was furious. He told me to leave the hotel before he called the hotel security and the police. I swore to him that Billy Ray called and invited me to his room. I'm sure he heard that line all the time from Billy Ray's female super-fans. Luckily, Billy Ray's hotel room door was slightly ajar, and the bodyguard asked him if what I said was true. Billy Ray confirmed what I told him, so he irately let me in.

I spent the next two to three hours talking to Billy Ray (he was a complete gentleman). We spoke about our lives, our families, relationships, etc. He had a very spiritually enlightened side to him which was a stark contrast from his "stage" persona. He spoke about the fact that some people called him an "overnight success" to which he said wasn't true since he spent over ten years playing in bars to become this so-called "overnight success." I told Billy Ray my rather desperate life story. When Billy Ray looked deeply into my eyes, he said something that changed my entire life...

Dreams

Billy Ray asked me *"What are your dreams?"* To which I quickly replied, *"I don't have any dreams. My life's about survival."* Billy Ray assured me I had a dream and that I needed to go out and discover what my dream was and never, ever give up on that dream.

One year, one small book, and one BIG Dream! I took Billy Ray's advice and went out in the world for the next year searching for this elusive dream. It wasn't so easy to find my dream. I read books, talked to people, but I could not for the life of me figure out what my dream was. I kept feeling sorry for myself and thinking, "Everyone has a dream except me."

Then, one day I was at Borders Bookstore (sadly, they went out of business) when a tiny book fell into my hands that changed my life: "How to Find Your Mission in Life" by Richard Bolles. Richard Bolles also wrote a very popular book titled "What Color is Your Parachute" in which one question helped me discover my dream:

"What do you love to do where you lose all sense of time?"

Finally! I knew the answer – I loved to write! When I was younger, I would write for hours and time would fly by. When I was writing, five hours seemed like five minutes to me. That's how I knew writing was my dream. I had absolutely no concept of time when I was writing.

One Road Leads to Many Others

In 1993, I headed down that road toward my dream – to become a writer. I joined writer's groups, attended writer's conferences, and read every book about writing that I could get my hands on. Then, I wrote a manuscript titled "Woman, take Hold of Your Power: 50 Unconscious Ways Women Give Up Their Power," which I tried to get published for over a year. I received rejection letter after rejection letter and was becoming quite discouraged. Finally, a big New York Publishing House called and said they wanted to ask me some questions. I was so excited! I thought to myself, "Oh my God, my dreams are finally coming true!"

The man from the publishing house explained that the book I wrote was a self-help book for women and he wanted to know what my "credentials" were. He asked if I had a Ph.D. I explained that while I didn't have a Ph.D., I had something better. He inquisitively asked, "What could be better than a Ph.D.?" To which I replied,

"Life Experience. I didn't write that book from theory, but from real life stories from my personal experiences and those of my friends."

He didn't agree with me and said, "Unfortunately the publishing business is very competitive and unless you have a Ph.D., we cannot take a chance on an unknown author. It's just business. I hope you understand."

I hung up the phone feeling disappointed and excited at the same time; disappointed that they weren't going to publish my book, but excited that I finally had some confirmation from a highly credible publishing house that my writing was good enough to get published.

I never did get that manuscript published by a traditional publisher, but I did fulfill my dream when I self-published that book several years later.

How I Got Writing Credentials Without Having Any Writing Credentials.

More than anything, I wanted to be a reporter so I could obtain these "writing credentials" that the publishing house spoke about. I figured I needed them to get published and to be successful. Since I had no credentials, I had to get very creative in order to get a job as a newspaper reporter.

My plan was hatched. I decided I would simply pretend to be a reporter, attend local events, write the story, take photos and then have my father give the written story to the editor of the newspaper during his morning walk. It was a subtle way of stalking the newspaper editor and getting in the back door.

The first week after I hatched my crazy plan, the editor published my story on the front page. At this point, I had never spoken with him. I was shocked and ecstatic. I did this for four more weeks in a row and every week he prominently published my articles in the newspaper. Finally, I got a call from the editor of the newspaper and in an irritating tone he asked, "What? Do you want a job or something?"

He was a large, intimidating and controversial guy from Scotland that some people loved, but a lot more people hated. I told him on the phone that I might want a job, so he invited me to come in and talk to him.

When I arrived at the newspaper headquarters, he asked me to shut the office door so no one could hear our conversation. He said annoyingly, *"You see all those reporters out there? Well, I have to do a lot of editing when they turn in their stories!"* I timidly replied *"Isn't' that what editors do?"*

"Yes, but my point is your writing is good and I don't have to edit it."

Wow! What a compliment! I was floored to say the least. Not long after, the editor of the newspaper offered me a full-time position with benefits as a reporter.

Unfortunately, when I learned the salary was half what I was making as a paralegal, I had to decline. Thankfully, we made a deal that I would be a freelance reporter for the newspaper, and he would pay me per article. It was perfect because as a freelancer, I could now get the "writing credentials" I needed as well as create a new stream of income to support myself and my three children.

The dream of becoming a writer led me to other roads I would have never imagined myself on – I became a motivational speaker, workshop leader, online entrepreneur, and book launch expert.

It's actually hard to believe I am a speaker as I spent seven long years overcoming my intense fears of public speaking (that's a whole other book). But deep down, I knew that if I was ever going to become a successful writer, I had to get over my fear of public speaking. I believed I was being judged harshly by others and didn't feel worthy enough to share my voice with the world. I finally overcame that fear and now I happily share my stories on stage in front of hundreds and sometimes thousands of people.

LISTENING TO MY INNER VOICE HELPED ME NOT JUST SURVIVE BUT THRIVE

Instead of listening to my fears that were trying to keep me safe and small, I began listening to soul and my inner voice. I began to appreciate my resourcefulness, creativity, determination, my ability to think outside the box, and my risk-taking skills, which some people refer to as "insanity" or "leaping without a net."

Living my Dream

I am living the life I dreamed of many years ago. I have a fulfilling business that I love. I work 20-25 hours a week and have a rewarding 6-figure income. Most importantly, I have FREEDOM. I am living my dreams of writing, coaching, and speaking which fills my soul. I talk to so many people on a weekly basis who are unhappy with their jobs and who are killing themselves to pay the bills, and I want to help them find and live their dreams.

John O'Donohue, Irish poet and Catholic Scholar, reminds us:

"To be born is to be chosen. No one is here by accident.
Each one of us was sent here for a special destiny."

So, what is *your* special destiny?

Confessions of a Serial Quitter

I have a confession to make. **I AM A QUITTER.**

That's right. I am an expert at quitting jobs.

Before I was 25 years old, I estimate that I had about 20 or 30 jobs. Sounds crazy, but it's true!

I repeated this pattern for many years, so it seems only natural to be writing a book teaching others how to *QUIT THEIR JOBS & FOLLOW THEIR DREAMS.*

By "quitting" things I didn't like, it actually brought me closer to what I did like.

I didn't set out in life to be a Quitter; it's just that I had a low tolerance for:

- Boring work
- Low pay
- Office politics
- Bosses (or anyone) telling me what to do
- Long hours
- Stress
- Long commutes
- Cubicles with no sunlight or fresh air
- Corporate BS

Maybe you can relate?

Every day, the majority of people I meet tell me how much they "hate" their jobs.

In my younger years, when I was a serial job hopper. I would see a job advertised that I thought sounded great, apply, get hired, and then realize a day, a week or even a month later, that I actually hated it!

Looking back, I'm glad I had such a low tolerance for *"job misery"* because I believe that trait is what has made me successful today. It forced me to try new things, take risks, get comfortable with uncertainty, fail, and helped me gain the clarity about who I was and what I liked and didn't like. Over time, this is what helped me discover my dreams and passions.

In his bestselling book, "Range: Why Generalists Triumph in a Specialized World," author David Epstein talks about generalists as people who find their path late in life, and who juggle many interests rather than focusing on one. He calls this exploratory time "sampling," and the people who do this are "samplers."

I didn't realize until I read his book and met him at the National Book Festival that I was a sampler. I was happy to learn that David's research shows people who try a lot of different things actually end up with more fulfilling and successful careers.

I'm glad I was a quitter of jobs (and careers and hobbies) and not afraid to be a sampler. As we go through this journey, I want you to keep in mind that it's okay to be a sampler and a quitter because that actually moves you closer to finding your passion and creating work you love.

In his book, David Epstein shares his doubts about changing careers and jobs:

"I was working on a scientific research vessel in the Pacific Ocean after college when I decided for sure that I wanted to be a writer, not a scientist. I never expected that my path from science into writing would go through work as the overnight crime reporter at a New York City tabloid, nor that I would shortly thereafter be a senior writer at Sports Illustrated, a job that, to my own surprise, I would leave. I began worrying that I was a job-commitment-phobic drifter who must be doing this whole career thing wrong. Learning about the advantages of breadth and delayed specialization has changed the way I see myself and the world."

David goes on to say that the challenge we all face is how to maintain the benefits of breadth, diverse experience, interdisciplinary thinking and delayed concentration in a world that increasingly incentivizes, even demands, hyper-specialization.

I'm giving you permission to be a sampler, to try new things, and to quit things that you don't enjoy.

Although early specialization has faster short-term benefits, David Epstein shows through his research that "slow bakers" or "late developers" are more successful long term and will increasingly thrive.

MULTIPLE INTERESTS AND MULTIPLE STREAMS OF INCOME

Having multiple streams of income is a great way to pursue different passions and interests and also to make more money than with just one stream. Moreover, it's good to have multiple streams in case one stream dries up, you have others coming in!

After I left the legal field, I started creating multiple streams of income.

Because I love teaching, I started my online business, Become a 6-Figure Woman, in 2005—www.becomea6figurewoman.com. I ran my online business part time while creating multiple streams of income. I created and sold digital online courses and also did private coaching. Over the years, I did a variety of things to generate income like website design, copywriting, and SEO (search engine optimization). These skills became very important later when I started my next business.

In 2013, I launched another business and website, www.bestsellingauthorprogram.com to help authors and entrepreneurs write, publish, promote, and profit from a bestselling book. I used all of the skills I had acquired from my legal, sales, and journalism careers to launch this new program. Using skills we've learned throughout our lives and then putting them together to create something new can be very lucrative. I call this "skill-stacking" and it can make you a lot of money.

When I'm not working on my client's books, I write my own books as well. I've published eight books as of the time of this writing.

I haven't had a 9 to 5 corporate job since 2000. I often work in my jammies or yoga clothes, my commute is from my bedroom to my office overlooking the beautiful Chesapeake Bay, and I feel blessed to get paid to do what I LOVE!

When you spend years in a job you hate, it feels so good to be your own boss and do what you love – and to also make money doing that.

I wake up without an alarm clock and start my day in a very relaxed way: meditation, journaling, yoga, a cup of English breakfast or Earl Grey tea, a leisurely walk in the neighborhood, and just ease into the day. I sometimes have lunch or dinner with my kids, family and friends, and go on mini-adventures and beach trips. I love spending time with my beautiful grand-daughter, Callie Rae!

I am so grateful to have a 6-figure income and to be living my dreams. I want to teach you how to do the same because I know how it feels to be STUCK in a job you hate and think like there's no way out. I can't wait to show you how to create a life and work you LOVE so that you can be paid for your passions, gifts and talents.

Even though I was miserable at the end of my 17-year legal career, I didn't leave voluntarily because of these three reasons:

1. Massive fears

2. Uncertainty about the future

3. Money worries

Fear, uncertainty, and money worries kept me stuck in a job I hated and "getting fired" was the universe telling me I was in the wrong job and that it was time for a change.

It's important to understand that just because you want to quit your job doesn't mean that you made a mistake taking that job, that you are a failure, or that you've wasted time in the wrong job.

Soren Kierkegaard, a German Philosopher once said:

"Life can only be understood backwards;
but it must be lived forwards."

I promise that you will use **ALL** of the skills you have learned so far in your life as you venture off in new directions to *follow your dreams*.

As I said earlier, I use many of the skills I obtained from my past jobs in my online business. In fact, I am thankful for all of my corporate-world skills like legal writing, legal research, as well as technology, communication, organizational, and sales skills. I am especially grateful I can type 100 words per minute as it comes in handy in the publishing field.

The key to creating a happy life is being able to recognize when you are off course from your authentic path (the one where you feel fulfilled, on purpose and passionate about) and to make small shifts that bring you back to your true, authentic path.

This book is designed to help get you back to that authentic path and rediscover what makes you happy, what brings you joy, and to recognize that you can be well paid for doing things you love. In fact, it's easier now more than ever to create work you love and that brings you deep fulfillment.

Most people spend their entire lives building somebody else's dreams...this book is about learning to put yourself first and to *START BUILDING YOUR DREAMS*.

Quitting your job is a huge risk, but it's time to get out of your comfort zone because:
COMFORT IS DEATH

So, together let's take the journey back to the real YOU...

The Pros and Cons to Quitting Your Job & Following Your Dreams:

Pros	Cons
Living More Authentically	Leaving a Secure position can be terrifying
Living a more meaningful life	The road will, without a doubt, be difficult
The opportunity to do what you LOVE!	You must face failure and rejection
Feeling Spiritually Fulfilled	Receiving Disapproval from others
Inspiring others to follow their dreams	Self-doubt
More Control of your Time and Income	Sacrificing the luxuries (for a while)
Living BIG	Living Little
Being Happy	Being Miserable

PART I - CLARITY

"Clarity about what matters provides
clarity about what does not."
~Cal Newport, author of Deep Work

Chapter 1 – The Four Distinctions – Job, Career, Hobby, Calling

"While your career is about a relationship between you and the world; your vocation is about the relationship between you and God. Vocation is a private vow. Your career is dependent upon other people, but your vocation belongs only to you. You can get fired from your career, but you can never get fired from your vocation."
~Elizabeth Gilbert, from the book "Big Magic"

Most people are searching for more purpose and more meaning in their lives. I'm sure it's why you are reading this book. There is a lot of confusion about purpose, passion and meaning, and I think it's because so many of us confuse these four words: **Job, Career, Hobby, and Calling.**

When I was in college studying law, I worked as a cocktail waitress at the Sheraton Hotel – that was my **JOB,** and it paid the bills. After I graduated from college, I worked for 17 years as a paralegal and legal secretary – that was my **CAREER**. I love baking and cooking – that is my **HOBBY**. My passion is writing, and that is my **CALLING**.

Do you see the distinctions I made?

Elizabeth Gilbert, author of the NY Times bestselling book, "Eat Pray Love" and "Big Magic," wrote a blog post about these four important distinctions between a job, a career, a hobby and a calling and I wanted to share her post with you as we begin our journey together…

Elizabeth Gilbert's blog post:

"Dear Ones - I get a lot of questions from people who are seeking purpose and meaning in their lives. And I get a lot of questions from people who are seeking career advice — especially about creative careers. And I get a lot of questions from people who are absolutely confused about where their energy is going in life, and why.

For anyone out there who is seeking purpose and meaning and direction in their lives, I thought it might be useful today to define and differentiate four very important words that relate to **HOW WE SPEND OUR TIME IN LIFE.**

Are you ready?

The four very important words are:

1. HOBBY

2. JOB

3. CAREER

4. VOCATION/CALLING

These four words are often interconnected, but they are NOT interchangeable.

Too much of the time, we treat these words like they are synonyms, but they are NOT. They are gloriously distinct and should remain gloriously distinct. Each is wonderful and important in its own way. I think a lot of the pain and confusion that people face when they are trying to chart their lives is that they don't understand the meaning of these words — or the expectations and demands of each word.

So, let me break down what I consider to be the definitions and differences.

1) **HOBBY** – A hobby is something that you do for pleasure, relaxation, distraction, or mild curiosity. A hobby is something that you do in your spare time. *Hobbies can come and go in life* – you might try out a hobby for a while, and then move on to something new. I grew up in a family where everyone had hobbies (my grandmother made rag rugs; my grandfather made jewelry out of old spoons; etc.) and I have hobbies myself. Gardening was my hobby a few years ago; now it's Karaoke and collage-making. You can tell when something is a hobby because your attitude toward it tends to be *relaxed* and *playful*. The stakes are SUPER low with hobbies. Sometimes you might make a bit of money out of your hobby, but that's not the point – nor does it need to be. Hobbies are important because they remind us that not everything in life has to be about productivity and efficiency and profit and destiny. Hobbies are mellow. This is a wonderful reminder, and the concept should relax you. Hobbies prove that we have spare time – that we are not just slaves to the capitalist machine or to our own ambitions. You don't NEED a hobby, mind you, but it's awfully nice to have one. Even the word itself is adorable and non-threatening: HOBBY! What a cute word. Go get one. You have nothing to lose, and it'll probably make you happier. Also, my grandparents would approve. Back before TV, everyone had hobbies. It's nice. No big deal.

2) **JOB** – You may not *need* a hobby, but you do absolutely *need* a job. Unless you have a trust fund, or just won the lottery, or somebody is completely supporting you financially... you need a job. Actually, I would argue that even if you DO have a trust fund or a winning lottery ticket or a generous patron, you should still have a job. I believe there is great dignity and honor to be found in having a job. A job is how you look after yourself in the world. I always had a job, or several jobs, back when I was an unpublished, aspiring writer. Even after

I'd already published three books, I still kept a regular job, *because I never wanted to burden my creativity with the responsibility of paying for my life.* Artists often resent having jobs, but I never resented it. Having a job always made me feel powerful and secure and free. It was good to know that I could support myself in the world, and that I would never starve, no matter what happened with my creativity. **Now, here's the most essential thing to understand about a job: IT DOESN'T HAVE TO BE AWESOME.** Your job can be boring, it can be a drag, it can even be "beneath you". Jobs don't need to be soul-fulfilling. Really, they don't. I've had all kinds of weird and lame jobs; it doesn't matter, you don't need to love your job; you just need to have a job and do it with respect. Of course, if you absolutely hate your job, by all means look for another one, but try to be philosophical about why you have this job right now. (Some good philosophical reasons for staying in a crappy job right now include: You are taking care of yourself; you are supporting your beloved family; you are saving up for something important; you are paying off debts. The list of reasons to have a job – even a bad job – goes on and on, and honor abides within all those reasons.) Don't judge yourself about your job and never be a snob about anyone else's job. We live in a material world and everyone has to do something for money, so just do whatever you have to do, collect your paycheck, and then go live the rest of your life however you want. Your job does not need to be how you define yourself; you can create your own definitions of your purpose and your meaning, pulled from deep within your imagination. A job is vital, but don't make it YOUR LIFE. It's not that big a deal. It's just a job – a very important and also not-at-all important thing.

3) **CAREER** – A career is different from a job. A job is just a *task* that you do for money, but a career is something that you *build over the years with energy, passion, and commitment.* You don't need to love your job, but I hope to heaven that you love your career – or else you're in the wrong career, and it would be better for you to quit that career and just go find yourself a job, or a different career. Careers are best done with excitement. Careers are huge investments. Careers require ambition, strategy, and hustle. Your career is a relationship with the world. I used to have jobs, but now I have a career. My career is: AUTHOR. That means: Professional Writer. When I think about my work in terms of my career, I need to make sure that I'm building good relationships in the publishing world, and making smart decisions, and managing myself well within a realm that is more public than private. I need to pay attention to what critics are saying about my work, and how my books are selling, and how well I'm meeting my deadlines. I need to tend to my career with respect and regard, or else I will lose it. I need to honor my contracts and my contacts. When I make decisions about my life, I need to think about whether this would be good or bad for my career. If I win an award, that's good for my career. If I get caught in a hotel room with a pile of cocaine and six exotic dancers, that's bad for my career. (Actually, now that I think about it, maybe that would be AWESOME for my career! Gotta look into that! HA!) Let me make something very clear about careers: **A career is a good thing to have if you really want one, but YOU DO NOT NEED TO HAVE A CAREER.** There is absolutely nothing wrong with going through your entire life having jobs, and enjoying your hobbies, and pursuing your vocation, but never having "a career". A career is not for everyone. A career is a choice. But if you do make that choice, make sure that you really care

about your career. Otherwise, it's just an exhausting marathon, for no reason. I really care about my career, but it's not the most important thing in my life. Not even close. The most important thing in my life is my....

4) **VOCATION** – The word "vocation" comes to us from the Latin verb "vocare" – meaning "*to call*". *YOUR VOCATION IS YOUR CALLING.* Your vocation is a summons that comes directly from the universe and is communicated through the *YEARNINGS OF YOUR SOUL*. While your career is about a relationship between you and the world; your vocation is about the relationship between you and God. Vocation is a private vow. Your career is dependent upon other people, but your vocation belongs only to you. You can get fired from your career, but you can never get fired from your vocation. Writing was my vocation long before I was lucky enough to get the career of an "Author" – and writing will always be my vocation, whether my career as an Author keeps working out or not. This is why I can approach my career with a certain sense of calm – because I know that, while I obviously care about career, I am not defined by it. When I consider my writing in terms of my career, I have to care what the world thinks about me. But when I consider my writing in terms of my vocation, **I TRULY DO NOT GIVE A FUCK WHAT THE WORLD THINKS ABOUT ME.** My career is dependent upon others; my vocation is entirely my own. The entire publishing world could vanish, and books could become obsolete, and I would still be a writer – because that's my vocation. That's my deal with God. *You do not need to make money from your vocation in order for it to have meaning.* Writing had meaning for me LONG before you ever heard of me, and long before anyone else wanted me to do it.

Vocation has nothing to do with money, with career, with status, with ambition. I often see people corrode their vocation by insisting that it become a career – and then making career decisions that destroy their vocation. (Amy Winehouse's career destroyed her vocation, for instance.) The day that I feel my career is destroying my vocation, I will quit my career and go get a job, so that I can protect my vocation. But I will never quit my vocation. Nobody even needs to know about your vocation, in order for it to have meaning. Your vocation is holy because it has nothing to do with anyone else. *Your vocation can be anything that brings you to life and makes you feel like your soul is animated by purpose.* Tending to your marriage can be your vocation. Raising your children can be your vocation. Teaching people how to take care of their health can be your vocation. Visiting your elderly neighbors can be your vocation. I have a friend who finds his vocation in picking up garbage off the streets wherever he goes; this is his gesture of love toward his fellow man. Searching for light and peace and meaning can be your vocation. Forgiveness can be your vocation. Brother Lawrence was a 17th century monk who worked his whole life washing dishes in a monastery (because washing dishes was his JOB) but his vocation was to see God in everything and everyone, and that is why he radiated grace. (Awesome vocation, by the way. People came from all over the world to watch Brother Lawrence wash dishes, because of the way he radiated divine love in every act. THAT'S vocation.) I admire the Roman Catholic Church for understanding the sanctity of vocation, and for teaching that the purest human vocation is LOVE. A vocation is the highest expression of your human purpose, and therefore you must approach it with deepest reverence. You can be called to your vocation by what you love (for instance: I love writing), or you can be called to your vocation by what you hate (for instance: I know people who dedicate themselves to social justice because of their hatred for violence and inequality.) If you don't have a vocation and you long for one, you can pray for one. You can ask the universe with humility to lead you to your vocation – but then you must pay VERY close attention to the clues and signs that point you toward your vocation. **Don't just pray and WAIT. Instead, pray and SEEK.** Everyone wants the lightning strike, but the path to your vocation is usually a trail of bread crumbs, instead. Look for clues. No clue is too small; no vocation is insignificant. Don't be proud; be attentive. **What brings your soul to life**? What makes you feel like you are not just a meat puppet – not just here to work hard and pay bills and wait to die? You cannot be lazy or entitled about your vocation, or apathetic, or fatalistic, or calculating. You cannot give up on it, if things don't "work out" – whatever that even means. You must work closely with your intuition in order to find your highest meaning in life. This is hard work sometimes, but it is divine work, and it is always worth it. (Here's a possibility, for instance: Searching for your vocation can be your vocation!) You can choose your hobbies, your jobs, or your careers, but you cannot choose your vocation; you can only accept the invitation that has been offered to you or decline it. You can honor your vocation, or you can neglect it. You can worship it, or you can ignore it. A vocation is offered to you as a sacred gift, and it is yours to care for, or to lose. When you treat your vocation as sacred, you will see your whole life as sacred – and everyone else's lives, too. When you are careless about your vocation, you will treat your whole life carelessly –- and other people's lives, too. Your vocation will become clear to you through the act of **PAYING ATTENTION** to your senses and your soul, and to what in the world causes you to feel love or hate. You will be led to your vocation, though the path is not always obvious. You must participate in its unfolding. Do not fall asleep on this job. Your vocation is **hinted** at through your talents, tastes, passions, and curiosities. Your vocation is calling you, even when you can't quite hear it. *("What you are seeking is seeking you" – Rumi*.) When you embrace a vocation, and commit yourself to that vocation, your mind becomes a quieter place. When you accept the divine invitation of your vocation, you will become strong. You will know that – as long as you are tending to your vocation – everything will be fine.

My feeling is that people look for purpose in life without understanding these four words: HOBBY, JOB, CAREER, VOCATION. People blend these four concepts, or mistake them, confuse them, or try to have all four at once, or pretend that they are all the same thing. Or people just generally get freaked out and confused, because they haven't thought these words through, or decided which ones are most important. (Or which ones are most important RIGHT NOW.) People generally want to know, "*What am I doing with my life?*", but they don't slow down long enough to really think about these four different aspects of this question – the four different possibilities for where our time and energy goes. People worry so much about their careers, for instance, that they often forget to pay attention to their vocations. Or people get so seduced by the grandeur of their vocations that they forget to have a job, and so they stop taking care of themselves and their families in the material world...which will only bring suffering. (Remember: Even Brother Lawrence had a job. He was not too proud to wash dishes.) Or people are so busy chasing social status and personal advancement that they forget to make time for the relaxing joy of having a sweet little hobby. And oftentimes people mistake a sweet little hobby for something that they think should be a job, or a career, or a vocation. **Don't try to blend what perhaps doesn't need to be blended. Don't mistake a job for a career, or a career for a vocation, or a vocation for a hobby, or a hobby for a job. Be clear about what each one is and be clear about what can be reasonably expected from each one and be clear about what is demanded of you with each one.**

Here's another thing I see happening: people get so embarrassed or resentful about their lousy day jobs that they forget to be grateful that they have a job at all – and this causes only more anxiety and confusion, which again, will make them stop paying reverent attention to their vocation, or enjoying their hobbies, or making plans for a career.

We live in a real world that is heavy sometimes with real-life obligations, but we also have souls that deserve care and attention. We can pay attention to our worldly ambitions and pleasures (hobbies, jobs, careers) without neglecting our mystical, otherworldly, beautiful and often impractical vocations. We can pay attention to all of it – but this requires sitting still at times and really thinking things through, with courage and dignity. And it requires an understanding of terms.

The important thing is to be sober and careful and attentive enough to know what you are REALLY talking about when you consider the question, *"What am I doing with my life?"*

It isn't easy to answer this question but understanding and respecting these four different words might be a start.

And when in doubt, at least *try* SOMETHING. As the wonderful poet David Whyte says: *"A wrong-headed but determined direction is better than none at all."*

Good luck out there, brave seekers!

Onward,

LG

****

My Own Confusion About The Four Distinctions

I love Elizabeth Gilbert's post because it helped bring clarity to my own life. I can see now how I tried to *blend things* that didn't need to be blended. At different times in my life, I tried to blend hobbies into jobs (jobbies) which didn't work out because it took all the fun out of it. I've also been resentful of some of the jobs I had because they weren't "lighting me up," however, I see now that I lacked gratitude for the fact that my job was actually supporting me and my family.

As I said earlier, my CALLING is writing. I do it in a variety of ways such as writing books, blog posts, online courses, articles, and talks. It took me a long time to figure this out, but I know in my heart and soul that I have been called to write. It's my *natural gift and it is what I LOVE doing!*

In this chapter, we are going to look back in your life to see how these four distinctions have played out.

First, I want to take what Elizabeth Gilbert said about "JOBS" in her post and make one more distinction between what I call a **FREEDOM JOB** and a **BONDAGE JOB**.

This is a distinction I feel is important to make because I've had both types of jobs and having a **FREEDOM JOB** is much better than being stuck in a **BONDAGE JOB**.

A **FREEDOM JOB** is a "drop-out" job that doesn't sap your spirits and suck up all your time and energy. You need time and energy to pursue your hobbies and to discover your calling. A freedom job covers most or all of your expenses and some extra but does not consume or define you.

A **FREEDOM JOB** is important because you need time, space and energy to explore your passions and curiosities. When you have a **FREEDOM JOB,** then you do what you have to do to pay the bills *without* giving away your soul. You want to save your energy for what you really want to do (or figuring out what you really want to do if you don't know what that is yet).

Remember, your vocation for a while might be figuring out what your vocation is; and that's okay. The point is: you need energy and space to figure out your passions, and a **FREEDOM JOB** will give you that.

My **FREEDOM JOB** after I was fired from the law firm was an outside sales job that I had for 10 years. I worked 20-25 hours per week, made six figures selling hot tubs, and had lots of time and energy to pursue my interests and passions. It wasn't draining to my soul like my legal job was at the end.

You can also think of your **FREEDOM JOB** like a bridge taking you from one side of the river to the other. The river you're heading to is a life of creativity, passion, fulfillment, and joy. It might not be your forever job, but it will take you where you want to go – MOVING you towards your dreams and your vocation.

A **BONDAGE JOB,** on the other hand, consumes your time, energy, and life force. A big part of why you might be feeling *stuck* when it comes to figuring out what your dreams are is because you don't have the time or energy required to do it.

Part of this journey is creating time in your life to daydream, try new things out, and discover renewed things about yourself. Unfortunately, if you're in a **BONDAGE JOB**, then your job has your time and energy.

Think about this:

It's hard to assess your life when your job is your life.

I'm not sure where you are in your life right now, but if you are working in a **BONDAGE JOB**, then the first goal for you is to transition from this **BONDAGE JOB** to a **FREEDOM JOB** so you can create space, time, and energy in your life to discover what you want at the deepest level of your being.

Elizabeth Gilbert said in her blog post:

> *"Everyone wants the lightning strike,*
> *but the path to your vocation is usually a*
> *trail of bread crumbs, instead.*
> *Look for clues. No clue is too small."*

To create your dream life, we need to find clues to your dreams.

I've created what I call "**Treasure Map Exercises**" throughout this book to give you deeper insight in putting together clues that will give you the answers you are seeking.

I recommend getting a special notebook or journal so you can do these exercises and record them all in one place where you can look back at them.

Let's get started with our first TREASURE MAP EXERCISE. When you see this image below throughout the book, that means there is an exercise coming up. Doing these exercises will help move you closer to creating your dream life. At the end, you'll put all the clues together and find your own treasure!

THE FOUR DISTINCTIONS IN YOUR OWN LIFE

It's your turn now to look at the four distinctions in your own life.

Answer the questions below in your notebook or journal. The goal is to take an inventory of your hobbies, careers, jobs, and vo-cations so that you can get a birds-eye view of them. Maybe you've never had a career, but only a series of jobs. That's okay. Maybe you don't know what your vocation (calling) is and that's okay too. Just write down what you have experienced in your life so far.

My hobbies are (or have been):

_____

_____

_____

_____

_____

My *BONDAGE jobs are (or have been):

_____

_____

_____

_____

_____

My *FREEDOM jobs are (or have been):

_____

_____

_____

_____

_____

My Careers are (or have been):

_____

_____

_____

_____

_____

My Vocations (Callings) are (or have been):

_____

_____

_____

_____

_____

Take some time to reflect on what you've written.

Do you think you've tried to blend things that didn't need blending like Elizabeth Gilbert spoke about in her blog post? Did you have a lot of bondage jobs?

I recommend doing this exercise for as many jobs, careers, callings, and hobbies as you can think of. This will give you a new perspective as you travel down memory lane and take a deeper look at your past.

Your past is what led you to this point in time right now. So, if you're feeling unfulfilled, unhappy, miserable, and miles off your authentic path, this will give you clues and the much-needed insight as to how you got there.

My father who is a big history buff says, *"If you don't know your history, you're bound to repeat it."* It's important to know your history to avoid repeating patterns.

I recommend the *Observation without Condemnation* approach when you're looking at your life and implementing changes. Don't condemn yourself for your past choices. You did the best you could with the knowledge, skills, and awareness you had.

As the wonderful Maya Angelou once said,

> *"Do the best you can until you know better.*
> *Then when you know better, do better."*

We are looking at where you've been so we can see what worked and acknowledge what didn't work so well. From that place, with a new perspective, we can make changes.

Once you've examined your own four distinctions regarding jobs, careers, hobbies and callings, in the next chapter, you are going to complete a **Job Autopsy** to deepen your understanding about your past jobs.

Chapter 2 – Performing a Job Autopsy

---

*A job has many parts to it like the tasks that we do,
the hours we work, the people we interact with, the salary,
the benefits, as well as intangible things like feeling
appreciated, respected and valued.*

At the end of my 17-year legal career, I was deeply confused about why a job I once loved became a job I absolutely despised.

It's easy to say, "I hate my job," but understanding *why* you hate your job will give you the insight you need to make changes.

My daughter was working in an outside sales job and was considering a job change. When I asked her why she hated her job, she complained about the hours being too early. I asked her if she was able to change the hours, would she want to stay at her job. Surprisingly, her answer was "YES." As she thought about it more, she realized there were several aspects of her job that she loved such as:

- Not being stuck in an office all day
- Driving a company vehicle
- Meeting new people
- Earning high commissions
- Generating her own leads
- Paid time off and vacations
- Great health insurance
- Stability

She ended up getting fired from this job because she was consistently late to meetings. As she contemplated her next move, she decided she wanted to start her own painting company because what was truly missing in her last job was creativity and freedom.

Before the sales job, she had worked as painter for five years for a government contractor, so she had the skills needed to start her own company. And now she is very happy painting as a subcontractor and has more freedom and creativity than she has ever had.

Doing a **JOB AUTOPSY** will give you a deep understanding about what you love and what you don't enjoy when it comes to work. Think of yourself as a private detective looking for clues from your past that you will use to greatly improve your future.

A **JOB AUTOPSY** can help you determine if implementing some changes at your current job would be enough to make your job more satisfying (at least for the time being) while you do this exploratory work.

You can make your current job more bearable and satisfying now while you look for another job.

MAYBE YOU JUST NEED SOME CAREER PATH RESUSCITATION (CPR)

Doing this deep work using the job autopsy exercises will help you figure out how you can breathe new life into your current job. For some people, making some changes at their current job will make things more bearable during this transition.

So today is the day that you are going to start taking back your power by gaining more satisfaction from your current job which is going to require two things on your part:

1. Purposeful action

2. Setting your intention

Beverly Kaye and Sharon Jordan-Evans, authors of "Love it, Don't Leave It: 26 Ways to Get What You Want at Work," say:

> *"Too often we leave for greener pastures elsewhere only to find Astroturf."*

You know my story now of how I had been a serial job-hopper for many years. I wanted to try new things and quite frankly, I think I liked the *chase* more than I liked the actual jobs I was chasing. However, the reality is I didn't know whether I liked a job until I actually tried it out.

Experience is what helped me figure things out.

Trying new jobs and experiences is a great way to gain more clarity. We get into trouble when we aren't happy at a job and we choose to stay there for years suffering needlessly.

Being a paralegal was my passion and career for many years and I loved it! I was a serial job hopper in the legal field because it was the best way I knew how to get a raise. And because I was a single mom living paycheck-to-paycheck, money for me was the driving factor.

In the late 1990s, I started feeling burnt out in the legal field; I had lost the passion I once had for my job and my job felt meaningless and stressful. I knew I wanted out but didn't know how to get out.

I didn't have any of the tools like the ones I'm sharing with you.

Many people change jobs in their chosen field only to find out it doesn't fix the deeper problem— that you've lost your passion and meaning in that field.

One of the things I learned about myself after leaving the legal field is that I am a people person, and I didn't enjoy long hours at the computer away from human connection. At the time, I was spending 80-90% of my day at the computer – no wonder I was so miserable!

What's interesting is that when I first began my career as a paralegal, I worked for a solo practitioner where I spent 60% of my day interviewing clients, doing new case intakes, interacting with clients, insurance adjustors, attorneys, court personnel, etc. I stayed at that job for over five years (which was a record for me). I loved so much about that job. So why did I leave the job that I loved at the small law firm?

MONEY

I went to the large law firms in Washington, D.C. because they paid more and offered better benefits, and that's when it happened:

CAREER CREEP

Marcus Buckingham, co-author of, *One Thing You Need to Know* defines Career Creep as:

"Following your initial success, one new responsibility is added, then another, then another, as your job slowly shifts beneath you, inching you further and further away from your strengths' path until finally, you wake up one morning and realize that the majority of your new job bores you, leaves you unfulfilled, frustrates you, drains you, or all of the above."

Sound familiar?

Over a period of several years, I started doing less and less of what I loved (interacting and engaging with people; legal writing and research, etc.) and more and more of what I didn't love (working on a computer, filing papers, making copies). Essentially, I traded in what I LOVED for more MONEY.

This is how I lost meaning: by following the money and making all my decisions based on this one factor.

When I got fired from the law firm at the end of my 17-year career, I can honestly say I was spending 95% of my day doing tasks I didn't like.

Because I was a struggling single parent of three trying to make ends meet, I couldn't just ditch my job because I wasn't happy. I had responsibilities and obligations. I felt trapped. I wanted more than anything to wave a magic wand and NOT to have to go to that dreaded job and still be able to take care of my family. I didn't quit because I didn't know what else to do to make money, so I settled for job misery.

I settled because I felt stuck; it felt like
I had NO other options at the time.

Do you feel stuck or like you're settling, and you know there is something more out there for you?

You're not alone.

Years ago, the Gallup organization began measuring the level of commitment employees felt toward their job and their employer. The numbers were startlingly low. Their research found that about one out of every five employees nationwide were truly excited about the work they were doing.

Over the years, these number have increased to an alarmingly high level. 80-90% of people say they are NOT happy at work.

Why have we settled for job misery?

PAUL STOLTZ GIVES US INSIGHT

Years ago, Oprah had a guest on her show that opened my eyes to what was happening in my life. His name was Paul Stoltz, author of *The Adversity Quotient*. According to Stolz, a person's Adversity Quotient (AQ) is the measure of *"one's ability to handle adversity."* Stolz says that if you don't have a high AQ, then you become easily overwhelmed and emotional, then pull back and stop trying.

In his book, Stolz states that people typically fall into one of three groups: *Quitters, Campers,* and *Climbers.*

1. **Quitters** are those people who have resigned from life and given up completely; they are bitter, depressed, and resentful. Campers are pretty much "retired Climbers" which means that they don't strive too hard or sacrifice as much as they once did.

2. **Campers** are only living 50% (or less) of their potential. They aren't really happy, and they aren't too miserable either.

They've found a tolerable place in life to "camp out" because on their way up the mountain they got tired and stopped.

3. Last, but not least, are the **Climbers**. Climbers are dedicated to constantly setting goals and achieving them. They make things happen, don't give up, learn from their mistakes, and move on. They are committed to a lifelong ascent up the mountain.

So, which one are YOU?

Quitters are at the bottom of the mountain, Campers are in the middle, and the Climbers are at the top.

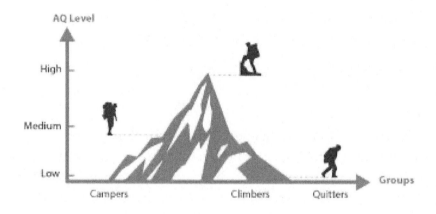

If you're reading this book, you're probably not a quitter. However, if you've stayed in a job you hate or that is unfulfilling for years, you might be a Camper.

Campers are living up to 50% of their potential. They don't have enough pain to change things, so they subconsciously camp out and accept the status quo.

We just suck it up and stay in a job we hate because it's a lot of work, energy, time, and risk to change it.

If you think you're in the Camper group, just know that you can decide right now to leave your campground (the status quo) and start climbing up the mountain.

IT ONLY TOOK ALEX ONE YEAR TO REALIZE HE WAS CAMPING

I recently hired one of my clients, 23-year-old Alex. He is a published author who has made almost $10,000 on the backend of his book, has started a successful podcast with over 5,000 subscribers, graduated from a top-tier college, and took a 6-figure job as a programmer/coder.

I happened to mention to him that I was looking for a project manager for my Bestselling Author business and he called me one day to see if I was still looking for help. I figured one of his classmates or friends needed a job. I was surprised to find out it was him.

I asked why he wanted to work for me when he had a successful 6-figure job at a big IT company, and he replied:

> *"This job was a great opportunity for me. But there is no way I'm going to sit in a cubicle for the rest of my life coding. I'm quitting my job to go travel the world."*

I was in shock. It took me 17 years and getting fired to finally have the courage to go follow my dreams and here is this 23-year-old "kid" who figured it out in one year! Very inspiring.

Alex is a smart young adult who saved up a year's salary to go follow his dreams. He also lined up a few consulting gigs (like working for me) to supplement his income as he travels. He plans to visit several states and countries. He's even subleased his apartment for six months and then will let it go completely.

I'm proud of Alex for following his dreams and exploring the world. That's the best way to learn about who you are and what makes you happy.

You can't replace experience with reading about experiences. You have to go out and do it and then step back, assess the situation, and make the necessary shifts.

20 QUESTIONS THAT CAN CHANGE YOUR LIFE

To figure out what you want (and don't want) in your work and your life, answer these 20 questions to gain more clarity about your current job (and you can use it for past jobs as well).

Remember, it's important to know
your history so you don't REPEAT IT.

Take the time to invest in yourself and answer ALL of the following questions.

You're worth it!

Get out your notebook and start answering the questions for your current job to start with and then you can go back later and do this for all of your jobs. Of course, if you're like me, you might need a second notebook!

Job Autopsy Questions

1. Are you a people person or a project person? Which role do you play in your current job? Which do you prefer?

2. What duties (tasks) do you dislike and would give them to someone else if you could? What percentage of your day do you spend doing these things?

3. What duties (tasks) are you passionate about at work? What percentage of your day is spent doing these things?

4. Of all the jobs you've had in your life, which one did you love the most, and why?

5. If there was one change you could make at your current job to make you stay, what would that be and why?

6. What would your ideal/perfect workday look like? Provide details for hours, location, pay, tasks, vacation time, etc.

7. Do you feel respected at work?

8. Do you receive praise and recognition at work?

9. Do you like the hours of your job?

10. Do you like the location where you work?

11. What kind of expectations did you have when you first took this job?

12. What has been your biggest disappointment?

13. Do you like and respect your boss, or do you work for a jerk?

14. Do you have fun at your job?

15. Do you like your co-workers?

16. Are there any new skills you could learn that would improve your job? If so, what are they?

17. Do you think you should be making more money for what you do?

18. Is there room for advancement in your current position?

19. Is your work life and home life in balance? If not, what exactly is out of balance?

20. What would you miss the most if you quit your job?

By taking the time to answer these questions, you have gained more insight as to what the exact source of your unhappiness at work is.

This is important because it helps you to visually see where you went off course. Remember that *Career Creep* is a very slow, insidious process and most people don't even notice it happening until they are completely miserable.

I suggest answering the above questions for ALL of your past jobs as well as your current job as this will help you begin to see patterns and clues.

The next step is to assess your answers to the 20 questions because this will lead to deeper clarity.

THE CLUES ARE HIDDEN IN YOUR ANSWERS

People person vs. project person. The solution to this is pretty obvious. If you're a people person spending 90% of your day working at a computer, doing research, writing or working on big projects, you are going to be miserable at work, and vice versa. Is there a way to change this? Can you speak to your boss about changing some of your duties? Maybe you could make a lateral move within the company. Explore your options.

Duties you dislike. What percentage of your day is spent doing things you dislike? According to author Marcus Buckingham, "...successful people spend 75% or more doing what they like to do." So, if 75% or more of your day is spent doing what you don't like, you are not going to be happy or successful in the long-term. Determine if some of these tasks you dislike can be delegated to others within your department. There is a saying that there is no dirty work. This just means that there is always someone who loves to do what you hate doing and vice versa. Again, this requires talking to your boss and seeing if some of the tasks you dislike can be reassigned and delegated to others who actually like them.

Duties that you are passionate about at work. If you're not spending at least 75% of your day doing what you love, then you will feel emotionally, mentally, and spiritually drained at the end of the day. The challenge is to figure out how to do more of what you love at work. Maybe you can switch responsibilities with another employee?

Favorite Job. Was it your favorite job because you loved your boss, you had great co-workers, or because you truly loved the tasks you spent the majority of your time doing? Sometimes it's been so long that we've forgotten what once made us jump out of bed in the morning.

Changing One Thing at Work. What is the one thing you would change at work that would make you stay? Is it the pay, the hours, the boss, the team you work with? Is there a way to alter this one thing? If you don't like the location, perhaps you can transfer to another city or state. If you don't like the hours, maybe you could job share or work from home. If you don't like the salary, perhaps you can ask for a raise or a different position. If you are afraid to ask for what you want, then there is no possibility of ever getting it.

Your Perfect Workday. Writing out the details of your perfect day will give you clues to your heart's desire. The key is to let your imagination run wild and not modify what comes to your mind during this exercise. We all have that practical and realistic voice inside of our heads that will try to squelch anything that seems too far removed from our current situation. I want you to ignore that voice for this exercise. THINK ABOUT THIS: You can be *practical* or *magical,* but you can't be both for this exercise. Choose to be magical during this exercise and let your imagination run wild.

Respect. We don't usually pay any attention to it if we are getting it, however, if we're not getting respect, then we don't feel valued or important. Feeling respected is a basic human need we all have. If you don't feel respected at work, try brainstorming ways that might make you feel more valued. Talking to your boss is the first step in asking for what you need.

Praise and recognition. Another need we all share is a need for recognition. To deny this need is to deny your humanity. In my sales job years ago, the company I worked for recognized the top sales representatives at an annual awards banquet. Even though some people probably won't admit it, I think everyone appreciates the kudos and recognition we receive from the company we work for and from management. If you aren't getting the praise you need at work, you could make suggestions for contests and achievement awards. Again, don't be afraid to ask for what you want. Stop settling. You will never be content with less.

Job Hours. Some hours may seem set in stone, but often if we let our boss know we're not happy with them, we find out they're not set in stone. My best friend works four 10-hour days instead of five eight-hour days. Both my brother and my daughter-in-law work from home five days a week and they love it. When I was working in my sales job 20-25 hours per week, making six figures, I had lots of down time, which gave me the freedom to work on some of my passions – public speaking, teaching, writing, building an online business (that's why I labeled my outside sales job as my **FREEDOM JOB**). There are lots of creative ways to change your hours. The trick is to be able to explain to your employer how it will benefit them as well. Make it a win/win proposition.

Location. Sometimes there's not much you can do about the location unless the company has other locations that interest you. Research to see if there is another location that would suit you better. What would your ideal location be? Companies can save a lot of money by not having the overhead of office space; therefore, many companies now allow employees to work from home.

Expectations. Life is full of expectations and life is full of disappointments. Is it possible you had some unrealistic expectations when you took this job? If so, what were they? Why did you have those expectations? Were you living in fantasy land? By acknowledging what your expectations were, you can see where you have been let down. You may have to do a reset when it comes to these inaccurate expectations.

Biggest disappointment. Maybe you worked long and hard on a big project only to have your boss take all the credit. Yes, disappointments are part of life, but if we don't communicate our feelings to the person involved, we may be carrying around a lot of repressed *resentments*. Those resentments may be playing a big part in why you want to quit your job. We need to clean up this area, so we can be sure the exact reasons we want (or don't want) to quit our jobs. In a marriage, there are lots of disappointments, but it doesn't always mean divorce. Explore this area carefully and be honest with yourself.

Working for a Jerk. You may not like this advice, but I'm going to say it anyway – it's better for your peace of mind to *accept* that you work for a jerk than to think you can change a jerk. 99.9% of the time you CANNOT change jerks, however, you can change how you interact with them. *How do you do this*? Staying under the radar is one way; having minimal contact with that person is another. Get advice from others who seem to know how to handle this person. Tell the jerk how you feel about their behavior and ask for what you need. You could also try focusing on the jerks' good qualities. *What*? You say they have no good qualities. You may have to search far and wide, but I can assure you they have at least one redeeming quality. Don't quit your job because of a jerk. Jerks come and go – hopefully they'll move on. I almost quit my 6-figure sales job once because the company hired a "jerk" manager that I despised. I was talking to my sales team leader and he gave me great advice – *"Jerks come and go, just wait it out and he'll be gone before you know it."* So, I waited, and within six months, he was gone. Hallelujah! I kept my 6-figure cushy sales job.

Fun Factor. Is FUN missing from your work? Some types of work just don't seem to be much fun, but I think you can always inject some fun into the workplace if you try. I've worked at many law firms that had softball teams, Friday happy hours, and summer picnics on private islands. Initiate some of these activities if you like. When I was working for a law firm in DC, one of best days I remember was during the Christmas holidays when I brought homemade rum balls to the office. Everyone who ate the rum balls got quite a buzz – all before lunch! Food and drink always makes people lighten up; so do office toys like silly putty, character slippers, stress balls, yo-yos, and more. Get Creative!

Co-Workers. Sometimes people act one way at work and are completely different away from work (hopefully for the better). At least make an attempt to get to know your co-workers in other settings and environments; this may transform your relationship with them.

New Skills. Wouldn't it be a shame to get passed over for a promotion because you lacked a simple certification or training? This happens in a lot of companies. It may require time and effort on your part. It will not only make you more marketable in the future, but it can often get you more money. Years ago, a friend of mine was making $30,000 less than the going rate for her position in the Human Resources Department of a grocery store chain because she didn't have her Master's degree. One day, she made the decision to go back to school part-time and get her Master's degree. It took her five years, but now she is making six figures. *What new skills can you learn at work?* When I worked for law firms, I took every free training course they offered, even if I wasn't currently using those specific skills or software in my job. I always knew down the road it would make me more marketable, would look great on my resume', and I might need those skills one day when I was finally able to quit my job. Remember, you may not always need these new skills right now, but if your company is paying for the training, I think it's worth investing your time to learn these new skills. SKILLS PAY THE BILLS!

Show me the Money. Of course, we all want to make more money, but sometimes we reach the top of the pay scale for a position. One of the many reasons I left the legal field was that I hit the top of the pay scale and there was nowhere else to go, except for the usual 2-3% annual salary increase. If you haven't reached the top, then it's time for you to ask for a raise. Before you do, make sure you come up with a valid list of reasons why you deserve a raise. Then ask.

Advancement. As a paralegal, I didn't have many options for traveling up the corporate ladder and getting a promotion unless I wanted to go back to school and get my law degree. Sometimes we can make lateral moves within the company.

Work and Home Life Balance. If your work life and home life are out of synch, it seems easy to blame it on your *big bad employer* who makes you work all those long hours for little pay. However, you agreed to it. Maybe it filled a void in your life, but now it is having negative consequences on you, your family, and maybe even your health. Implement new boundaries about what you are NOT willing to tolerate and get your life back in balance.

What would you miss if you didn't have your job? If you said "Nothing," then it's pretty clear that you absolutely need to quit your job. Most of us, however, can list a few things or people we would miss if we left. Making this list will help you gain perspective. Sometimes we think we want to quit our jobs when in reality, we just want to alter them a bit.

So how do you know when it's time to leave your job? Here are a few clues it's time to leave:

Now that you've taken the time to do this transformative work and gain insight, you should have a sense of where you've been and how you ended up in your current job.

You may have discovered that by making some changes, you can tolerate your current job for a while, and create something you are passionate about on the side (a side hustle). Often, we can create something new on the side to get in a good financial place so we can quit our jobs permanently and do what we love!

Just know that YOU are responsible for your own workplace satisfaction, NOT your employer. To believe that your workplace is solely responsible for your happiness is to give your power away to your employer.

We take our power back when we take action and ask for what we need. If we don't get it, that's okay because then we can make a decision to leave or to stay. We are not victims unless we give our employers all our power and stay stuck in a job we hate for the rest of our lives.

Congratulations on doing the deep work! You dug deep into your job history and you have a better sense now of what is making you happy or unhappy when it comes to work.

Next, in Chapter 3, we are going soul searching instead of job searching...

Chapter 3 – More Soul Searching, Less Job Searching

> *"A person doesn't know what he can do unless he tries.*
> *Trying things is the answer to finding your talent."*
> *~Howard Finster*
> *(Artist, who started painting at age 59)*

The truth is most of us would rather go *job searching* than *soul searching*.

Why?

Because it's easier to skip soul searching and just go find another job; this way we don't have to ask ourselves the really hard questions like…

- What brings me alive?
- What does my soul want to do?
- What brings me joy?
- What needs to die so my dreams can live?

It is easier to live a *default* life than an *intentional* life.

After I left the law firm, I didn't know what I was going to do, but thankfully I was 100% certain I didn't want another job that left me feeling empty and unfulfilled.

Coming from the fast-paced legal environment, I was not accustomed to having downtime and I certainly didn't have time for soul searching. I had become comfortable with job misery. Intuitively, I knew I needed downtime to create my dream life, but I also felt guilty and stressed out for having so much free time when everyone in my life did not.

MEDITATION NOT MEDICATION

A couple of months after leaving the law firm, I experienced my first panic attack. I thought I was having a heart attack, so I asked a friend to take me to the emergency room. After extensive testing and an EKG, they determined that my heart was fine.

The doctor asked me if I had any stress in my life, to which I replied, *"No, I don't have any stress, everything is fine."*

I suppose because "high stress" was the norm in my life at the time, I didn't realize that all the changes were causing more stress.

THE MORE THE DOCTOR INQUIRED ABOUT MY LIFE, HERE'S WHAT HE DISCOVERED:

- I was fired from my job at the law firm.
- I had no financial resources except a few months' severance pay.
- My ex-husband refused to pay child support, and I was constantly fighting with him to help me pay the bills and take care of the kids.
- My older brother and best friend was diagnosed with AIDS and was dying.
- The house I was renting was going to be sold, and I didn't have another place to move to since I had no job and no money in the bank.
- I didn't know what I was going to do with my life.

The doctor determined that I did indeed have a lot of stress in my life, and he wanted me to see a psychiatrist. I had never been to a psychiatrist, so I took his advice and went to see one.

The psychiatrist he sent me to gave me a bad feeling right away. After a short conversation, he told me I was at high risk for suicide and that I needed to be on anti-depression medications right away.

I knew immediately this was not true.

I wasn't depressed, and I had never once thought about suicide. I realized he didn't know me, and he didn't know what he was talking about regardless of his degree and credentials on the wall in his office. Thankfully, I listened to my intuition and left his office as quickly as I could.

LISTEN TO YOUR OWN INTUITION

Doctors are not Gods. Unfortunately, many people treat them like they are. They are human beings with degrees and specialized training, but they don't have all the answers. If your gut is telling you something different, seek a second opinion.

Since I was a child, I have hated medications. I remember being five years old and my mother would try to give me over-the-counter medicine and I refused to take it. I felt that medicine was poison to my body. So when the doctor told me I needed to take this medicine (or I might die), I knew that was NOT what I needed.

I'm not suggesting or telling you to NOT take medicine you have been prescribed. However, for me, it was not the right option as I was not depressed or suicidal.

During the appointment, I even asked the psychiatrist what other options there were to medication and he said, "*There are none.*"

I left his office and never returned. My instincts told me there was another option, so I headed to the bookstore to see what I could find.

I discovered a book called "Wherever You Go, There You Are" by Jon Kabat-Zinn which was about *meditation*. After doing some research, I discovered that there were many studies done about the physiological benefits of meditation including reducing anxiety and stress.

I DECIDED TO TRY MEDITATION INSTEAD OF MEDICATION

Meditation didn't work instantly, as I still was having panic attacks, but slowly over the next year, it worked. I never had another panic attack again.

It was challenging to get my mind to slow down and stop worrying and obsessing about the future. I started with two minutes a day and worked my way up to 20 minutes a day. As I began to practice meditation daily, my life changed drastically. I reconnected with my intuition and I started making more positive and informed choices from that place.

Positive choices like this led me to Unity Church which shifted my mindset and led me on a new spiritual path. I discovered the book "A Course in Miracles," which changed my life, and I began studying every self-help book I could get my hands on.

I also sought out a counselor (a Licensed Clinical Social Worker) to help me work on issues I had from my past. I loved therapy because it gave me so many new tools to use in my life that I did not have before. My therapist helped me remove the blinders and see things I wasn't aware of.

As I began to increase my faith, I took a 12-week class at Unity called the 4T Prosperity Course. During those 12 weeks, I had several financial windfalls come to me. I won't go into all the details, but I was beginning to have more faith and less worry.

I was still job-searching because it made me feel better studying the help wanted ads and submitting resumes, but the reality was that soul-searching was what I needed the most.

SOMETIMES WHEN WE'RE NOT SURE OF WHERE TO GO, WE HAVE TO GO BACKWARDS AND LOOK FOR CLUES

When I was a little girl, I loved to put on neighborhood shows. I would organize the *"entertainment"* which consisted of songs, skits, dances, and puppet shows. I loved being the center of attention. Ironically, the older I got, the more self-conscious I became until one day I woke up and I was the opposite of the center of attention; I was more like a wallflower. I kept to myself and only spoke to others if I was spoken to. It took me many years to get back in touch with this lost part of myself.

The longer we stay in a job or career we hate, the more removed we are from our innate joy, passion, and dreams until we can't even remember what they are. We literally have dream amnesia. Sometimes all we know is, *"I'm just not happy"* and *"There must be more to life than this."*

We may have material objects, we may even have cash, but on the inside is an empty feeling that whispers *there must be something more*.

Finding out exactly what that *something more* is the work we all must do if we are in a job that does not fulfill us. Finding what *you* need to feel fulfilled *is* work only you can do. The answers are inside of you.

Marcus Buckingham, author of the book "One Thing You Need to Know," says:

"Some people will tell you that it doesn't matter if you like your work; you just have to be good at it. Question this advice. You may well be good at some activities you don't enjoy, but your ENJOYMENT is the fuel you require to keep practicing the activity. Lacking this enjoyment, your performance will likely plateau."

Years ago, I met a man named Burt who mentored others in becoming professional speakers. Burt shared a personal story with me about how he had been a real estate guru for years earning *big dollars* in the real estate business. Thankfully, he realized one day that what he was really making was *empty dollars* because the real estate business did not *fulfill* him. Changing people's lives through speaking and being able to reach large groups of people is what Burt truly craved in his life. It gave his life meaning, and he decided that was more important to him than all the *empty dollars* in the world!

Once you are fully grounded in who you are – physically, emotionally, spiritually, and mentally – this knowingness will lead you to trust in your intuition and to follow your heart.

DON'T LISTEN TO THE WELL-MEANING ADVICE OF OTHERS

An ex-boyfriend of mine once asked me why I wanted to leave my *secure* job at the law firm to start my online business when I was already making *good money* with great benefits and was living a pretty comfortable life (according to him). He said I was living a life that most people only "dreamed about."

At first, I felt guilty for wanting something more and for not following the crowd. I thought to myself, "Maybe he's right, maybe I'm a bad person for wanting more. Maybe I should be happy with what I have when so many people have so much less than me."

Thankfully, I realized pretty quickly that my thinking was misguided.

OUR DESIRE FOR APPROVAL IS THE PATH AWAY FROM WHAT OUR SOUL CRAVES

When people we care about question something we are doing and that challenges the status quo, we pull back from our true desires because we want to fit in, and we have a deep need for their approval. Our survival instincts (our primitive brain) tells us we need that approval, or we will die. **This is NOT true.**

If you don't get approval from those closest to you, I can assure you that you won't die. It might feel like it though because you respect their opinions and it's scary to leave the "crowd," but the alternative is to lead a life of quiet desperation, and I don't think that's what you want, or you wouldn't be reading this book. It isn't easy to go against what other people think is the right path for you, but the truth is, only your soul knows what the right path is for you.

LISTENING TO WHAT YOUR SOUL AND HEART WANTS WON'T ALWAYS BE THE POPULAR CHOICE

You have to be okay with not getting acceptance and approval from those closest to you. Keep your dreams to yourself and don't share them with others because many times those voices and opinions will deter you from making positive changes and taking a new path.

In her bestselling book, "The Artist's Way," by Julia Cameron, she talks about *blocked friends* and *poisonous playmates.*

Blocked friends and poisonous playmates don't want us to change, to put ourselves first, to set aside time for play, daydream and do creative work or even to nurture ourselves. They want you to choose them and not yourself.

We often play nice and don't want to hurt other people's feelings which is why so many people default to giving their time and attention to others instead of themselves.

If you want to create a life you don't want to run away from, it's critical you become vigilant about where your time and energy goes, and also with whom you share your dreams and ideas.

Here are a few guidelines about sharing your dreams and ideas:

- Make sure your friend or family member is nurturing and not toxic. No poisonous playmates here.

- Make sure your friend or family member is supportive of you and not jealous. No green-eyed monsters allowed.

- Make sure your friend is not a blocked creative and is pursuing their own dreams and goals. No blocked creatives here.

- Make sure your friend or family member is not a drama llama. You need peace, not drama, to create your dream life.

Surround yourself with supportive people who want your highest good and are your biggest fans. Not everyone in your life will be that support system that you need, so make sure to protect your dreams and ideas from the non-supportive people.

Our small self wants to keep the status quo and not make waves. Of course, I didn't want to upset anyone when I left my legal job, but I had to do what was best for me.

I could have stayed in my legal job for the rest of my life and "settled" for a mediocre life that was unfulfilling, uninspiring, and unbearable; but deep down something was reassuring me that I deserved to be happy. At the end of the day, it didn't matter what other people thought I should be doing. What mattered is how I felt about what I was doing.

WHY IT'S BETTER TO WOBBLE THAN SETTLE

In the movie *The Wizard of Oz*, it took a tornado and an upside-down house to get Dorothy on the yellow brick road and back to her true home. When we are thousands of miles off our authentic path, sometimes it takes an act of God to wake us up from our deep sleep.

Getting fired from my job at the law firm felt like a life-changing tornado had entered my life, but it actually turned out to be exactly what I needed as it pushed me in the direction of my dreams. The day finally came when my need for security was overpowered by my desire for having a life on my own terms. The cost of that goal was "uncertainty."

We don't just snap our figures and have it all figured it. It's a process that takes time and I find most of the time we stumble into clarity.

Being open to learning and committed to growing is the key to finding that clarity in your life.

> *"Being yourself is not remaining where you are or being satisfied with what you are. It is the point of departure."*
> *–Sydney J. Harris*

There is something deep inside of you that feeds your soul. *Do you know what it is?*

I think a part of us knows what feeds our souls, but unfortunately, we've either ignored it, abandoned it, or simply forgotten whatever "*it*" is by making up excuses about how impractical, self-indulging or childish it would be to follow "it."

This is flawed thinking.

What Brings You Alive?

During one of our weekly sessions, my therapist said, "I don't know what it is Michelle, but when you were talking about writing, teaching, and your online business…it was like you were high on life."

I was on an adrenaline high because those topics (writing, speaking, my online business and creativity) are what feeds my soul. I get very excited and animated when I talk about these subjects. Her comment made me feel good because I knew how many years I didn't know what fed my soul and how far I traveled to get to this knowing place.

If you don't know what it is that feeds your soul, some of the exercises in this book will point you to new directions to explore. Think of it as a trip down the yellow brick road that will eventually lead you back home!

In order to discover what feeds your soul, it is important to:

- Create a written mission statement to help clarify your goals.
- Know your strengths.
- Recognize your demons.

- Be honest about what you enjoy doing and especially what you DON'T enjoy doing.
- Have a purpose for what you will be doing.

A MISSION STATEMENT WILL HELP YOU LEARN TO SAY NO

A mission statement is a written statement of your purpose and reason for being.

I highly recommend the book, "The Path: Creating Your Mission Statement for Work and for Life" written by Laurie Beth Jones. Years ago, I taught a class at Unity, and it helped me and my students get more clarity in our lives.

Laurie Beth Jones has created a very easy formula for writing your mission statement. First, she suggests that you choose three verbs that excite you because every mission must have "action"; then, choose your core values (what you stand for) and the group or cause, which most moves you (who you came here to help). A+B+C=D

I wrote the following mission statement years before I left my job at the law firm and long before I was following my dreams:

"My mission is to inspire, educate and
motivate others to believe in themselves
and to find their true purpose in life."

Once I had a written mission statement, new "opportunities" came along to test me to see if I was focused and committed. Reading and re-reading my mission statement helped me to say NO when new opportunities came along that didn't move me closer to my mission.

Having your own written mission statement will get you more focused so you're not living a life of default but living a life of design.

If you are bored, restless, and hate your job, these are all signs that you are **NOT** living your life on purpose. As I said, first you must discover who *you* are before *you* get the answer to what your purpose is.

TREASURE MAP EXERCISE: SOUL SEARCHING

STEP 1: Make a list of your 10 favorite activities that bring you the most JOY (enJOYment). (*Examples*: Sitting at the Ocean; Writing; Decorating; Baking; Organizing; Storytelling; Burning Candles; Running; Painting). If you get stuck, think about activities you engage in where you lose all sense of time. *Even if you haven't done these activities for a while (months or years), write them down. *Don't think about how to make money with these activities, just write 10 things that bring you JOY.

"It is in his pleasure that a man really lives...
It is from his leisure that he constructs the true fabric of self."
~Agnes Repplier, an American Essayist

STEP 2: Now, choose two of these JOYful activities you would like to earn money doing.

For example, I love sitting at the ocean and I love writing. Years ago, I was cleaning out my closet when I stumbled upon some old journals written during various vacations to the beach when my kids were younger. I began reading them and thought to myself, *"This writing is really good. I can't believe I wrote this. My writing is so different (better...deeper...more alive) when I'm at the ocean than when I'm at home."*

Then, at that exact moment in time, I turned the TV on to "Good Morning America" and saw William Haley being interviewed about his father, Alex Haley. Alex Haley wrote the bestselling book *Roots* that sold over one million copies in the first year and was turned into a miniseries that was watched by an astonishing 130 million people. *Roots* also won both the Pulitzer Prize and the National Book Award. In the interview, William Haley was sharing that his father said he did his best writing when he was near the water. Alex Haley would often hop on board a freight or cargo ship and take long trips to do his writing. The crux of the story was that whenever his dad needed to write he made sure he was near the water because it got his creative juices flowing.

After seeing this interview, I had an "aha" moment. I decided to offer a class called "Ocean Writing" and through a series of synchronistic events and listening to my heart OceanWriting.com was born!

I combined my two passions – "writing" and "being at the ocean" – and created a successful writers' program that I teach annually. Pretty cool that I created a way to get paid to sit at the ocean, huh?

Now that I've given you an example of how to get your creative juices going, what two Joys from your list above can you combine to come up with a unique business?

During one of my workshops, I had a woman in my class who combined the stock market with horoscopes and created several business ideas like a board game based on the financial tendencies of particular horoscope signs. Brilliant!

The point is to think outside the box.

If you want to find work that feels like PLAY, you do have to PLAY.

STEP 3: List two or three combinations of things that bring you JOY from your list above to come up with a unique business. (REMEMBER: Have FUN with these exercises. Play with your imagination and give yourself the gift of exploring without any commitment).

Let me give you an example of a real business that combines two unrelated passions…

I was watching "Cupcake Wars" when I saw two young entrepreneurs who started a bakery in Las Vegas called, "**Showboy Bake Shop**" where they combined their love of show business and good cake!

The owners, Stephen Lowry and Jared Sullivan's, had a background in stage, film and design. They also both loved baking.

Can you see how powerful it is to take two of your passions and come up with a unique business.

STEP 4: List your favorite combination of these two activities that can be a unique business.

STEP 5: Pick your favorite way of providing a service to others from the list above.

STEP 6: List 10 specific action steps you can do now to take this idea to implementation.

Remember: We are just imagining and playing to see what shows up—there are no right or wrong answers.

Nine Lives Game

You've probably heard that cats have nine lives. Perhaps that is why cats are so laid back and calm. They know when their current life ends, they're coming back again. For a moment, let's pretend that you have nine lives, too.

STEP 1: If you had nine lives and could be nine different people—what would you be? Examples: Writer, Gourmet Chef, Professor, Race Car Driver, Athlete, Mayor, Chocolatier. Don't use your logical mind; use your creative mind and give yourself permission to dream!

Barbara Sher, author of "I Could Do Anything if I Only Knew What It Was" (excellent book that I highly recommend) says we've been trained to *believe that we only get one choice in our lives.* This isn't true at all. We have an endless number of choices; so, what we really need to *learn is how to manage these choices.*

Once you have chosen your nine lives, then answer the questions below which will help you manage your choices better. The point is, we can't do everything all at once, but if we manage our time better, we can do a lot more than we are doing right now.

STEP 2: Review your list, then answer these questions:

- Which of the nine lives above can you focus on this year?
- When that one is complete, which one can you focus on next year?
- Which of the nine lives can you focus on for 30 minutes to an hour each day?
- Which one can you do on occasion?

STEP 3: Make a 3-year JOY plan. Which JOYs can you focus on each year?

Strengths And Talents Finder

Often, when we are good at something – when it comes natural to us and doesn't require effort – we don't think of it as our strength because we take it for granted. Sometimes, we mistakenly believe that everyone can do this particular skill.

Writing has been one of those skills that I took for granted for a long time. I thought everyone could write and that everyone enjoyed writing. I found out that was not true.

The exercise below is a skill assessment to put your strengths and talents on paper so you can look at them more objectively. Usually people see traits in us that we don't see in ourselves.

Many years ago, I joined Toastmasters to overcome my fear of public speaking. Other members would tell me after I gave a speech how "great" my talk was and how "confident" I was when I spoke.

At the time, I had a tremendous amount of fear and couldn't understand what these people were talking about. In fact, I thought they were all crazy! They were seeing something in me that I wasn't able to see in myself.

Sometimes we are blind to our own talents. That's why we need other people to help us see our blind spots.

STEP 1: Write five skills you use in your current job that you like:

STEP 2: Write five skills people say you are good at:

STEP 3: Write two skills you enJOY the most from both of the above lists:

STEP 4: List 10 businesses you could start using these two skills:

Richard Bode, author of *Beachcombing at Miramar* says:

It astounds me when I think of the courage it takes to live, to behave as we want to behave, to be who we want to be. The world is filled with those who would keep us from singing the songs we want to sing, painting the pictures we want to paint, skimming the stones we want to skim. Some are bosses, some are officials of oppressive regimes – and some are our mothers, fathers, teachers, husbands, or wives, who for whatever reasons, try to stifle the life force that makes us who we are. But we have this choice: We can empower them, or we can empower ourselves.

That is a powerful statement. Bode was a middle-aged man who left an unhappy marriage and a long career with a NY public relations agency giving up a chance to become a millionaire in order to live a more authentic life. Although when others mentioned to Bode how courageous they felt he was by leaving his highly successful job, Bode says, *"I can no more say I acted with courage when I quit that job than I can say a man who is suffocating acts with courage when he tries to breathe."*

Bode quit his job, sold his belongings, placed his cash in a shoe box, and became a "beachcomber" to seek the truth about his life – that was his dream. He wrote two books about what he discovered through this process, which I absolutely love! Both books are inspiring and motivating – which we all need daily doses of.

Quitting Your Job and Following Your Dreams is not an easy path – although others may see it that way. Bode says that many people think that being a beachcomber is "the easiest job in the world." He disagrees and explains in his book that being a beachcomber is a demanding job that calls for *discipline* and *zeal*.

NEWS ALERT! So does the path you have ventured onto.

Now it's time to look at our shadow side that may be sabotaging our dreams…

MAKE FRIENDS WITH YOUR DEMONS OR ELSE

Pia Melody, author of *Facing Codependence* says you have to, "Hug your demons or they will bite you in the ass."

If you don't embrace what is dysfunctional in you, then you are doomed to repeat it and stay in the past. Notice she didn't say "change," she said "embrace." There is a big difference.

What demons have you been ignoring that are holding you back from your dreams?

In her book, "The Dark Side of the Light Chasers," author, Debbie Ford explains how important it is to our personal growth to "unmask those aspects of ourselves, which destroys our relationships, kills our spirit and keeps us from fulfilling our dreams."

Carl Jung, noted psychologist, said the shadow is those parts of ourselves we try to hide and deny.

"What we don't own, owns us."

So, what are some common shadows we try to hide, deny, or repress?

- Fear
- Greed
- Ugliness
- Impatience
- Being Manipulative
- Being Disorganized
- Being Judgmental
- Anger
- Emotional problems
- Laziness
- Selfishness

In our wholeness, we possess both sides of each trait which means that you are at times both strong and weak; patient and impatient; generous and greedy. When any of these traits are not balanced and in check, they can be blocks that prevent us from living our dreams.

> *Balancing our shadow selves by fully owning them*
> *will help clear the path to your dreams.*

If you do not feel worthy of living your dreams, or having the desires of your heart, then there is an internal block that needs to be addressed. If this is an area in which you need help, then I recommend reading Debbie Ford's book mentioned above and spending time with a good therapist or counselor that can help you work on those parts of yourself that you are rejecting.

Nathaniel Brandon, author of many amazing books on self-esteem, says:

> *"Productive achievement is a consequence and an*
> *expression of healthy self-esteem, not its cause..."*

In order to self-realize your dreams, it's important to feel good about who you are because when you do, your *daily behaviors* will be in line with those feelings.

Your daily behaviors either contribute or take away from your goals and dreams.

Write It Down If You Expect It To Ever Happen

Once you begin to get clarity about your future dreams and aspirations, it is imperative that you write them down. Henriette Anne Klauser, author of "Write it Down, Make it Happen," says:

> *"Writing down your dreams and aspirations is like*
> *hanging up a sign that says, 'Open for Business.'"*

We have lots of thoughts running through our minds daily. According to the National Science Foundation, the average person thinks an average of 1,000 thoughts per hour and has approximately 12,000 thoughts per day. Some statistics are even higher. The thoughts that are repeated are what mold and shape our lives.

This is extremely important.

The successful people in life choose the same thoughts daily, and those thoughts are positive, uplifting and constructive.

So not only do we have to become more aware of the thoughts we have every day, but when we want to create something new in our life, we need to send out a signal to the universe about our dreams – writing down your dreams and goals will begin the process of attracting the people and circumstances needed for you to achieve those dreams and goals.

"A Course in Miracles" says:

> *"The moment you set an intention,*
> *the Universe conspires to assist you."*

It is comforting to know you are not alone; you are being guided and supported. I strongly believe if you have the desire in your heart, then you also have the abilities and capabilities within you to make those desires a reality.

MY DESIRE TO MAKE 6 FIGURES DROVE ME

Working as an outside sales representative in an all-commission job selling hot tubs, I earned $60K the first year which was the "average" for salespeople in the company. Within 18 months of joining the company, however, I was able to double my income! Other sales reps in the company wanted to know my "secret" to making a six-figure income and doubling my income.

The secret is this: I *tracked* my income weekly. In the past, I used to keep careful *track* of my bills and guess what? My bills grew bigger and bigger. This time, I *tracked* my income in an Excel spreadsheet that I would print every time I had a sale. I had a yearly goal to make six figures, and within 18 months, I achieved that goal!

What you "focus" on grows. Just like plants need water to grow; your dreams need daily focus in order to grow, too.

ORGANIZING YOUR LIFE AND YOUR GOALS

In his book, "The 26-Hour Day" by Vince Panella, a time-management expert, the author advises that there is no such thing as time management until you write down where you are now in your life and where you want to be in six months. Do this for every area of your life such as:

- Health
- Finances
- Family
- Relationships
- Spirituality
- Travel
- Home
- Business

Then, transfer the information from your notes on to index cards that you read each morning when you wake up. The idea is that it puts your goals in the forefront of your mind each day and your to-do list is based on these written down goals. Without the goal-setting exercise, your to-do list is pretty much worthless.

I have done the exercises in his book and they work! After doing this for six months, I achieved many of the goals I wrote down on the note cards. Then, I reviewed the cards and created new ones for the next six months. My to-do list is based on my goals and that is what moves me closer and closer to reaching my goals every day. I do this every six months.

Make your TO-DO list based on your goals.

HOW CATTLE RANCHERS MOVE CATTLE

I recently heard a story about a cattle rancher who had to move large herds of cattle from one location to the next. This was before they had fences, so there was nothing to contain the cattle. He said that the cattle would go way off course so to bring them back, they would tie a donkey's leg to the leg of the cattle. The cattle would try to break free from the donkey by jerking around. Every time the cattle did this, the donkey would move one step closer to home.

The donkey had something the cattle did not. **Intention**. The donkey wanted to return home because the donkey knew where the food and water was. So, one step at a time, the donkey would bring home cattle that were miles off course.

The moral of the story is that even if you take one small step per day towards your goals, at the end of the year, you will be 365 steps closer to achieving your goals. Nothing is impossible; only the limitations you create in your mind.

The other side of the coin is: It's NOT easy! If it was easy, everyone would be living their dreams instead of a 90% job dissatisfaction rate!

If you don't give up, you will achieve much more than if you never try.

STOP! Write down the goals you want to achieve in the next six months. Do not read anymore until you have your goals in black and white in front of you. Tell the Universe what you want! Include the following areas of where you are now and where you want to be:

- Health
- Finances
- Family
- Relationships
- Spirituality
- Travel
- Home
- Business

Your RAS Is Helping You Sort It All Out.

Did you know there is a system inside of you to help you attract what you want?

It would be impossible to sort and process all of the information available to us. The good news is that in your brain is something called a *Reticular Activating System* (RAS) to help you with all of this. An RAS is basically your own personal assistant who will bring "relevant" information to your attention. So, what is "relevant" information?

Let's say you are at a football stadium watching a game with thousands of other fans. There is a lot of noise from the fans cheering, people talking, announcements, and music. Suddenly, a voice over the loudspeaker calls your name and your attention is on full alert. Your RAS has been activated. Your RAS acts on your behalf as a filter to bring to your attention *relevant information* and helps you leave behind the rest. By repeating thoughts daily and writing down your dreams and goals, you are providing your RAS something to work with.

Several years ago, I was on a conference call with Jack Canfield, co-author of the *Chicken Soup for the Soul* series. During this call, Jack mentioned how important it was to be vividly clear about what you wanted and to write it down because he said this is what *"PRO-GRAMS YOUR UNCONSCIOUS."*

Let's say you have a goal along with an affirmation that says, "I want to own a Lexus." Since the reality is that you don't currently own a Lexus, according to Canfield, a *structural tension* is created in your brain. The brain always wants to resolve any structural tension. In order to do that, you will begin to draw to you what is needed to achieve the goal, which will in turn, resolve the structural tension.

That's why this book has lots of exercises for you to write your answers down, so it brings those ideas to the front and center of your attention. **Writing down your goals is key!**

Soul searching is NOT a one and done event.
It's a life-long process.

We are always changing and evolving. Just like in nature, nothing stays the same. We are either dying or growing.

Our goal is to evolve and become a climber, not a camper. When we make positive choices that are led by our souls, then we create a life we don't want to run away from. That's why taking the time to do the exercises in this book and soul searching is such an important part of the process. It's about getting to know yourself again.

Now it's time to take some of your answers in this chapter and start testing things out with fun action and activities...

Chapter 4 – Vocation Vacations

"The secret to success is to make your Vocation a Vacation."
~Mark Twain

This chapter is all about test driving some of your vocation options before you go all in.

After my son Jason graduated from high school, like many people, he was trying to figure out what he wanted to do with the rest of his life. One day after visiting the local college, he became interested in massage therapy. He looked at the curriculum and decided *100%, without a doubt,* he wanted to become a massage therapist.

I was about to invest $10,000+ for the program when the thought popped into my head that I should take him to talk to a friend of mine who was a massage therapist. This way, he could get a massage, talk to her about the business side of things, and then decide if this was something he really wanted to do. I guess my gut was telling me that we needed to be 100% certain this was the right path for my son so we both didn't waste a lot of time and money.

The day before Jason was supposed to enroll in the massage therapy program, I took him to my friend's house where he received a full body massage and then he asked the massage therapist questions about the business. I was so excited as we left her house because it seemed to me that things went well.

As we left her house, I asked my son what he thought about everything and was quite surprised when he replied, "I could never be a massage therapist. I could never do that to strangers!" I was so thankful I made that decision and did not invest $10,000 in tuition only to find out down the road my son really wasn't happy with that choice.

FAST FORWARD TO TODAY

Today, my son has found his passion in sales. He is one of the top sales professionals at Lexus and recently won the *Presidential Award*! Every year, he earns bonuses, and they send him on a trip to Mexico. My son is super smart and super successful – he makes six figures, owns his own home (which will be paid off in seven years), owns a brand-new Sea Ray boat, and is married to the love of his life. I'm also happy to report that he absolutely loves what he does for a living. Imagine if he had gone through the massage therapy school and then felt guilty because of the money I invested on the tuition and stayed with that job for the wrong reasons. He would have been miserable to say the least.

This is becoming more and more common – people go to college or university to get a degree, only to find out **AFTER** graduation that they don't like their chosen field. They end up staying in jobs for years and decades because of the money they invested in their education and the student loans they have to pay back.

LAWYER TURNED WINDOW SALESPERSON

Another example of someone in the wrong career is my former attorney who absolutely hated practicing law but was extremely good at it. He handled a case for me years ago, and I can honestly say, I've never seen a better trial lawyer. We won a very difficult case. However, as a practicing attorney, he was miserable.

As fate would have it, a series of unfortunate events happened that caused him to lose his license to practice law. Or maybe these weren't unfortunate events but synchronistic events, designed to bring him back to his authentic path. The great news is he's now a top sales representative for a well-known window company, and he loves it. He told me that he's much happier selling windows than he ever was practicing law.

This is why I like the idea of "test driving" your dream job. I know now that's what I was doing in my younger days by taking a variety of jobs and trying them out for a while. I was just "test driving" jobs to see what I liked.

JUST FOR LAUGHS, HERE ARE A FEW OF THE JOBS I SAMPLED:

- **WWF Wrestling Girl** – Yes, that's right! I used to walk up the WWF wrestlers in the 1980s! I walked up a guy by the name of "Playboy Buddy Rose" and hung out with well-known wrestlers like Andre the Giant, Mr. Perfect, Bob Backlund, and other wrestling celebrities at the time.

- **Cocktail Waitress** – This was such a fun job! I met a lot of celebrities who stayed at this Sheraton Hotel during my time there. I also worked at the J.W. Marriott Hotel in D.C. and that was fun as well.

- **Private Process Server** – This was an interesting job serving people who were evading service. I became quite good at figuring out creative ways to get people served. One time, I went to a bar where the defendant was hanging out and I had the papers I was serving wrapped in a Christmas gift box. I pretended to give him a Christmas present and got him served. At the time, I only had to touch his body with the papers. He could tear them up, throw them away, or walk away from them, but he was served.

- **Jewelry Store Salesperson** - I hated this job because I hated retail and I couldn't stand waiting around for people to come into the store.

- **Cashier at McDonald's** – This was my first job at age 15½ and I had fun working there with my older brother, Michael.

- **HVAC sales rep** – I knew nothing about HVAC, but they convinced me I could sell their products, and they were wrong. I didn't have the knowledge required to sell this product and I wasn't good at climbing ladders and going on top of tall buildings.

- **Real Estate Magazine Presenter** – I travelled to various real estate offices and sold advertising space in an industry magazine. It was fun for a while, but not enough pay.

- **Freelance Instructor for Community Colleges** – As a subcontractor for the College, I was sent to various locations to teach business writing. I really wanted to teach creative writing and public speaking. It paid the bills, but I didn't enjoy it.

- **Newspaper Reporter** – I mentioned this job earlier. I loved chasing and writing stories, but I didn't love the pay. It served its purpose and got me the writing credentials I needed to do other things.

- I had many more jobs! These were just a few.

When I was a serial job hopper, everyone around me thought I was crazy. My ex one time called me a "Job Whore" because I had 2-3 jobs at a time and was always changing jobs.

I suppose I looked very unstable; constantly changing jobs, however, without trying out jobs, I really didn't know what I liked and didn't like. They seemed like good jobs, but you never know until you actually work in a job if you will enjoy it or not.

I guess it's kind of like dating. The point of dating is to see if you want to be with that person long term. I was just dating jobs instead of people!

PIVOT PLANET TO THE RESCUE

Luckily for you, there is a company, *Pivot Planet* (**www.pivot-planet.com**) that can arrange for you to "test drive" your dream job or dream business. After all, it would be a great misfortune to quit your job only to find out down the road that you really didn't like what you thought was going to be your *dream* job or *dream* business.

Career coaching is a popular way to help you figure out what direction to take. That is a great idea, however, I like the concept of working with Pivot Planet that provides virtual mentorship with real people in real careers. Here is an excerpt from their website:

- Since 2004, Pivot Planet's founder, Brian Kurth, and his Vocation Vacations career mentorship team have provided thousands of one to three-day in-person mentorship experiences to people exploring a new career or a path not taken.

- For as little as $50 per hour, Pivot Planet connects people around the world looking to "pivot" from an existing career to a new career or enhance their current job skills with expert advisors working in hundreds of fields. These advisors offer affordable, one-on-one video and phone sessions. Pivot Planet also offers the option of in-person mentorship with some of its advisors.

- Pivot Planet goes beyond connecting online, career coaching or corporate outplacement.

- Pivot Planet is the resource for finding real-life career and start-up business advice shared by experienced advisors who can answer your questions and offer insights into their profession. Anywhere. Anytime."

I love it! I wish this program had been around when I was in my 20's! It would have saved me from taking a lot of jobs I ended up hating.

Hobby or Jobby?

Remember what Elizabeth Gilbert said about blending hobbies with jobs. Sometimes the two should not be blended.

My friends and family always comment how great I am at cooking and baking. Many people have suggested that I start my own catering business, but I know myself well enough to know that I enjoy cooking on a small scale (as a hobby) and that I would never be happy spending eight or more hours a day in a hot kitchen doing prep work and cooking for large parties or as a job. I know without a doubt that cooking is just my hobby.

Often, there is a fine line between a hobby and a vocation.

Sometimes we ruin our hobbies
by trying to turn them into businesses.

It's not a mistake to try, but don't invest too much into it. My rule of thumb is go and make your first $100 doing whatever "it" is and then reassess that decision and see if you actually enjoyed the experience before you take a deep dive into it.

I've known many people over the years who say they want to have an online business, but they really hate being at the computer and despise technology. Therefore, it wouldn't be a good fit, and they would be miserable having an online business.

I've also met people who say they want to write books, but when it comes to actually writing the book, they don't like the process of sitting down to the blank page and doing the actual writing.

It doesn't mean you can't start an online business or write a book if you hate the process; you can absolutely outsource the parts of the business you're not good at. For example, many of my authors use ghostwriters to get their book written.

It's important to look at the difference between a hobby and a dream job. Our dream job (or business) should involve things we enjoy doing that may (or may not) be hobbies, and our hobbies may be things we can make money at.

So, how do we know if we should
make our hobby our dream job?

Well, one way would be to test it out.

Get a part-time job before leaving your full-time job to see if you really like it. You could also volunteer at an organization where you would like to work.

If your dream job is working for yourself, find someone else who is doing something similar to what you want to do and ask them if you can work for them as an intern to see if it really is your dream job.

I encourage you to "test drive" your dream job or hobby-based job with **Pivot Planet** as part of your exploration for the next chapter in your life. Some of the advisors they have (and there are hundreds are):

- Travel Writer
- Chief Technology Officer
- Actor
- Dog Daycare Owner
- Digital Strategist
- Make-up Artist
- Magazine Editor
- Distiller
- Music Producer
- Filmmaker
- Fitness Trainer
- Non-profit Director
- Home Stager
- Pet Resort Owner
- Pastry Chef
- Pastor
- Publisher
- Psychologist
- Professional Poker Player
- Private Investigator
- Wine Tasting Room Owner

And the list goes on and on! Check it out yourself: **https://www.pivotplanet.com/browse**

This is a great way to try out your ideas before taking the plunge!

Find creative ways to try out your dream jobs (or businesses) using some of the things you listed in Chapter 3 (Remember: Go Soul Searching NOT Job Searching).

Maybe you thought you really wanted to be a veterinarian, but after trying it out, you discovered you really want to be an animal trainer. Or perhaps you thought you loved organizing people's closets only to discover you'd rather organize their finances.

Go where your excitement is, however, also make a mental note that every hobby that excites you (or everything you are curious about) is NOT automatically going to be your dream job or dream business! Sometimes what we do for a few hours a month as a hobby would make us crazy if we had to do it eight hours a day as a job.

Explore your choices by trying them out *before* making a final decision.

Pivot Planet Founder Brian Kurth says:

"Think of it as a risk-free way of sampling your dream without quitting your day job. It's a taste that gives you a chance to determine... do I want to pursue this?"

WHAT'S YOUR FANTASY?

Go back to Chapter 3 and review your answers to the Nine Lives Game (*If you had nine lives and could be nine different people – what would you be?*). After reviewing your list, I want you to write your top three choices below. These should be the ones that get your juices flowing!

MY TOP 3 LIVES FROM THE 9 LIVES GAME ARE:

1. _____
2. _____
3. _____

CHOOSE ONE OF THE THREE LIVES TO FOCUS ON.

Write what your perfect day would look like if you were living this life.

Write the details in your journal! Here are some details you might think about:

- Where you are living?
- What time of day or night do you work?
- Do you work from home?
- Do you travel?
- Who is around you?
- Who works for you?
- How do you spend your day?

- How much money do you get paid?
- How do you get paid?
- Who are your dream clients?

Remember, our dreams and visions are first created in our mind's eye. This is a safe place for you to explore your fantasies. Sometimes as adults, we forget how to *daydream*. To create a life we truly love, we must re-learn the forgotten art of daydreaming and fantasies, and most importantly, we must be SPECIFIC.

Fairy Tales Help Us Learn About Who We Are

Most of us heard some or all of these Fairy Tales:

- Little Red Riding Hood
- Cinderella
- Sleeping Beauty
- Snow White
- Hansel and Gretel

The common denominator in these fairy tales is that they all have lots of obstacles and happy endings, right?

Fairy tales are important because they speak to our subconscious. They remind us to ask questions, to never give up in our quest for happiness, to retain the wonderment of childhood, to utilize our imagination, and that dreams can, and do, come true.

Fairy tales also help us dig deep within ourselves to discover new things about ourselves, how to overcome problems (even seemingly impossible ones), and they tell us that if we follow the right path, then our dreams can come true.

In the book, "Modern Fantasy: Children's Literature, Discovery for a Lifetime" by Barbara D. Stoodt-Hill and Linda B. Amspaugh-Corson (Prentice-Hall, 1996) the definition of fantasy is:

"...fantasy always includes at least one element of the impossible, one element that goes against the laws of the physical universe,

as we currently understand them; it concerns things that cannot really happen, people or creatures that do not really exist. Nevertheless, each story must have its own self-contained logic that creates its own reality."

You can choose to be practical or magical, and it's time for you to be magical!

The book goes on to say:

"Fairy tales are unbelievable stories featuring magic and the supernatural. Fairies, giants, witches, dwarves, good people, and bad people in fairy tales live in supernatural worlds with enchanted toadstools and crystal lakes. Heroes and heroines in these stories have supernatural assistance in solving problems."

Although the fairy tale may have a happy ending, usually obstacles arise somewhere in the middle of the plot. There is the "impossible" element that must be acknowledged.

Don't deceive yourself by seeing only the "good part" of your dream job or business. Fairy tales are designed to mirror real life struggles.

Don't delude yourself, because the truth is ...

There is no perfect job or business.

As human beings, no matter what role we are in, we have both weaknesses and strengths. Fairy tales help us see the positive as well as the negative. They help us see the dark and the light. This is extremely important or else there is a good chance we might delude ourselves into seeing only the good without seeing the obstacles and struggles that we are sure to encounter as we move towards our dreams. It's important to name our potential obstacles.

NAME 3 POTENTIAL OBSTACLES YOU MIGHT FACE IN YOUR DREAM JOB OR BUSINESS:

1. _____

2. _____

3. _____

PLAY OUT THESE 3 OBSTACLES IN YOUR MIND AND ON PAPER IN GREAT DETAIL

What would be the parts of your dream job that you really don't like?

Understand that there is never going to be a job or a business that you love doing 100% of the tasks. If you spend at least 75% of your time doing what you love, you will be happy and joyous.

Write down below at least three things you don't like about your dream job/business. Be brutally honest with yourself.

WRITE DOWN 3 THINGS YOU KNOW YOU WON'T LIKE ABOUT YOUR DREAM JOB/BUSINESS:

1. _____
2. _____
3. _____

If you talk to others who are in the line of work you are considering, or if you hire an advisor on **Pivot Planet**, make sure you ask them what part(s) of their jobs they don't like.

MY FRIEND QUIT THE SAME JOB THREE TIMES

My good friend, Jenny, was in mortgage banking for many years and loved the part of her job that involved doing the numbers, taking loan applications, finding the right loans for people, but she HATED the part of the job that involved having to go out in the field to sell the product. Even though she was good at "sales," she intensely hated "cold calling." Jenny explains that lots of people go into this type of business—mortgage banking, then face the fierce competition and rejection and become dismayed. Jenny got in and out of mortgage banking three different times because she says, "the money was so good."

The first time Jenny quit mortgage banking, she got a job as a waitress, then did some temp work, and decided to go back into mortgage banking because she knew the money was there. The second time she quit mortgage banking, she sold the home she owned and was living on her equity. When the money ran out, she went back into mortgage banking again because she got a great offer she couldn't turn down. Inside though, she was miserable.

She left once again and got a job as a secretary. Again, being lured by the money, she went back into the mortgage business one final time. That third and last time, she knew she would never return because she finally acknowledged to herself that being in the mortgage banking was:

"Like sandpaper rubbing against my soul."

Jenny finally realized that the money she was earning was not worth selling her soul!

Jenny reminds us:

"People get stuck in the money part, and in chasing the money. Yes, we need money to survive, but you can't put a dollar figure on the JOY in your heart. You become rich in your soul when you do what you love, and nobody can take that away."

The next step in this journey is clearing out the old to make room for the NEW...

PART II – CLEARING

*"The wisdom of life consists in
the elimination of non-essentials."*
~ Lin Yutang

Chapter 5 – It Takes an Intermission to Find Your Mission

Tama Kieves, author of "This Time I Dance! Trusting the Journey of Creating the Work You Love," said this after taking a 10-day vacation at a beach away from her high stress job as an attorney:

> *"I could not assess my job and my life while in the thick of the job that was my life."*

You must find a way to remove yourself, if only for a few days, from the job that drains your energy and dampens your spirits and go to a space where you can rest, reflect, revamp, and reconnect to what you truly want your life to be.

If you can get to a faraway beach or the mountains, that's great; but if you can only get to the local park that has a lake and a bench under a shaded tree, then by all means, go for it! Tama suggests:

> *"Consciously let go of what tires you. And what inspires you will take its place."*

Where you go to rest isn't as important as just stepping out of your life for a few hours or a few days (or more if you can) to regain a fresh perspective. It's amazing when I go on vacation or away for a girl's only weekend, how I am able to have a different view of my life and business.

After I left the legal field, I was fortunate to find a job doing outside sales (my **FREEDOM JOB**) that was much more aligned with who I was. It gave me a lot of free time to follow my curiosities, get back to daydreaming, and allowed me to use my imagination and recharge. I was blessed because I only worked 20-25 hours a week doing outside sales and was making six figures; it gave me the freedom I craved because my bosses were 350 miles away from me; and most importantly, it gave me the space I needed to start exploring my buried dreams.

I've learned that the longer you spend disconnected from your passions and your true self, the longer it takes you to reconnect and recover. There's a lot of rest time, sleep time, and time-outs needed!

My outside sales job, with its minimal hours and high pay, was a stepping stone job on my journey to living my dreams. Even though it was a great job, after a decade, the Universe started giving me signs that it was time to pack my bags and head in a new direction.

The quiet voice within me said, "It's time to move on. Don't get too comfortable. That wasn't your final resting place!"

I'm grateful that I heard the voice and that I listened. I've learned that when I don't LISTEN to my inner voice, it creates a lot of unnecessary pain and drama.

Just as I was hearing the voice telling me it was time to move on, the housing market crashed. The company I worked for filed bankruptcy and ended up firing the entire sales team.

That was my BIG sign to move on and to take my online business full-time.

ARE YOU LISTENING TO THAT QUIET VOICE?

If your life is filled with endless activities, chores, and a job that doesn't fulfill you, it's easy to miss the shhhh-ispers (as I like to call them.)

Oprah says God speaks to us in *whispers*. She also says if you don't listen to the whispers, you'll get hit with a brick upside your head, and if you don't listen when the brick comes, then the walls will come tumbling down around you, and if you still don't listen, then the house will come crashing down.

When things are off course in our lives, the Universe is always trying to get our attention with "WAKE UP CALLS" – they are literally calling to WAKE YOU UP to your SOUL! Sometimes they are drastic in the form of health issues, family issues, job loss, relationship change, etc. You can't ignore the signs because they will only get louder and louder.

Time outs are an essential part of this journey. It's your next step to creating the life of your dreams. Start planning your TIME OUTS now! The sooner you do this, the less pain you will have to endure.

LIST 3 WAYS YOU CAN CREATE TIMEOUTS IN YOUR LIFE

1. _____
2. _____
3. _____

EXAMPLES:

- Cut down or remove activities that you volunteer for that you really don't want to be doing.

- Take a vacation or mini-vacation to the beach by yourself.

- Carve out some time for solitude in your house to reflect and do your soul's work.

- Take a few hours out of your weekend to be by yourself and do nothing.

MENTAL TIME OUTS

Years ago, I was having trouble falling asleep and staying asleep. My mind was always on full speed, and I didn't know how to slow it down. Luckily, I discovered meditation and the numerous mental and physical health benefits I learned about persuaded me to give it a try. There were many studies done on the physiological benefits of meditation that I couldn't overlook; it was a great way to calm down my monkey mind.

Slowing down my overactive mind for two minutes seemed like an eternity in the beginning. I knew it wouldn't be easy, but I stuck with it and I can tell you whole-heartedly that meditation changed my life. I am a huge advocate of meditation as I truly believe it will help you take a quantum leap toward your dreams.

Now, I practice meditation at least 20 minutes a day in the morning; and sometimes in the evening. It has helped me hear my own quiet voice, and it also drowned out the voice of others.

Recently, I made a pact with God that whenever God was thinking of me, to show me a sign, which I chose to be a red cardinal.

Right after I made that pact with God, I was sitting outside in my backyard, under a shaded tree in late August writing this chapter. Just as I wrote the words, "Meditation changed my life," a beautiful red cardinal landed a few feet from my lounge chair. Actually, the red cardinal is back. I can see this beautiful creature as I am writing these words to you.

God, your Higher Power, the Universe, whatever you like to call the creative life force of everything that is, can easily be found in quiet spaces and in nature. So, if you want to connect with this Higher Power, create some space in your mind and in your life to hear the whispers. Creativity flourishes when we give it space. I believe this is where "million-dollar ideas" come from because nature abhors a vacuum.

Meditation has a way of bringing us back to the present moment. We learn through practicing meditation to pay attention on purpose and without judgment.

One of the books that helped me learn about meditation that I mentioned earlier was, "Wherever You Go, There You Are" by Jon Kabat-Zinn. Here are a few words about meditation from Jon's book:

"Meditation is simply about being yourself and knowing something about who that is. It is about coming to realize that you are on a path whether you like it or not, namely, the path that is your life. Meditation may help us see that this path we call our life has direction; that it is always unfolding, moment by moment; and that what happens now, in this moment, influences what happens next."

You are the co-Creator of your life! How powerful is that?

"A Course in Miracles" says:

*"There are no neutral thoughts –
we are always creating on some level."*

Do you want to be present to this creative process of your life?

Meditation is a tool that will engage you and wake you up to the authentic you and to your life's path.

One warning, though, DON'T use meditation as an escape to be fully engaged in your life or to avoid the parts of your life you'd rather not deal with.

You might also need to take an intermission from technology to create more time and space in your life.

HOW TO BREAK UP WITH YOUR PHONE

While at a book festival recently with my father, I picked up the book, *How to Break Up with Your Phone*, by Catherine Price. I actually thought I would give it to my kids, but once I started reading it, I realized I needed it more.

Because I have an online business, I felt like I was attached at the hip to my phone, computer, laptop, and iPad. I also was experiencing increased back and neck issues which was from spending way too much time at the computer and on my devices.

A FEW INTERESTING STATISTICS I LEARNED FROM THIS BOOK:

- Americans check their phones on average at least 47 times per day. For people between 18 and 24, the average is 82 (the numbers are consistently on the rise).

- On average, Americans spend more than 4 hours a day on their phones. That amounts to about 28 hours a week, 112 hours a month, or 56 full days a year.

- Nearly 80% of Americans check their phones within a half hour of waking up.

- Half of us check our phones in the middle of the night.

- We're checking our phones so much that we're giving ourselves repetitive strain injuries such as "texting thumb," "text neck," and "cell phone elbow."

- Nearly 1 out of every 10 American adults admits to checking their phone during sex.

Once I started reading this book, I realized there was an imbalance in this area of my life, and I needed to make some changes.

In 2017, a *Stress in America* report by the American Psychological Association said two-thirds of American adults agree that periodically unplugging or taking a DIGITAL DETOX would be good for their mental health.

The triggers that helped me realize I needed a DIGITAL DETOX were:

- You are absolutely burnt out in the industry.

- You spend 75% of your day doing tasks you hate, and there is absolutely no way to change this.

- You cannot be true to your soul in this job.

- Your skills are no longer necessary in your job.

- The nature of the job you are in does not align with your dreams.

- Your dreams can never be fulfilled while at this job.

- Your job is very stressful and is negatively affecting your health.

- Although you've tried to make changes, everything stays the same.

- Your core values are NOT in alignment with your employer's values.

- My back completely went out on me for almost a week after being glued to the computer working on client projects.

- My body felt stiff all the time.

- I would watch webinars and read eBooks on my phone in the middle of the night, then was not able to fall asleep.

- My sleep patterns were interrupted.

- When I didn't check my phone dozens of times a day, I felt anxious like I was missing out on things (FOMO – FEAR OF MISSING OUT – is real).

- After I installed a screen-time tracker I saw that I was in fact spending four hours plus on my iPhone daily and additional hours on my desktop computer and laptop.

- My attention span was getting shorter and shorter.

- My memory seemed weaker.

- My brain felt "tired" all the time like I had brain fatigue and brain fog.

- I could not find the time to create content for my online business and write my own books!

I couldn't understand how I was the boss of my 6-figure business and I couldn't find the "time" to work on my own book projects.

The number one culprit I discovered was FACEBOOK!

It was easy for me to make the excuse that I was on Facebook because of my "online business," but the truth of the matter was that I was doing mindless scrolling, watching videos, watching webinars from sponsored ads, and not doing any "work".

So, I deleted the Facebook app from my iPhone.

And guess what happened?

I found 2-4 hours a day to create content (writing blog posts, online courses, and books) and it's been amazing ever since.

At first, I thought I would have FACEBOOK withdrawals, but the opposite happened – I felt FREE!

And not only did I feel FREE, I felt grateful I discovered the book "How to Break Up With Your Phone" because I didn't know just how insidious this technology problem I had was and how it was stealing away my dreams one post, one scroll, one email, one tweet, and one text at a time!

Until I became aware of the problem, I was operating in default mode which is how many of us operate especially when it comes to technology.

WHAT I LOVE ABOUT CATHERINE PRICE'S BOOK IS HOW SHE BREAKS IT DOWN INTO TWO PARTS:

1. **The Wake Up** – Educate readers about how our iPhones are designed to addict us and what they are doing to our sleep, our memories, our attention spans, and our lives.

2. **The Breakup** – How to breakup with technology (not in an all-or-nothing event but create a new healthy relationship with technology that does not steal your life away).

In her book, Catherine Price, says:

"In order to maximize the amount of time we spend on our devices, designers manipulate our brain chemistry in ways that are known to trigger addictive behaviors. Most of these techniques involve a brain chemical called dopamine. Dopamine has many roles, but for our purposes, the most important thing to know is that, by activating pleasure-related receptors in our brains, it teaches us to associate certain behaviors with rewards (think of a rat that gets a pellet every time it presses a lever). Dopamine makes us feel excited – and we like feeling excited. Any experience that triggers the release of dopamine is therefore something that we'll want to experience again."

So basically, we are bombarded with these online triggers (likes on our Facebook posts, shares, multiple likes on Instagram, etc.).

Unfortunately, phones and apps are deliberately designed without *"STOPPING CUES"* to alert us when we've had enough. This is why it's so easy to accidentally binge and not realize you have a problem.

Our brains just want more dopamine
– again and again and again!

So, this isn't about a lack of willpower on your part, this is about technology designers deliberately manipulating our dopamine responses to make it extremely difficult to stop using their products.

Remember, this chapter is about removing things from your life in order to create more time in your life to explore, imagine, and design your dream life.

I fully believe that technology is a double-edged sword. It has advanced society in many ways, but it's also negatively affecting the way we relate to people, interact with one another, and can cause physical problems when we binge on technology.

The truth is that it's easier to check Facebook or Instagram or write a Twitter post than it is to work on your dreams or, in my case, write a book.

WHY?

Because we all have an inner demon called "**RESISTANCE.**"

Stephen Pressfield, author of "The War of Art" says this about resistance:

"There is an enemy. There is an intelligent, active, malign force working against us. Step one is to recognize this. This recognition alone is enormously powerful. It saved my life, and it will save yours."

We all have resistance when it comes to pursuing our dreams, our art, and our passions.

The more barriers we can remove like **technology addiction**, the more successful we will be.

If you feel like you are spending too much time on your devices, I suggest reading Catherine Price's book and creating a new relationship with technology that gives you the time and space you need to create your dream life.

RITUALS AND INTERMISSIONS

Carl Jung knew how to create daily rituals and take intermissions in order to do deep work.

According to journalist Mason Currey, author of "Daily Rituals," Jung would rise at 7 a.m. and after a big breakfast, he would spend two hours of undistracted writing time in his private office. His afternoons would be filled with long walks in the countryside and meditation. In 1922, Jung built a two-story stone house retreat he called *the Tower*. Jung once said,

> *"In my retiring room, I am by myself..." and*
> *"I keep the key with me all the time;*
> *no one else is allowed in there except with my permission."*

There was no electricity at *the Tower* and Jung was in bed by 10 p.m. Jung went on to say,

> *"The feeling of repose and renewal that I had*
> *in this tower was intense from the start."*

The tower was not an escape from work, but more of a space to advance his work. In order to do his deep thinking, he needed to be alone with his thoughts.

It might sound strange, but we live in a noisy world and we need to be alone with our thoughts in order to do our deep work.

In his bestselling book, "Deep Work," Cal Newport defines the term deep work as:

> *"Professional activities performed in a state of*
> *distraction-free concentration that push your cognitive*
> *capabilities to their limit. These efforts create new value,*
> *improve your skills and are hard to replicate."*

Jung built a *tower* of stone in the woods to promote deep work and the payoff was massive.

It isn't easy to prioritize our own *deep work*, but if you want to create your dream life, it's absolutely imperative to do so.

In order to get my writing done, I have to organize my life in such a way that I get lots of long, consecutive, uninterrupted time by myself.

When I was checking my emails, Facebook, Twitter, text messages, etc., I was trading my time as well as my dreams for this technology-induced dopamine fix like an addict. My time was fragmented, and as a result, so were my dreams.

I've developed a new relationship with these devices by adding some new rules.

HERE ARE SOME OF MY NEW TECHNOLOGY RULES:

- No Facebook app on my phone; I check Facebook 1-2 times per day when I'm at my desktop computer.

- No phone next to me when I'm writing content (books, blog posts, courses) as it is distracting.

- No phone in bed with me at night.

- No watching videos, webinars or reading on my phone in bed two hours prior to going to sleep.

- Unsubscribe from email lists I no longer needed so I only get emails from people I want, and that gives me more time to read and enjoy those emails.

- No phone during meals with others.

- Deleted all apps I was no longer using.

- Have only apps and tools on my phone's home page that improve my life without stealing my attention.

- Turned off all notifications.

- Leave my phone on vibrate all the time.

Once you balance the time you spend on technology,
you will free up more time to work on creating a life
you don't want to run away from.

We all need white space to "hear the still small voice." That's why taking an intermission, creating rituals, meditating and unplugging from technology will open the communication lines from your soul to your heart and to your head.

In the next chapter, we're going to talk about "energy vampires"; those people, places and things that steal away our energy, time and attention and show up as distractions that prevent us from living our dream life.

Chapter 6 – Removing Energy Zappers

"A high-quality life has much more to do with what you REMOVE from it than what you add to it."
~Cheryl Richards, author of "Standing Up for Your Life"

Energy zappers come in a variety of forms such as: unfinished projects, negative people, physical and emotional clutter, an unhealthy lifestyle, and any activities that don't move you closer to your dreams, mission, and purpose (even if you haven't figured that out yet).

To create the time and energy required to transition out of your 9 to 5, you need to identify and remove as many of the *energy zappers* in your life as possible.

Years ago, I made a list I titled "**Top 10 Things that are Draining my Energy**" and on that list was:

1. Non-profit paperwork (I had a non-profit at the time)
2. Office Clutter
3. Paper Clutter
4. House Projects
5. Dry Cleaning
6. Yellow Page Ad
7. Garage Clutter
8. Horseback Riding Lessons
9. Boyfriend issues
10. Son's bills

For a year, I worked on removing many of these top energy drainers from my life, and in 12 months, I removed 8 out of the 10. I was very proud of myself! Eventually, I removed ALL of the top energy drainers.

Many times, these *energy zappers* are deep subconscious blocks that manifest as self-sabotaging distractions that keep us from moving forward, evolving, and growing. Often, we feel like these energy zappers are beyond our control, and we are helpless victims who cannot change the situation.

One distraction I have in my life that is a repeating pattern: dysfunctional relationships with men. Jealous boyfriends, clingy boyfriends, emotionally unavailable boyfriends, partying boyfriends, narcissistic boyfriends, etc.

As I looked back on my life, I realized that I allowed these unhealthy relationships to occupy too much time in my life and more importantly, I was so distracted by trying to fix these relationships that I wasn't working on my own life and my own dreams. I used my personal energy trying to fix men instead of building and creating my own dreams! I was putting others needs ahead of myself.

In fact, one time I was a speaker at a women's conference in Florida, I had an epiphany during one of the written exercises we were doing: every time I was creating something BIG in my business and in my life, I got involved in a dysfunctional relationship with a man. It seemed like an *unintentional* distraction (like I was a victim of circumstances), but I had to face the truth that I was choosing these types of men, and I was wasting a lot of time on them. I allowed these distractions for a myriad of unconscious emotional reasons (which I have worked on in therapy), and by doing the hard inner work. As a result of doing this work, I am now living my dreams full out.

I finally recognized this pattern in my life and sought support to heal the emotional issues that caused me to be attracted to these types of men. I am happy to say, I am a *RECOVERED JERK MAG-NET!* I now have strong boundaries around my time and my life. I am focused on my dreams and do not allow dysfunctional relationships and distractions to block my dreams.

I don't want you to think that this process was easy or fast; it was not. It took years to work on these underlying emotional and spiritual issues regarding relationships and my long-held patterns, but it was worth the time, money and energy I spent getting support and help in order to heal.

Recently, I spent over a year working with three different healing professionals that helped me get to another layer of my deep-seated patterns and issues. It was one of the hardest years of my life breaking these emotional patterns.

Think about things that are going on in your life right now that seem like they are beyond your control. Now, I want you to write them down. We will look at them more closely in a minute.

Let's begin with your Top 10 List of Energy Vampires

List whatever pops into your mind without thinking too hard about it. What are the top 10 energy vampires in your life right now? Don't worry about how long they will take to remove, just write down the top 10 things (top of mind) you feel are preventing you from living your dreams.

For example, the "house projects" item I had on my top 10 list took me almost two years to complete. Mainly because I procrastinated about the work that needed to be done. If I had just done the repairs as they came up, I wouldn't have had such a long list. When I made my top 10 list many years ago, I decided I needed to declutter every room in my house. My office alone took three months to do!

Removing energy vampires in your life is an important part of the process in creating your dream life and that's why I wanted to devote an entire chapter to it. Remember, this section is about CLEARING things out. We need to clear out the old in order to make room for the new.

We all have blind spots, and my goal is to help awaken you to the energy that is being extracted from you every day that you could be using to follow your dreams and create a life you love.

Let's take a look at each category and begin the process of identifying your biggest energy zappers so you can take action to remove them.

Vision without action is a daydream.
Action without vision is a nightmare.
~Japanese Proverb

UNFINISHED PROJECTS

What unfinished projects are lurking around in your home and in your life? Do you have tax returns that need to be filed from three years ago? Do you have a room that you started painting and never finished? What about that pair of slacks hanging on the treadmill in your bedroom that needs a new button? Or the half-finished craft projects in boxes you were going to get to last Christmas?

The goal is not to get rid of your to-do list once and for all because that is an unrealistic goal. The immediate goal is to remove the projects that have been on your to-do list for too long. You know, the ones you've been procrastinating about for months, if not years!

The purpose of your to-do list is to better organize your time, so important tasks and appointments don't slip your mind. A lot of people do the easiest tasks first, crossing them off the list and then transferring the dreaded tasks from week to week and from list to list. *Sound familiar?* I know. I've done this many times myself.

If you're serious about quitting your job and following your dreams, you're going to have to free up all that psychic energy that is being drained from you by these energy zappers.

Every day, review your top 10 energy zappers that you wrote down and start removing them from your life. Simplify your life so you can focus on what's important to your heart and soul.

ACTIVITIES THAT DON'T MOVE YOU CLOSER TO YOUR MISSION

Remember the mission statement you wrote down in Chapter 3. If you didn't do the exercises, GO BACK AND DO THEM NOW. Having a mission statement will make your life easier because it will act as a guiding light to help you know when to say "*YES*" to requests and when to say "*NO*."

In 1999, shortly after I wrote my mission statement (*My mission is to inspire, motivate and educate others to believe in themselves and find their true purpose in life*), I received a call from a friend who had a "business opportunity." Because I am very curious by nature, and the fact that I am a recovering people pleaser and don't like telling people NO, I typically would spend lots of time listening to what others had to say about these "business opportunities." I can't tell you how many network marketing activities I became involved in until one day I grew tired of these companies changing the structure of their compensation plans; I finally realized I wanted to build my own business and dreams instead of someone else's.

On this particular phone call, with my mission statement hanging on the wall right in front of me in my office, I listened for a few minutes, but when this person asked me to spend more time on a conference call with her boss to give me "additional information" about the business opportunity, I kindly declined. I told her that the opportunity she mentioned was not in alignment with my mission. I also explained that I needed to stay 100% focused on my mission and goals.

I have done this repeatedly since then. As you probably know, there are a lot of great business opportunities, projects and ventures you could get involved in; but the question for you to ask yourself is: *Is this opportunity, project or venture moving me closer to my mission or not?* If the answer is NO, then only go back to the activities that will help advance you towards your mission.

Always keep in mind, however, that it is okay to explore and test things out as we discussed earlier with vocation vacations and test driving jobs to find clues that will help you create a new future. Use your mission statement as a guiding light to make decisions.

REMOVING EMOTIONAL AND PHYSICAL CLUTTER

I am by no means an expert in emotional clutter, unless you want to count the fact that I've carried my own emotional baggage around with me for years and I spent many more years in therapy unloading it.

So, how do you know if you have emotional clutter? There are clues.

First, look to your relationships.

Ask yourself, "Is there a lot of drama, hurt, pain and disappointment?"

If the answer is YES, that is **Clue #1** that you haven't fully released the past including the pain, resentments and grudges that we all hang on to. Once you release these, your life will become much calmer and more peaceful. If your relationships are not peaceful and conflict-free, then you probably have unfinished business somewhere in your past. When you clear up that unfinished business, the emotional clutter will be released and will no longer be an obstacle to creating the life of your dreams.

Emotional clutter is like a blocked artery to the heart. My advice is do the deep work (the work you don't want to do) to process it or it will kill your dreams and visions.

In order to clean up my own emotional baggage, I worked with a trained therapist, an energy healer, read self-help books and worked with a spiritual counselor who helped me find the buried emotional blocks I wasn't even conscious of. This was important work in my journey to living my dream life. I also worked with a practitioner who specialized in trauma, emotional issues and grief work.

A great book I recommend about healing and resolving past trauma is "Waking the Tiger" by Peter A. Levine

In his book, Levine lays out the steps needed to heal trauma from life's events.

He also makes an important point that trauma can come from any of the following experiences:

- Victims of physical and mental abuse
- Soldiers and war-related events
- Natural disasters such as earthquakes, tornadoes, floods and fires
- Accidents and falls
- Serious illnesses
- Sudden loss
- Surgery and other medical procedures
- Large-scale social traumas
- Mass shootings
- Difficult births

A trauma is anything that causes a frozen residue of energy in our bodies, minds and souls that has not been resolved and discharged. This residue remains trapped in the nervous system where it can wreak havoc on our bodies and spirits causing long-term alarming, debilitating symptoms such as PTSD.

So it's important to know that if you find yourself stuck and unable to move forward in your life, you may need to heal past traumas.

Clue #2 is that you have a strong emotional reaction (over-reactions) to certain situations that happen in your life.

Clue #3 is that certain situations keep repeating themselves.

Unfortunately, sweeping the emotional clutter under the rug isn't an option when you are creating your dream life because these dramas and traumas will repeatedly block you from your dreams.

Often, when we look back at our lives and create a timeline of events, we begin to see a pattern emerging.

So, what can you do about emotional clutter?

It would be nice if we could just visit the doctor, go under anesthesia, and have all our emotional baggage removed in an outpatient visit. We live in an instant gratification world but removing emotional baggage does not happen instantaneously.

HERE ARE A FEW SUGGESTIONS BASED ON MY OWN EXPERIENCES:

- Visit a therapist and start talking about it; you would be amazed at how freeing it is to simply talk about it and release your past.

- Do forgiveness work with a trained therapist or counselor.

- If you've done a lot of "talk" therapy, then work with an energy healer who might be able to help you remove emotional blocks in your body.

- Go to a spiritual counselor who is an expert at identifying and removing emotional blocks.

- Visit a "Re-birther" to see what pain from your past is blocking you in your present; I did this, and it helped me tremendously.

- Purchase a journal and write it down. Remember, what doesn't get ex-pressed becomes de-pressed. Get it all out!

- Cry all the tears you held back over the years. Holding back our emotions is not only damaging to our emotional health but it is damaging to our physical health as well. When we hold back our tears, they are stored in our bodies and fester in our bodies until we find ourselves at the doctor complaining about things like ulcers, insomnia, and high blood pressure. Rent some sad movies and give yourself permission to cry it all out.

- Face the fears that are holding you back from moving forward in your life–fear of failure, fear of success, fear of the unknown, fear of rejection, fear of change (this is a BIG ONE!), fear of being judged, fear of not feeling deserving or worthy. Fears are what keep us playing it safe – they keep us "camping out," and they keep us stuck in status quo mode. Anyone who is successful has faced their fears to achieve higher levels of success. You never know your potential unless you bite off more than you can chew. In the past, I've scheduled classes to teach before I ever put the program together because I knew it would motivate me to action and enable me to overcome my fears at the same time. I took action in spite of my fears, and you can do the same.

- Tell the truth to yourself and to others.

FINDING MY VOICE

After working with an energy therapist for several months to remove some long-standing emotional blocks in my body, I discovered that my throat chakra was completely closed off.

During one session, I sensed and actually visualized a golf ball lodged in my throat. At the time, I was in an on-again off-again eight-year relationship. One of my complaints in the relationship was my boyfriend was obsessed with golf. It wasn't the golf per se that bothered me, but rather how he avoided intimacy and emotional connection with me by using golf as an escape. The golf ball represented all the times during our relationship that I did not speak my truth.

I believed I had to hold back my voice to preserve the relationship. My fears that the relationship would end kept me silent. The more I held back my true feelings and thoughts, however, the more emotionally disconnected we became until finally a crisis occurred causing us to separate.

In her book, "Silencing the Self," author Dana Crowley Jack discusses a condition called the divided self.

"The woman begins to experience two opposing selves; an outwardly conforming, compliant self, and an inner, secret self who is enraged and resentful. Trying to live up to external standards, a woman creates a 'dark double' – an accompanying shadow self that undermines her attempts to be a loveable woman."

Through Speaking Circles® and personal therapy work, I became more consciously aware of my own divided self. I began to notice the thoughts I had were very different, if not completely opposite, to the words I spoke.

Ironically, in my intimate relationships, I was striving for more intimacy using deception as the means to get there. As I began to wake up, I discovered that one of my unspoken needs in my relationships was "security," and in exchange for security I repressed my voice. My needs became distorted, and the price I paid was a loss of self-worth and an inability to show my true, authentic self within the relationship. The distance between who I appeared to be and who I really was grew larger every day.

As young children, one of our needs is to be accepted and loved; as a result as we get older, we sometimes had to repress our true thoughts and feelings in order to get these needs met.

For many of us, showing emotion was unacceptable. I was not allowed to show anger or hurt, and I was taught to play the nice girl role all the time regardless of how I truly felt. One of the phrases my mother often said during my childhood was *"Children should be seen and not heard."*

Repressing our truth and our voice is the birth of the divided self – the *"conforming, compliant self'* and our dark double.

If any of this sounds familiar, ask yourself, *"What is the pay off?"*

Check in often throughout each day to see if your thoughts match the words you are speaking. If they don't match or are not even close, you may be operating from your divided self.

Make friends with your divided self; find out what she is trying to gain. We can speak our truth and get our needs met, but it isn't always easy. And sometimes we speak our truth, and the relationship ends. If that happens, then the person you were in the relationship with wasn't comfortable with you being your true self.

Do you really want to be in a relationship where you aren't able to be the real and authentic you?

I SPOKE MY TRUTH AND THE RELATIONSHIP ENDED

I am happy to say I ended a four-year on-again, off-again relationship when I realized the more truth I spoke in this relationship, the worse things got until finally I could no longer take all the drama, stress and anxiety in my life. I had enough. I was tired, drained and I finally made a conscious choice to choose myself and my dreams over this drama filled, high-conflict relationship with an extremely narcissistic and manipulative man.

Staying emotionally balanced isn't a one and done event; it's an ongoing process we have to work on throughout our lives. Some tools that help me stay emotionally balanced and peaceful are meditation, yoga, journaling, walking, exercise, organizing my *stuff*, taking mini vacations, being near the water, getting together with my friends, seeing my children and grandchildren, and talking to a counselor or therapist if needed.

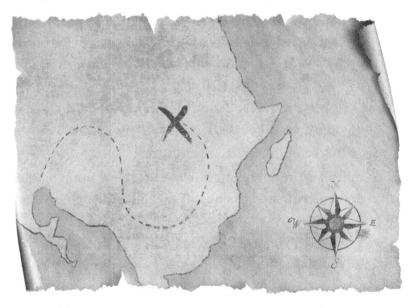

Write down some activities that keep you emotionally balanced or that appeal to you and start doing them.

PHYSICAL CLUTTER

Just as emotional clutter can block the energy required to live our dreams, so can physical clutter. It can affect us physically, mentally, emotionally and spiritually. As we begin to clear up the clutter in our homes and in our lives, we release the "stagnant" negative energy, which creates space for new energy to come into our lives.

There are so many excuses about why we don't want to get rid of our clutter; here are some common excuses not to clear out the clutter:

- **I might need this someday.**
- **It has sentimental value.**
- **I have so much, I don't know where to begin.**
- **I don't have the time, money or energy to declutter.**

These all seem like valid excuses, but the fact is your clutter is keeping you from your dreams.

You do have a choice, though. You can remove the clutter or remove the possibility of ever achieving your dreams. It's that serious. You've got to get rid of the old to make room for the new. This process involves a lot of faith and trust.

So, what exactly is clutter? According to Karen Kingston, author of "Clear Your Clutter with Feng Shui," there are four categories:

1. Things you do not use or love.

2. Things that are untidy or disorganized.

3. Too many things in too small of a space.

4. Anything unfinished.

We addressed "Unfinished Projects," already so we have three additional areas to look at.

First, I encourage you to systematically go through each and every room in your home and begin to get rid of things you do not use or love. As Marie Kondo, author of "The Life Changing Magic of Tidying Up," suggests "remove things that don't spark joy."

I redecorated my bedroom several years ago and it was difficult to get rid of knick-knacks and so-called "decorations" that had been there for the past 10 years or more. I didn't "love" many of these items, but they seemed like they were a part of me because they were around for so long. They almost seemed like extensions of the old me. I made the tough decision before I began the project that when I looked around my room, I only wanted to see things that I absolutely loved and that sparked JOY.

Consequently, my house is decluttered and the items in it represent the true me. I only display things in my home that bring me great joy and happiness. Photos of my children and grandchildren; angel and butterfly décor; my Buddha lady statue, candles, several pieces of custom art that I love; homemade pottery; books that are meaningful to me; and a small writing desk. I can honestly say my home is a serene and peaceful environment. A place for me to retreat to when I am feeling stressed or overwhelmed, or when I simply want to relax and feel warm and safe.

I want you to feel that way about your home when you walk through the front door and when you go into any room in your house. If you don't feel that way, then it's time to start filling up boxes for a yard sale, donation, or the trash.

Clearing up your clutter isn't always about removing things from your house. It is also about *organizing the stuff you are keeping*.

When I was in outside sales, I saw a lot of houses and sometimes there was so much clutter in these homes, there wasn't a place for me to sit down to talk with the homeowners. It takes time, money and energy to organize your stuff, but once it's done, your life will work better because you'll spend less time looking for things that are lost in piles of stuff.

I can see why Marie Kondo has sold millions of books on organizing our stuff and removing clutter because our "stuff" is literally taking over our lives.

Joshua Becker, author of "The More of Less," says:

"When we embrace minimalism, we are immediately freed to pursue our greatest passions. And for some of us, it's been a long time since we've had access to the resources required to chase our hearts' greatest delights, however we define those delights. Living with less offers more time to spend on meaningful activities, more freedom to travel, more clarity in our spiritual pursuits, increased mental capacity to solve our most heartfelt problems, healthier finances to support causes we believe in, and greater flexibility to pursue the careers we most desire."

A minimalist lifestyle can be custom created to focus on what's important to you. It doesn't have to be extreme like selling everything you own and living in a tiny house. It's just about finding balance so you can spend less time taking care of your stuff and more time on your dreams and passions.

Put a box by the front door and every day try to find one or two things to give away and start removing the clutter, or buy Marie Kondo's book and go all in.

REMOVING NEGATIVE PEOPLE

When I began to reclaim my authentic self and speak more of my truth, my whole world began to change. It was as if I was an actress in a play and as one scene ended, a new scene began only some of the old characters were replaced with new characters.

There appeared to be a natural clearing out of relationships in my life that did not support me speaking my truth. This doesn't mean when you begin to speak your truth, you will automatically lose relationships in your life; however, chances are good that there are a few people in your life who are more comfortable with you when you don't speak your truth.

Harriet Lerner, author of "The Dance of Intimacy," says:

"People need us to be a certain way for their own sake,
and for the most complex variety of unconscious reasons.
Being real means being who you are in relationships regardless
of what others need, wish or expect you to be."

If you've been wearing a mask in your relationships as I was (the mask of people-pleasing and avoiding conflict), when you remove the mask, there will be an adjustment period as people are not used to you speaking up and telling your truth; some people will drift out of your life because they were more comfortable with you when you wore the mask.

Speaking your truth always involves taking a risk. I had a friend I knew from high school for over 30 years. As I took small risks in our relationship and began telling her more of my true thoughts and feelings, she became more withdrawn from the relationship. Suddenly, a huge crisis was created, and my friend dropped out of my life completely.

Intimacy in relationships means being able to share our true thoughts and feelings to another human being. My client and author of "Keep Your Sexy Sacred," Sabrina Lawton says the word *Intimacy* means "In To Me SEE." I love that!

It's easy to show only our "best selves" in relationships, but we are out of balance and not operating within our authentic self if we are not also expressing our weaknesses and vulnerabilities. This is the key to emotional health and well-being.

Another aspect of speaking your truth is you may find yourself in more conflicts for a short time while others adjust to your new self – which is not really a new you at all, but simply a "truer" version of the you that you've always been.

In nature, there is a constant recycling of life and death – a natural replenishing. As you begin to find your true voice, try it on with different people in your life.

Take baby steps and remember to speak your truth while connected to your heart and with compassion. It takes courage to remain true to yourself and not everyone – even those closest to you – will always support you in reclaiming your authentic self. Let nature do her work; she will always replenish what she takes away.

Trust.

AN UNHEALTHY LIFESTYLE

Adelle Davis once said,

> *"As I see it, every day you can do one of two things: build health or produce disease in yourself."*

Which one are you up to these days?

It seems to me what she is really saying is, if you aren't taking care of yourself daily, eventually that neglect will catch up with you in the form of disease.

Unfortunately, many people don't value their health until it is taken away from them. The foundation of your happiness and your future is built on taking care of yourself NOW.

Years ago, I met a man on a sales appointment who was having all of his teeth pulled and replacing them with dentures. He was probably in his late 40's or early 50's, and I remember the comment he made to me that day, *"This is a result of 20 years of neglect."* He didn't go to the dentist because he didn't *like* the dentist; so in the end he suffered a huge loss.

One of my favorite sayings is: "If you do what is easy, life will be hard. If you do what is hard, life will be easy."

Everyone knows what is required to take care of ourselves; in fact, it's pretty simple – proper nutrition, exercise on a regular basis, low-stress, plenty of sleep, and balance.

So, if we all "know" this, why do many of us neglect these areas in our lives? The most common excuses are lack of time, discipline and/or the energy to do something about it.

There's a Spanish proverb that says:

> *"A man too busy to take care of his health is like a mechanic too busy to take care of his tools."*

Your body is the tool you need to achieve your dreams. Your body takes you from place to place, and that requires a certain level of energy. If you aren't taking care of your body, the energy levels won't be there to sustain your dreams. This is a life and death issue; either your dreams live, or they die.

Which one do you choose?

Creating the life of your dreams requires a tremendous amount of energy. Anthony Robbins says this about energy:

> *"The higher your energy level, the more efficient your body. The more efficient your body, the better you feel and the more you will use your talent to produce outstanding results."*

I believe the type of people we choose to surround ourselves with is also important to our long-term success as well as the types of books we read. So, if you want to get healthy, start hanging out with healthy people and read books frequently about health to inspire and motivate you. Of course, hanging around healthy people and reading books about good health won't do anything for you if you don't take action and implement healthy habits.

When my energy levels get low, I know it means I've neglected my morning routine.

HERE'S WHAT MY MORNING ROUTINE LOOKS LIKE NOW (IT HAS EVOLVED OVER THE YEARS):

- 20 minutes of meditation
- Yoga
- Daily three-mile walk
- Lifting Weights
- Gym 2-3 days a week
- Reading a chapter or more from my spiritual books
- Journaling three pages every day
- Listing five items in my gratitude journal
- Drinking a Green Smoothie, Fresh Juice, Overnight Oats or an Acai' bowl
- A warm shower
- 30-minutes spent in nature and in the sun
- Creatively expressing myself

Actor Matthew McConaughey has a great rule: "…to break one sweat a day… whether that's going for a run, whether that's dancing, whether that's making love – just break a sweat a day."

In fact, researchers at Duke, Harvard and Stanford have shown that exercise is not only good for your body, but it is a powerful antidote for depression and anxiety. According to Duke, the researchers found that adults who worked out for 45 minutes a day (30 minutes of aerobics and 15 minutes of warm-up and cool-down) did equally as well as the group who took the prescription medication. They also did a six-month follow-up on these groups. Those who exercised fared better than those who took the medication and had a lower chance of relapse (8% vs. 38%).

The key to transforming your life is to live an examined life.

We all have bad habits because we're often living our lives in default mode. When we want to change our life and get out of the default mode, a great way to do that is by changing our habits.

In his book, "Atomic Habits," author James Clear shares the story of how the fate of British Cycling changed one day in 2003. At the time, professional cyclists in Great Britain had endured nearly 100 years of mediocrity until they hired Dave Brailsford as the new performance director. Since 1908, Great Britain had only won a single gold medal at the Olympic Games and had failed in the Tour de France.

Brailsford was committed to one strategy: "**THE AGGREGATION OF MARGINAL GAINS**" which was the philosophy of searching for tiny margins of improvement in everything you do. Brailsford said,

"The whole principle came from the idea that if you broke down everything you could think of that goes into riding a bike, and then improve it by 1 percent, you will get a significant increase when you put them all together."

So that's what Brailsford and his team began doing – making small adjustments.

Here's some of what they did:

- **Redesigned the bike seats to make them more comfortable and rubbed alcohol on the tires for a better grip.**
- **Asked the riders to wear electrically heated over-shorts to maintain ideal muscle temperature while riding.**
- **Used biofeedback sensors to monitor how each athlete responded to a particular workout.**
- **Tested various fabrics in a wind tunnel and had their outdoor riders switch to indoor racing suits, which proved to be lighter and more dynamic.**

- Tested different types of massage gel seats to see which one led to the fastest muscle recovery.
- Hired a surgeon to teach each rider the best way to wash their hands to reduce the chances of catching a cold.
- Determined the type of pillow and mattress that resulted in the best night's sleep for each rider.
- Painted the inside of the team truck white, which helped them spot little bits of dust that would normally slip by unnoticed but could degrade the performance of the finely tuned bikes.

As these small improvements accumulated, and the results improved exponentially. Just five years after Brailsford took over, they won 60% of the gold medals available in the 2008 Olympic Games consequently dominating the road and track cycling events. Several cyclists went on to win the Tour de France; this became regarded as the most successful run in cycling history.

How does this happen?

According to James Clear, here's the answer:

"It is so easy to overestimate the importance of one defining moment and underestimate the value of making small improvements on a daily basis. Too often, we convince ourselves that massive success requires massive action.

Whether it is losing weight, building a business, writing a book, winning a championship, or achieving any other goal, we put pressure on ourselves to make some earth-shattering improvement that everyone will talk about.

Meanwhile, improving by 1 percent isn't particularly notable – sometimes it isn't even noticeable – but it can be far more meaningful, especially in the long run. The difference a tiny improvement can make over time is astounding.

Here's how the math works out: if you can get 1 percent better each day for one year, you'll end up thirty-seven times better by the time you're done.

Conversely, if you get 1 percent worse each day for one year, you'll decline nearly down to zero. What starts as a small win or minor setback accumulates into something much more."

We're not looking for perfection in any of the areas of your life; we're looking for small advancements. A 1% a day improvement will create huge changes in your life over time.

One of the best books I read about small changes many years ago was "The Slight Edge" by Jeff Olson.

Small changes = Big results

The changes in my life happened over a period of years. It's easy to look at successful people and miss the 10+ years they spent training and working on their craft.

Don't underestimate the power of small consistent actions to take your towards creating your dream life.

In the next chapter, we are going to be looking at one of the biggest obstacles to people being able to live their dreams – Money $$$$

Chapter 7 – The Less You Pay, The More You Can Play

Money is a double-edged sword. We need it to survive, we need it to enjoy life, we need it to help others and we need it in order to be generous. Unfortunately, we also use money in emotionally unhealthy ways when we aren't fulfilled and living our lives on purpose, which causes us to have fewer options and bigger obstacles to overcome while pursuing our dreams.

In this chapter, we will look at ways to reduce your expenses and get out of debt so you can buy back your time.

We've discussed the differences between a BONDAGE JOB and a FREEDOM JOB. The main difference is a FREEDOM JOB gives you a paycheck but doesn't consume your time, your energy, your soul or define you. A BONDAGE JOB sucks all of your energy, time and consumes your soul.

Tama Kieves, author of two brilliant books, "This Time I Dance" and "Inspired & Unstoppable," was a Harvard Lawyer on the partnership track at a high-profile law firm in New York City who courageously quit her job and started waiting tables at the Paradise Café so she could write. Kieves would often write in cafés, walk in the park, journal, read and in many ways, peel off the dead layers around her heart and her intuition. She chose to wait tables because she wanted to work *desk-free*. According to Tama, for every notch of status she gave up, she gained a world of freedom.

IT'S TIME TO PUT YOUR LIVING EXPENSES ON A DIET

Years ago, I owned a 5,000 square foot, million-dollar home, which I absolutely loved. I bought it when my kids were teenagers, and it was a great family home. I purchased it with my then fiancé, and when we split up, all the bills for the million-dollar house fell on me.

After a while, it became a burden to take care of the 5,000 square foot house financially and physically. After five years, I sold that house and downsized to a 2,300 square foot one level rancher in my dream neighborhood overlooking the Chesapeake Bay. My space is quiet, serene, and I'm gazing out at the water as I write these words. It's the perfect place for me. I decreased my monthly expenses by over 60% so I could reduce my stress, focus my energy, spend time doing what I love, and enjoy my life.

One of the homes I lived in years ago had an in-law suite in the basement, and I was able to rent out that space for income. There's a show on HGTV about turning regular properties into income-producing properties. With the increasing popularity of services like AirBNB, you may be able to rent out some space in your home to generate cash. Or maybe you can do a low-cost remodel and create an in-law suite or area to rent out if you own your home.

Instead of looking at cutting your living expenses as hard work, let's look at it as a fun adventure.

In his book, "The More of Less: Finding the Life You Want Under Everything You Own," author Joshua Becker and creator of www.BecomingMinimalist.com says:

"Now, resisting consumerism won't give us happiness in itself. An absence is just a nothingness. What matters is what we fill the empty space with. But we have to start somewhere. Resisting consumerism can keep us from being deceived and can give us the possibility of finding real happiness, whatever that might look like for each of us."

Cutting expenses won't automatically bring happiness; it's about filling the empty space with meaning. Every day I get to do things that are meaningful to me – meditation, journaling, going on long walks in my neighborhood by the water, reading books, writing books, creating content for my online business, spending time with my kids and granddaughter as well as family and friends. When

I was trapped in my corporate job, I didn't do anything meaningful to me. I was too busy with work responsibilities and by the time I got home, I was exhausted.

HERE'S A FEW STORIES FROM JOSHUA BECKER'S BOOK TO INSPIRE YOU:

1. Leo Babauta, a minimalist with six children, had recently moved from Guam to San Francisco with only the contents of one suitcase for each member of the family. Leo credits minimalism with helping him get out of debt, lose weight, stop smoking and leave the job he couldn't stand.

2. Tammy Strobel lives with her husband and cat in a 128-square foot home in Portland. The Strobels' had racked up over $30,000 in debt and embraced minimalist living as a means of overcoming it. But they fell so in love with their new life that they continued living in a Tiny House even after they had retired their debt, becoming ambassadors for this housing option.

3. Annette Garland is an Irish freelance journalist based mainly in Southeast Asia. She spends most of her time in Malaysia, travels frequently to Australia and Indonesia goes to India when she can, visits Ireland and France once a year and has plenty of other countries on her itinerary for the future. It is minimalism, she says, that enables her to do all of this. Annette has no permanent home and no car. She's been a web-working nomad since January 2013, when she decided to leave France. She calls herself an *"anywhereist."*

Do any of these stories inspire you and make you think deeper about what you really want for yourself and your life?

Sondra and Markus Ray are authors of over 20 books, workshop leaders, and trainers who recently shared with me that they don't "own" anything. No house. No car. They do rent a lovely loft apartment in Washington, D.C. with a few belongings to make it homey, but not owning things gives them freedom to travel to exotic places like India, Bali, Australia, and so many beautiful places around the world to teach their seminars. They love their freedom and wouldn't trade it for anything.

I'm not the travelling type, so travelling around the world doesn't appeal to me. However, I don't own a home right now because I don't want all the unexpected expenses that go along with owning a home.

In fact, I recently heard about a study that said the happiest people don't own homes. I can tell you that's been true for me.

Lots of well-meaning people tell me renting a house is like throwing money down the drain and they remind me of the tax write-offs I'm not getting, but guess what? I have a rent payment I can afford, and I have no unexpected expenses. And if I decide I want to move, I can pick up and go somewhere new. I feel that I have freedom living here, and I love it. The other interesting thing about the house I'm renting is that the woman who owns it is 107 years old! I feel her spirit and her energy in this house. Lots of love and happiness. She told her family she doesn't want to sell her home because she might move back one day! I'm thankful she's allowing me to rent her home and enjoy it as my own. A house like the one I'm renting on the water in an upscale neighborhood would be close to a million dollars to own, but I get to rent it at a fraction of the cost.

Creating your dream life isn't about giving up everything. It's also not about holding onto everything and just trying to better organize it. Instead, it's about reducing your debt and possessions to a level that will set you free. Only you know what that level is.

DOWNSIZING YOUR DEBT

On average in the United States, we see over 5,000 advertisements per day telling us to buy more. We also consume twice as many material goods as we did just 50 years ago. The average home size has tripled and contains about 300,000 items. We own more televisions sets than there are people in the house. We have so much stuff that one out of ten Americans rents off-site storage.

We also have a personal debt problem and the average person has over $15,000 in credit card debt and the average mortgage balance is over $150,000.

You don't need statistics though to recognize that you have too much stuff or too much debt.

Let's look at some of the benefits we will reap by reducing expenses, debt, and possessions:

- **Less stress because you'll have less excess.**

- **More money – spending less and reducing what you pay out leaves more money to play.**

- **More time and energy – now you'll have more time to follow your passions and interests and pursue things that have meaning for you.**

- **Less distraction – our things are competing for our attention. When we remove some of those things, we can place our attention elsewhere.**

- **More freedom – physically, psychically, and financially. Stuff weighs us down and makes us feel heavy. Removing stuff makes us feel lighter.**

- **More happiness – more joy and happiness because we have more time and energy to spend on meaningful activities as we learn that things don't and never will make us happy.**

We already talked about reducing clutter and possessions (energy zappers), so now we are going to focus on reducing your living expenses.

Think about it this way – for every dollar you reduce in your living expenses, you get an increase in your freedom account.

Less bills = more thrills!

You can live on a lot less than you think.

Often, we fall into default mode which is high-consumerism mode and as a result we have a high amount of debt which limits our freedom. By shrinking your expenses, you increase your opportunities.

Maybe you still feel that cutting down your expenses and material consumption seems more like deprivation or restraint, or even scarcity, but I promise it will be financial liberty and the path to real freedom.

"When we're bored in our lives, in our job and we have cash, that's a dangerous place to be. Often times, we fill the hole in our lives with extravagances, vanity, excess and insanity that feel like wealth – but the truth is it's not wealth, it's DEBT and STRESS. This debt and stress is stealing away the time you could be living a more meaningful life with and creating work you love." ~Tama Kieves, author of "This Time I Dance"

We shop on autopilot and think we "need" what we're buying when the truth is the line between our needs and our wants has been blurred.

When we're in the wrong career, we turn reckless and distract ourselves with things we don't need. Reducing your expenses is the price to pay for your freedom and your ticket out of job hell.

It's time to get creative and play the game of reducing your expenses to get back more freedom in your life.

LOOK AT EACH CATEGORY AND TAKE AS MANY ACTIONS AS YOU CAN WITH THE GOAL TO REDUCE YOUR LIVING EXPENSES BY 25% OR MORE:

MORTGAGE:

- Refinance your mortgage for a better rate.
- Drop your private mortgage insurance (PMI).
- Sell your house and move to something more affordable.

RENT:

- Downsize; do you really need that 3,000-5,000+ square foot house? I know I didn't.
- Get a roommate or rent out part of your house.
- Negotiate with your landlord to reduce your rent or handle repairs for a reduction of rent.

UTILITIES:

- Turn your thermostat down and use space heaters or window air conditioners instead of heating and cooling the whole house.
- Sign up for the energy saving day that your local carrier usually has.
- Don't leave lights and televisions on when not in use.
- Take shorter showers, and don't leave the water running.

AUTO:

- Refinance your auto loan and reduce your payment.
- Sell your car privately and buy a less expensive used car.
- Swap out your lease.
- Evaluate whether you even need a car.

CABLE AND INTERNET:

- Get rid of extras – premium channels, multiple boxes and DVRs, etc.
- Disable your cable – use Netflix or other lower cost options.

CELL PHONE:

- Sign up for automatic payments and save a percentage of the payment.
- Change or remove your insurance.
- Switch your plan or carrier and see if the new carrier will buy out your contract.

HOMEOWNERS INSURANCE:

- Shop around to at least 3-5 companies to get the best rate.
- Bundle your home and auto insurance.
- Look for discounts like having a home security system.

GROCERIES:

- Make a digital list on your phone and keep a budget so you don't overspend.
- Choose store brand items.
- Join the store's loyalty program to get discounts.

EATING OUT:

- Order a meal that you can make into two or three meals.
- Split an entrée with the person you're dining with.
- Scope out specials such as happy hour food discounts, weekly deals.
- Use a meal delivery service and save money on eating out all the time.

STUDENT LOAN DEBT:

- Sign up for an income-driven repayment plan.
- Ask for a deferment or forbearance.
- Refinance your student loans.

CREDIT CARD DEBT:

- Ask for a lower interest rate.
- Transfer your balance.
- Consolidate your credit cards.

MEMBERSHIPS AND AUTOMATIC PAYMENTS:

- Review your automatic renewals and cancel ones you are not using.
- Memberships to big box stores are great if you have a large family, but if you're not going there weekly, then cancel it.
- Cancel your gym membership if you don't use it.
- Cancel your newspaper and magazine subscriptions if you aren't using them.

JOIN A BARTER CLUB:

- Join a barter club and barter your services if you own a business.
- Eat out using barter dollars.
- Use barter dollars for anything you're paying cash for (I am in a barter club and I love it!)

You can cut your expenses by 25% if you work at it consistently. Write out all of your living expenses and your automatic payments and go through them one by one. It helps to see things visually. Also include those quarterly payments, annual payments, and one-time payments.

Remember: The less you have to pay...the more time you have to play.

Let's talk about debt now.

DEBT IS A THREAT TO YOUR DREAMS

Debt is the #1 threat to living your dreams. It hijacks your future and keeps you trapped in situations in which you might not want to be. When you have debt, you pay interest and instead of your money working for you, you are allowing someone else to use your money for their own benefit.

Dave Ramsey, who is the author of numerous books on finance and runs *Financial Peace University*, recommends the following baby steps to get control of your money:

1. Save $1000 for your starter emergency fund.

2. Pay off all debt (except the house) using the debt snowball.

3. Save 3-6 months of expenses in a fully funded emergency fund.

4. Invest 15% of your household income in retirement.

5. Save for your children's college fund.

6. Pay off your home early.

7. Build wealth and give.

Learn more at: www.daveramsey.com/dave-ramsey-7-baby-steps

THE LAST THING YOU WANT TO DO IS QUIT YOUR JOB AND BE STRESSED OUT ABOUT MONEY.

Dave Ramsey recommends having three to six months of living expenses in the bank as an emergency fund, paying off all debt, and then working on putting your money to work for you through mutual funds.

Chris Hogan, author of the book "The Everyday Millionaire," has now helped hundreds, and maybe thousands of average everyday people become millionaires. It's never too late to start no matter what your age.

We live in a consumer-driven world that teaches us to buy things we want (not need) on credit, but when you do that, you're trading in your future for temporary enjoyment.

Chris Hogan says,

"If you live fake rich now, you'll retire real broke later."

So, getting out of debt, having an emergency fund, and investing in your future is critical to living your dreams and having freedom.

In the next chapter, we will talk about reducing your hours at work and/or weaning yourself off your job to give you more time to explore and follow your dreams...

Chapter 8 – Weaning Yourself Off Your 9-5

Several years ago, I was teaching a workshop based on this book, "Quit Your Job and Follow Your Dreams," when a middle-aged woman raised her hand and said "Michelle, I'm an attorney. I make six figures, have great benefits like health insurance, two months of paid vacations, a 401k, but what I really want to do is start an acting studio on the beach in Florida. I can't figure out how to do that? I'm not a risk taker like you."

My answer:

"Following your dreams isn't an overnight event. It is something you transition into."

Of course, it isn't easy leaving a 6-figure job, or any job that pays the bills and gives you great benefits, but if you're miserable every single day of your life, then you need to come up with an exit strategy.

In this chapter, we will talk about transitioning out of your job before making the BIG LEAP out of it permanently.

There are so many creative ways to create your dream life:

- **Ann Patchett worked as a waitress at TGI Fridays and wrote in her spare time.**
- **Elizabeth Gilbert kept multiple side jobs in order to pursue her passion of writing books and didn't actually quit her jobs until a year after Eat, Pray, Love became a huge success.**
- **Toni Morrison would wake up at 5 a.m. to work on her novels before going off to her real-life career in the publishing world.**

Many successful entrepreneurs kept their day jobs until their dream business was profitable and they could afford to quit.

Elizabeth Gilbert shares some advice about anyone who is pursuing their passions and creativity:

"People don't do this kind of thing because they have all kinds of extra time and energy for it; they do this kind of thing because their creativity matters to them enough that they are willing to make all kinds of SACRIFICES for it."

Yes, your dreams require sacrifice.

This chapter is about transitioning out of your current job until you can afford to quit.

PART-TIME WORK CAN CREATE MORE SPENDABLE INCOME

Before I left the legal field completely, I went from full-time to part-time which provided the perfect transition out of the corporate world.

The process was very serendipitous; I had received a call from a head-hunter looking to place someone in a part-time position working 5:30 p.m. to 1:30 a.m. three nights per week in the word processing department of a huge law firm. Just 18 hours per week!

At first, I thought she was crazy. As a single parent with three children, I couldn't afford to only work part-time. To my surprise, when I looked at the numbers, I discovered I would have more "spendable income" working part-time than I did working full-time for 40 hours per week.

So, I took the leap and left my full-time job and worked part-time for the next five years. This schedule gave me the freedom I was craving and the time I wanted to spend with my kids, as well as the chance to explore my dreams.

To make this work, I created multiple streams of income:

- I supplemented my part-time income at the law firm selling candles for a company called Party Lite (an in-home party business).

- I took a part time nanny job that paid well.

- I rented out a portion of my house for extra income.

- I rented out my one-car garage to a man who had an antique car who needed a safe place to store it.

- I delivered pizza kits for a non-profit organization with my kids on the nights I wasn't working.

You may wonder how I had more "spendable income" working fewer hours. At the time, I was paying $1000 a month in daycare, about $150 per month to commute into D.C., as well going out to lunch almost every day, purchasing business attire, and being in a much higher tax bracket.

My full-time job paid $45,000+ a year with benefits. The new part time job paid $18,000 a year. Here are the hard numbers:

- My part-time job at the law-firm ($18,000/year)
- Rental income from my roommate ($7,200/year)*
- Income from the candle business ($5000+/year)
- Nanny money ($5,000+/year)
- Pizza Kit money ($3,000+/year)

I also reduced my expenses:

- Day care ($12,000/year)
- Commuting costs ($2,000/year)
- Business Clothing ($2,500/year)
- Lunches Out ($2,400/year)
- Lower tax bracket – priceless!

In the end, it all balanced out and I was able to make ends meet.

Remember that the sacrifice is temporary and it's a path forward to living your dreams and getting your life back.

Some people might be uncomfortable renting space in their home due to privacy issues. I did give up some privacy to be able to maintain the level of income I needed to pay the bills.

When you're serious about your dreams and your freedom, you will be resourceful and creative.

Think outside the cubicle prison you're in.

Working part-time was the perfect way for me to transition out of the legal field and it opened up so much energy, time and space in my life to explore and find more clues to my dreams.

The hardest part is letting go of the security that you have with your job. It's like taking away the safety net and that can be very scary.

"The magic begins when we courageously leave what we've known to trust and hope for something more."
~**Nicole Williams, author of "Earn What You're Worth"**

I coached a woman many years ago who was making about $40,000 a year working for someone else. She knew that with her skills and talents, she could start her own business doing the same thing and double her income in the first year. Why didn't she do it? Job security.

She knew for while she would not have a steady paycheck, and she understood there was a lot of risk involved. That's why it's so important to budget, pay off debt, reduce living expenses, and create other sources of income to minimize the anxiety and fears you will undoubtedly have about making this transition.

FAITH ALSO HELPS WHEN MAKING THE TRANSITION

Faith is knowing deep inside that you are being guided and ultimately being taken care of.

Don't, however, use faith as an excuse for not taking action.

You have to be an active participant and co-creator in your life. Don't complain about your life but then do nothing to change it. Many people make excuses for why they aren't living their dreams and remain stuck.

Kyle Maynard, a star high school wrestler who is also a congenital amputee (all four limbs), says, "I think excuses are a way for people to give up and get away from their dreams."

If you hear any excuses coming out of your mouth, remind yourself how important your dreams are and how committed you are to making them a reality.

You can be committed to having freedom even if you don't know exactly what that looks like; you just know it's not working with your current employer and living your life like you are now.

GOING PART-TIME WITH YOUR CURRENT COMPANY

Start looking within your company for part-time opportunities. Find out what the salary cut would be and make plans to supplement the cut in pay. Remember to consider that you will also be cutting expenses associated with the full-time job so you will be saving money.

Make it a habit to review and monitor jobs online. When the time is right, you will find that perfect part-time job to transition out of your full-time job; this is the quickest way out of the 9-5 corporate grind in my opinion. Finding ways to supplement the reduction in income is key. We will talk more about multiple streams of income in Chapter 10.

3 STEPS TO WEAN YOURSELF OFF OF YOUR FULL-TIME JOB:

1. Reduce your expenses; live within your means
2. Switch from a full-time job to a part-time job
3. Create multiple streams of income

Transitioning from your full-time job to a part-time job (either with the company you are with now or with a new company) will give you the time freedom to pursue your dreams while making enough money to pay your bills.

To work part time, you must take action to reduce your expenses, live within your means, and create multiple streams of income to replace some of the lost income.

WORKING PART-TIME IS LIKE HAVING ONE FOOT OUT OF THE DOOR TO YOUR OLD LIFE

Working part-time is a stepping-stone on the journey to your dreams. Don't underestimate the power of this step.

I had my "FREEDOM JOB" selling hot tubs for almost 10 years while I was building my online business. I didn't have a solid plan; I was following my heart, my curiosity and my passions. That FREEDOM JOB was a stepping stone to the life I have now.

If you have your finances in order and can pay your bills, you will be fine. I don't want you drowning in a sea of unpaid bills and having creditors chasing you down so you can "follow your dreams."

No Starving Artists here!

THINGS TO CONSIDER WHEN TAKING A PART-TIME JOB

- Ask yourself, "How much of my day will be spent doing things I love and doing things I dislike or hate?" You want at least 75% of your time spent doing things you love and only 25% doing things you dislike or hate. If not, you're going to be very unhappy, and that unhappiness with spill over into your energy reserves and deplete the energy you need to pursue your dreams. So even if the money is tempting, don't do it!

- Are you a people person or a project person? Is the job in line with this preference? Make sure it is or you will be miserable.

- Can I pay all of my bills with the income from the part-time job? If the answer is No, figure out how you will supplement that income.

- Will I have the time to work on my dreams? Don't take a job that has so much responsibility that you can't sleep at night or concentrate on your dreams.

- Most part-time jobs do not offer health insurance, so do some research and find a policy that works for you. I have health insurance with Care First that is a few hundred per month. Is it the greatest insurance out there? No. But, I eat healthy, exercise, get plenty of sleep, have minimal stress and have fun so I rarely go to the doctor. In fact, I have the type of insurance that they only sell to "healthy people" (so I'm told).

- Determine what you will do with any retirement funds you have (i.e., roll them into another account).

- Save enough to cover at least 6-12 months expenses before you transition to a part-time job. This will reduce a lot of anxiety, fear and stress.

- Once you've found that part-time job that seems perfect for you and your circumstances, select a date and go for it!

CONGRATULATIONS! You are on your way to living life on your own terms!

"There is only one success –
to be able to spend your life in your own way."
~Christopher Morley (1890-1957) American Novelist and Poet

CONTINUE WORKING TOWARDS YOUR DREAMS WHILE YOU HAVE YOUR PART-TIME JOB

I did this for years by working different freelance jobs before I could go full-time with my online business. I always made sure that the "jobs" I took would not consume so much of my time or energy that I didn't have the time and energy for my dreams.

Some of the part-times jobs I had were a freelance newspaper reporter; I taught classes for the Community College; I coached clients part-time as an independent contractor.

HOW LONG DO YOU HAVE TO STAY IN THIS PART-TIME JOB?

It's all up to you. The quicker you get your finances under control, reduce your living expenses and debt, build a savings account that can sustain you while you are building your dream life, create multiple sources of income, then the quicker you can leave your part-time job.

All of these factors will determine how long you have to stay in your part-time job.

We all have different rhythms and different goals. Don't let others set the clock for you. You will know when it's time. If you allow yourself quiet time every day, you will begin to hear the voice inside that will guide you to the next right step. You will hear the call. Trust it! It will never lead you astray.

Marjory Zoet Bankson, author of "Call to the Soul: Six Stages of Spiritual Development," says: "At the core, listening for the call is about restoring our relationship with self, with the world around us and with God."

She goes onto say:

"Each time that a call has run its course, leaving us empty and bereft of purpose, we can trust that something new will arrive... because we have experienced this barren desert time before...

because we know we are in the space between calls, when the whisper of purpose is too soft to hear."

It's okay to be in between calls, but don't stay there too long. When we start experiencing those "barren desert" feelings, we know it's time to move on.

Think of living your dreams as a river you have to cross. To get to the other side of the river, there are stepping stones.

In this book, each chapter is a stepping stone to help you get to the other side.

*The next section of the book is "Creation,"
and it is about Creating Your Dream Life!
You've done the work of gaining clarity and clearing things out.
Creation is the next and final step in the process.*

PART III – CREATION

"Take a small step in the direction of a dream and watch the synchronous doors flying open."
~Julia Cameron, author of The Artists Way

Chapter 9 – The Passion Test

"When you are clear, what you want will show up in your life,
and only to the extent you are clear."
~Janet Bray Attwood, author of "The Passion Test"

Your passions are important because they are what light you up!
When you get clear on your passions, the magic starts to happen,
and synchronistic events line up to make your dreams come true.

Everyone has a different perspective on what the word *passion*
means to them. Some people say it is their interests and/or hobbies,
others say it is their obsessions, and still others believe it is the
things we are really good at.

Over the years, I've used different tools to help me clarify what
is important to me and what I am passionate about.

The Passion Test

Janet Bray Attwood and Chris Attwood, co-authors of "The
Passion Test: The Effortless Path to Discovering Your Destiny" say
that our passions are "the most important things you can think of
which would give you a life of joy, passion and fulfillment."

Janet and Chris created a tool called the Passion Test® which is
a two-part test that helps people discover their purpose, destiny,
and ways to create work that feels like PLAY.

It's important to clarify our passions because when you get clear
on exactly what they are, you can align your goals with them and
begin to create and design a life you truly love.

Passion Test – Part One

Write down your top 10 - 15 passions (the most important things you can think of which would give you a life of joy, passion and fulfillment) by filling in the blank to the following sentence:

"When my life is ideal, I am

_____."

It's important to begin each passion with a verb related to being, doing or having. Close your eyes and picture your ideal life and then write your list.

Some examples of passions are:

When my life is ideal...

- I am travelling the world first class.
- I am working with an enlightened team.
- I am making a difference in the lives of others.
- I am speaking to large groups of people.
- I am a multi-millionaire.
- I am a bestselling author.

- I am being of service to thousands of people.
- I am having fun.
- I am helping others create and live their vision.
- I am working for myself in my own business.
- I am living in a beautiful home on the water.
- I am hosting writers retreats twice a year.
- I am teaching online programs that help others.
- I am painting in my studio every day.
- I am hiking in nature 3-4 x per week.

We're not looking for details of *how* you will make this happen, it's just about the feeling of joy and fulfillment when you are doing these things.

Okay, now it's your turn...

When my life is ideal, I am...

_____.

Write the top 10-15 things that come to your mind.

Passion Test – Part Two

Once you've written your top 10-15 passions, then you will select your top five passions by reviewing each one on the list and choosing the ones that are most important to you.

Start with #1 and #2. Which one is more important? Let's say it's #2. Then, compare #2 to #3 and choose which one of those is more important. If it's #3, then compare that one to #4. Go through the entire list until you end up with your top five choices.

Magic really does happen when we get clarity in our lives. It's easy for people to say *"I hate my job..."* but when you ask someone specifically what else they want to do, most people don't have an answer. When you do these exercises, you will know what is important to you, and then you can start setting your goals based on your passion list.

Repeat this exercise every six months since you are constantly evolving and growing. What was important six months ago, might have been achieved or maybe it just isn't as important as it was and something new might take its place.

Once you are done, write your top five passions on notecards or post-it notes and place them in strategic locations in your home.

Here are some location suggestions:

- **Your bathroom mirror**
- **Next to your computer**
- **In the kitchen where you prep and cook food**
- **Next to the remote control where you watch TV**
- **In your car on the dashboard**
- **On the refrigerator**

Doing this will keep your top five passions in the forefront of your mind. Otherwise, in a few weeks, you might have amnesia about what you wrote down.

Why does this happen?

Because life happens. Life is always moving, and we are busy with multiple things. It's easy to write down our goals, but it's easier to forget them.

When you read through your passion list several times a day, they will be ingrained deep inside of you. So, when you are making decisions, you can now ask yourself... is this going to help move me forward in the direction of my passions? Is this in alignment with my passions?

STOP RIGHT NOW AND PLACE YOUR INDEX CARDS OR POST IT NOTES IN AT LEAST FIVE PLACES.

Serendipity happens when we get clear on what we want. You do not have to figure out the "how" on anything on your list; you never know what will show up in your life.

CREATING MARKERS AND SIGNPOSTS

Janet and Chris recommend once you have your top 5 passions, that you begin to create markers (a signpost that you are living your passion).

For example, let's say your passion is becoming a bestselling author.

Your markers would be:

- **I've written and published my book**
- **My book is on a bestsellers list**
- **I am earning income from my book**

So, take the time NOW to write out your markers and signposts of what will happen when you have achieved that passion.

After leaving the legal field, I read a transformational book by Barbara Stanny called "Secrets of Six Figure Women." Stanny had an inspiring story, and she interviewed over 150 women to compare the characteristics of women earning six figures to those of women who were not making six figures.

This book inspired me so much because after 17 years in the legal field, the most I ever made was $50k per year. In fact, I can tell you, before reading that book, when I was in the corporate grind, I never thought about making six figures and I didn't even know it was possible.

After reading her book, I did something very important. I wrote the following sentence 100 times per day.

I AM MAKING 6 FIGURES DOING WHAT I LOVE

I knew in my career at the time, I was not going to earn six figures, but I really didn't know what I could do to make six figures. I just knew that I wanted to become a 6-figure woman.

I was passionate and obsessed about becoming a 6-figure woman. I didn't focus on the *how*, I just kept writing *"I am making 6-figures doing what I love."*

And guess what?

Within 18 months, I was making six figures working 20-25 hours a week in an outside sales job selling hot tubs! How amazing is that?

It was just like my serendipitous meeting with Billy Ray Cyrus in 1992, when I became obsessed with the thought *"I am going to meet Billy Ray Cyrus, he has something important to tell me that will change my life."*

I was obsessed with this thought and I truly *believed* it. Most of my friends and family thought I had lost my mind and was delusional about meeting Billy Ray; until of course, I met Billy Ray and he changed the entire trajectory of my life.

We all have two voices inside our heads; one that begs us to be practical and the other that wants us to step out on the ledge and be magical. Your soul chooses the magical path and that always feels scary.

When it comes to being practical vs. dreaming big, most people start with being practical and they end up limiting themselves.

Sometimes the reason we try to be "realistic" or "practical" is because we are afraid that if we dream too big, we will be disappointed and heartbroken if we don't achieve our dreams.

So, I'm going to challenge you to DREAM BIG anyway, and trust that serendipity will arrive to help you bring your dreams into fruition.

When I wanted to leave my job at the law firm, the guy I was dating (a very pragmatic and conservative guy) gave me dozens of reasons NOT to follow my dreams. He said my job at the law firm was a job that I should feel lucky and blessed to have and that so many people would love to have a job like I had.

In a way, he was putting this guilt trip on me and trying to kill my dreams. In fact, after that conversation, I started calling him a "dream killer." I could see his point of view knowing he started at the bottom of a company and worked his way to the top and was now making six figures. He just didn't understand the entrepreneurial and creative spirit that lived inside of me. The job at the law firm felt like a prison to me, and no matter how practical his advice was, I was never going to be happy in that prison. Thank God I didn't listen to him. In fact, we broke up shortly after that because I didn't feel supported or encouraged by him.

I've noticed that other men I've dated seemed jealous about my success, my freedom and my lifestyle. They tried to make me feel bad about what I was doing. I no longer date those types of men. Remember, I'm a recovered jerk magnet!

Be careful who you share your dreams with – there are a lot of *dream killers* and *poisonous playmates* out there. Being in a coaching group or mastermind with like-minded people is great support as you go towards creating and living your dreams.

Now that you have your top five passions,
in the next Chapter we are going to talk about
creating multiple streams of income...

Chapter 10 –
Multiple Streams of Income

Tom Corley, author of "Rich Habits," studied the habits of millionaires during a five-year study of the rich and poor. Here's what he found as it pertains to most self-made millionaires and their income streams:

- **65% of self-made millionaires had three streams of income.**
- **45% of self-made millionaires had four streams of income.**
- **29% of self-made millionaires had five or more streams of income.**

Having multiple streams of income is the same idea as diversifying your investment portfolio. When one income stream suffers, the others make up for it.

In my last job in the legal field, they hired a new Human Resources Administrator to secretly *clean house.*

What I mean by *clean house* is she was specifically hired to get rid of the high-paid employees without laying them off or firing them so they would be ineligible to collect unemployment or receive severance pay. Unfortunately and unfairly, the law firm was *cleaning house* through fear, intimidation and harassment.

Within weeks, co-workers in my department who had worked there for 5-20 years all left. I recognized right away what was going on and thought to myself, *"They can get rid of me if they want to, but I'm not leaving here without some severance pay."*

The new Human Resources Administrator was a tall, heavy set, angry, intimidating, and very scary woman who made my heart pound just by walking in the room. I had many confrontations with this woman, and the harder she tried to intimidate me, the stronger and more resilient I became. I kept a detailed journal of everything that was happening. When I gathered enough evidence, I filed an in-house harassment complaint with our corporate office. Within 24 hours, the intimidation and harassment stopped, and the investigation into my complaint began.

After a month, I was called into a formal meeting where I was told it was determined that I did NOT have a valid complaint and that this woman was not, according to their investigations, guilty of harassment.

After working for attorneys for more than 17 years, one thing I knew for sure was they were scared to death of lawsuits from disgruntled employees and would do almost *anything* to avoid them.

In the meeting, I was informed that my department was being restructured and my work hours were changing. Interestingly, the days and hours they offered were ones they knew I would be unable to work because of my three young children.

When I declined the offer, they told me I was free to go look for another job and that they were giving me severance pay! It wasn't a lot of money, but at that time in my life, it was perfect because it gave me some paid time off with benefits to transition out of the legal field completely.

When one stream of income dries up, you better have other streams of income flowing in!

You never know when one source of income is going to dry up.

According to the special series on the Oprah show years ago titled "Debt Diet," 75% of Americans are living paycheck-to-paycheck. That's a tremendous amount of stress! There is another way to live…

DO WHAT SQUIRRELS DO

Every Fall, the gray squirrel spends the majority of its time gathering nuts and seeds so that it will have enough food to last throughout the winter.

Did you also know that the squirrel buries its food in hundreds of different locations?

Before the squirrel buries the nuts, he cleans each nut which leaves a unique scent so he can find the nut later in winter. If a fellow squirrel or another animal finds the stash, the squirrel will have food buried in other locations.

So, what do squirrels and nuts have to do with quitting your job and following your dreams?

Well, if you look to one job as your only source of income and something happens to that job, you are going to be seriously out of luck and highly stressed. The solution to this problem is to have multiple streams of income – in other words, have a lot of nuts buried in the ground!

The founder of Entrepreneur Magazine, Chase Revel, says that it is much easier *to earn $1,000 per month from 10 small businesses than it is to earn $10,000 per month from one big one.* I like "easier," how about you?

Since getting laid off from the law firm in 2000, I have maintained multiple streams of income in my life – usually 4-8 streams. Here are some of the streams I've had over the past 15 years:

- **Royalties from My Books**
- **Income from My Bestselling Author Programs**
- **Public Speaking Engagements**
- **Coaching Income**
- **Sales from Digital Courses and Information Products**
- **Website Design Services**
- **Copywriting Services**
- **Income from Events And Retreats**

Some people say that their energy feels scattered when they have too many projects going on at once. I somewhat agree with that. Most projects require more energy in the beginning when you are getting everything set up; once the project gets going and you have systems and automation in place, then you should be able to start working on creating another stream of income (project); especially if it's passive like selling a digital online course.

Of course, this isn't always the case. Some projects require energy from beginning to end, but I believe the bulk of that energy is used when you are getting the project off the ground.

EMBRACE WHAT YOU LOVE

Others may criticize or make fun at things that interest you. That's the beauty of being human—we are all unique, and we must respect each other's differences enough to let others be who they are. We must also give ourselves permission to love what we love. Some of the things I love are decorating, cooking and baking, feng shui, baking, writing, arts and crafts, and bike riding.

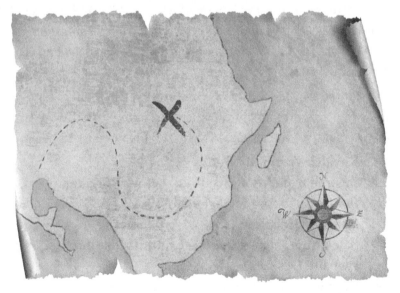

- What are five talents/interests that you LOVE?
- What are five services that you could provide to others using these talents/interests?

*Remember, people have to want these services. Just because we love something, doesn't always mean there is a market for it, but it's worth exploring.

START A BUSINESS FOR UNDER $100

There's a great book by Chris Guillebeau, *The $100 Startup: Reinvent The Way You Make a Living, Do What You Love, and Create a New Future*. The essence of Chris's book is the $100 Start-Up Model – profitable businesses typically run by one person with little start-up capital.

You need skills to pay the bills, and many people already have skills for which others are willing to pay.

Go to www.fiverr.com and you'll be inspired when you see how people are using their skills to get paid – skills like graphic design, editing, copywriting, cover design, voiceovers, logo design, branding, legal help, videography and so much more.

I started my business www.bestsellingauthorprogram.com in 2013 with my first client, and within two years, I was making six figures from that program. I had the skills people wanted: writing, publishing, formatting, technology skills, and launching books to multiple #1 bestsellers lists on Amazon. I've also launched books to the Wall Street Journal and USA Today bestsellers lists!

SOMETIMES YOU CAN'T FIND THE PERFECT JOB IN THE MARKETPLACE, SO YOU HAVE TO CREATE IT YOURSELF.

There's a reason why so many freelance sites like fiverr.com, up-work.com, readsy.com and others exist. Before the internet, the employment pool was more localized and people were considered for positions geographically. Now the employment pool is global. I've had assistants from other countries which is amazing.

If you have a marketable skill, there are people ready to hire you. Maybe you're an expert at Excel spreadsheets; if you are, there are people like me who would love to hire you to create custom spreadsheets for their business.

THE FASTEST WAY TO MAKE MONEY.

The fastest way I've found to make money is to offer a **Done-For-You Service**. I've learned that if you offer to give a man a fish or to teach him how to fish, the majority of time he will want you to give him the fish.

THE FOUR ARCHETYPES OF CREATING INCOME

Cathy Heller, author of *Don't Keep Your Day Job* talked about these 4 archetypes in a recent podcast I was listening to and I immediately connected with them, so I wanted to share those with you here since we are talking about how to create multiple streams of income.

1. **Creator** – You are the creator and maker of what you sell. It can be a physical product or a service, but you make it, and you sell it.

2. **Teacher** – Once you've mastered something and you begin to teach it you can 10x your income. Cathy Heller took her success as a musician and started teaching her strategies to aspiring musicians and was able to 10x the amount of money she was making as a "Creator". I've found the same thing to be true in my business. Once I've mastered something, I make more money teaching it. So teaching is a great way to earn bigger money.

3. **Curator** – This is where your pull together people, events or projects. For example, I have an independent publishing company and I publish books for clients, so I am a curator. Take your passion and figure out a way to be a curator of it.

4. **Investigator** – You love your topic so much you get paid to be an investigator of it. You might start a podcast, write a blog or a book about it. Someone who comes to mind as an Investigator archetype is Vani Hari, creator of the popular blog, www.foodbabe.com and author of "Feeding You Lies: How to Unravel the Food Industry's Playbook and Reclaim Your Health." She is an investigator who gets paid to do research! How can you be an investigator?

HAVING ONE STREAM OF INCOME IS RISKY

It's important that you do NOT put all your nuts in one basket. If one source of income doesn't work out, it's important to have other sources. I know I sound like a broken record, but it's that important. Remember, the average millionaire has 3-5 streams of income!

For so many years I lived paycheck-to-paycheck, so I know first-hand what it's like to live with exorbitant amounts of fear, stress and insecurity. It's no fun. I don't want you to have a false sense of security when it comes to your job because that false sense of security can lead you right to the poor house.

When I was in my 20s, I worked for a solo practitioner, a personal injury attorney who absolutely adored me. I loved working for him; he was quirky, funny, crazy in a good way and had a big heart. I wore many hats in that small office which caused me to mistakenly believe that the office could not function without me.

I thought I was irreplaceable—I was wrong!

I was by no means the perfect employee. I had my faults, and one time while my boss was out of town, I decided to go pick up a mattress for one of my kids on my lunch hour. I told the receptionist to cover for me in case the boss called, and she agreed. My mattress errand took much longer than I anticipated; hours later, when I finally returned to the office (in the days before cell phones), I learned that my boss was calling every thirty minutes to talk to me. I was shocked when I got back to the office and was fired on the spot!

That experience taught me many valuable lessons:

- **Everyone can be replaced.**
- **There is no such thing as job security.**
- **Have money in the bank for a rainy day because the storm is on the way.**
- **Life is less stressful when you have multiple streams of income.**

Look at Richard Branson, a British adventurer, who is a master at creating multiple streams of income.

At age 17, Branson started a Student Advisory Center, which was designed to help young people. At age 20, he founded a record mail-order company known as "Virgin" and then opened a record shop in London. He later founded a recording studio known as "Virgin Records." (He later sold Virgin Music Group, for $1 billion). Years later, Branson founded "Virgin Atlantic Airways" which is now the second largest British international airline. Branson had a television reality show and has broken several world records. The man is an amazing creator of combining his passions with providing high quality services to others.

Zig Ziglar once said,

> *"You can have everything you want if you help enough other people get what they want."*

Branson not only has fun doing so…he makes lots of money!

Phil Laut, author of "Money is my Friend" makes a very good suggestion about how long you should try out a new idea:

> *Now that you have an idea of what you can do to make your favorite money-making idea a financial success, ask yourself whether you are willing to stick with it, no matter what it takes, until you receive your first $100 from it. After receiving your first $100, you can decide whether you want to continue or not.*

Good luck happens when you're in action.

PICK YOUR FAVORITE PROFIT PATH

My motto is: "Work less, make more."

What I've found so fascinating about running an online business is how you can make money while you sleep, and if you're sick or take a day off, it doesn't matter – you can still make money!

Some ways to make money online:

- **Affiliate Marketing (selling other people's products)**
- **Selling crafts and homemade items on sites like Etsy**
- **Selling Information Products like an Online Course**
- **Publishing Books on Amazon**
- **Coaching**
- **Consulting**
- **Training**
- **VIP Days**
- **Done-For-You Services**
- **And MORE!**

No matter how old you are, where you grew up, what kind of job you have, or what your hobbies are, you are an expert in something. Maybe you breed toy poodles or run profitable day care centers or create beautiful art or race cars. If you collected the information in your area of expertise and packaged it into an e-book or as an online course or in a coaching program, then you could begin making money with your knowledge!

Many of my clients who I've helped publish and launch their books to the #1 bestsellers list are now making thousands of dollars from their books in a variety of ways.

Their book is just the gateway to their other products and services.

Remember, you don't have to know everything there is to know about a subject, but if you know more than the average person, then you're probably an expert.

MAKING MONEY BY ACCIDENT

I want to share with you a funny story about a guy named Tom Antion who I met years ago at the National Speakers Association (NSA). Tom sold a variety of information products and taught classes about making money on the internet.

Tom taught people that they could either develop a product and then find the market for the product OR look for an already existing market and then create a product around the market.

One day, Tom stumbled upon an already existing market.

Doing some research on keywords, Tom discovered that there were over 13,000 searches per month for the keywords *"how to write a eulogy"* and over 11,000 searches for the keywords *"how to write a wedding toast."* Now Tom doesn't know anything about either of those topics, but what Tom does know is how to create information products and make money on the internet from them.

Once Tom saw that there was an already existing market for information products on eulogies and wedding toasts, Tom went to a popular site called "Elance" (now upwork.com) to find and hire a freelance writer to write two e-books: one on eulogies and one about weddings toasts. He paid the freelance writer less than $400 for each job. He then put up a simple template website for less than $50 and he began selling his e-books for $17.00.

That may not sound like a huge amount of money, but the market was already there. He took some simple, inexpensive steps and created a unique product.

Guess how much each site generates?

His eulogy site generates about $35,000 a year and his wedding toast site generates about $40,000 a year. Not bad for doing the work once and letting the money roll in month after month, year after year.

Could an extra $75k a year help you quit your job?

BUYER BEWARE

A lot of programs show you how to make money online. Some of them are legitimate, and some of them are scams. You must do your *due diligence* when it comes to "making money online" programs. Buyer Beware.

I believe the reasons most people are not successful when they attempt to start an online business are:

- **They are not at the right stage in their online business and it does not match the program they are purchasing.**
- **The person's skillset does not match what is required for that type of business.**
- **The lifestyle the person wants does not match the type of business they are attempting to start.**

Don't sign up for a $10k coaching program from a guy that says he's making $1 million dollars a month if you've never even made $1 online. There is a huge gap between where you are and where the teacher is. You most likely wouldn't even understand the industry lingo used and the learning curve would be too great for you to overcome. You would be setting yourself up for failure.

It would be better to find someone who is doing what you want to do and who is just a little further along than you are and learn from that person.

We will talk about investing in yourself shortly; it's important to do, but you have to invest in the right things.

5 STAGES OF AN ONLINE BUSINESS

- **Stage 1 - $0 to $20k – Baby**. Involves learning new skills, understanding the platform, building a website, email list, and developing and testing a service, product, or program to sell.

- **Stage 2 - $20-50k – Toddler**. You've learned the environment, the skills needed, the industry lingo, and you've laid a foundation, and this is where you get more clarity on what you want to do with your business.

- **Stage 3 - $50-$100k** – Adolescent. You've grown up quite a bit. You are committed and you know what it takes to run an online business. You know your strengths and your weaknesses. At this point, you may get some support for your business – a virtual assistant, a tech person, a copywriter, a funnel specialist, an operations manager, etc.

- **Stage 4 - $100k to $1m** – Adult with Authority. You've proven yourself online because you learned how to make six figures! Now you can decide if you want to stay at this level and run a small boutique online business or grow your business. You have increased the value you offer in the marketplace. You are investing in marketing and have a small team.

- **Stage 5 - $1m and up** – Mature Adult. You have a great team that runs your business with systems, automation and accountability. You are charging a high-ticket premium and may have multiple programs.

Do you see how if you hire a mature adult to coach and mentor you when you are at the baby stage, the material and teachings will be far too advanced for where you are at? There are things you need to learn at every stage of starting and growing an online business.

Remember the movie *The Karate Kid*? If not, it's worth watching. In the movie, Daniel, the main character, leaves his hometown and moves to Southern California with his mom but quickly finds himself the target of a group of bullies who study karate at the Cobra Kai dojo. Luckily, Daniel befriends Mr. Miyagi, an unassuming repairman who just happens to be a martial art master himself. Miyagi takes Daniel under his wing, and trains him using unconventional methods which become the foundation for preparing him to compete against the brutal Cobra Kai.

In business, you need to build a strong foundation to build your business upon. There is a lot of training that has to happen and that takes time.

So, if you are at stage 1 or 2, then you should hire someone who is at stage 3 or 4. If you're at stage 4, then you can hire someone who is at stage 5.

Now that you understand the stages of an online business, let's talk about some of the ways you can make money online.

Three Popular Ways to Make Money Online

Selling An Online Course.

Selling an online course is one of the most popular ways to make money online, but it is not as easy as it used to be or that experts make it out to be. I started my online business in 2005 because I was teaching live workshops and it was difficult to get people to come out of their homes and to attend. I decided to put up a website and teach virtually, before it was as popular as it is now. Currently, it's a very crowded marketplace. It's not just about developing an online curriculum; you need to have an email list and a social media following and run paid ads to drive traffic to an automated webinar to sell your course. Everyone is running Facebook ads, and it's very expensive and has a steep learning curve. If you have a large social media following and an email list already, and you can tap into that, then this could be a good business model for you. For beginners with no platform, no list, no social media and no online experience it will be hard. Which leads to the next business model…

Offering an In-Demand Service

Offering an in-demand service will be the fastest and simplest way for you to make money online. It's actually the reason I have a 6-figure business with my Amazon Bestselling Author program. My main program is a **Done-For-You Service**. I went from making

$3-$5k a month coaching and selling online courses to $25-$50k+ per month offering a premium service that high-level entrepreneurs, coaches, speakers, executives, and trainers want.

If you have a skillset like copywriting, graphic design, administrative skills, editing, or sales, you will be able to quickly start offering your services to already established and successful business owners like myself. I've grown a team slowly. Right now, in my business I have a Virtual Assistant who does administrative work, organization tasks, some graphics work and sets up book launches for me. I also have a Publishing Assistant who edits, formats and publishes books for me. I just added a Project Manager to organize my business and a Tech person to take care of the websites for myself and some of my clients. So, think about what skill you have that could add value to an already existing online business owner.

Coaching Is Very Lucrative

I attribute my successful 6-figure online business to the coach I hired in September 2014, Jason Nyback. Coaches are amazing! If you want to be a coach, you don't necessarily have to be certified, although that can help, but you should have a very specific niche. Don't try to be a general "Life Coach" because Life Coach Schools are certifying thousands of people and it's a crowded marketplace.

If you have knowledge or expertise in a specific area, then you can coach others who need help in that area. Let me give you some examples of niche coaches I found at the Life Coach school run by Brooke Castillo:

- **Binge Eating Coach**
- **Real Estate Coach**
- **Weight Loss Coach**
- **Autoimmune Coach**
- **Feminist Confidence Coach**

- **Money Coach**
- **Mindfulness Coach**
- **Menopause Coach**
- **Running Coach**
- **The Deep Dive Coach (one of my clients)**
- **Female Entrepreneur Coach**
- **Non-Profit Career Coach**
- **Adoption Coach**
- **Introvert Coach**
- **Stop Over-Drinking Coach**

The benefit of being associated with a coaching school and certification program is that you can use their structures, systems and support in your own business. Also, they may refer clients to you.

Those are my top three suggestions for starting and running an online business. Just know there are many other business models for you to consider.

Other Ways to Make Money Online

Affiliate Marketing

You can make money selling other people's products. This requires you to build an email list to market to, develop a relationship with your list, and find quality programs with good affiliate commissions to offer to your list.

Membership Sites

These always sound fantastic in theory – get 1000 people to pay you $50 a month and you have a $50k per month business. It's not as easy as it sounds. You have to constantly create new content and build a large following. I've done it, and I don't care for this business model.

Live Retreats

These sound great as well, but they are challenging to organize and get people to commit to attending. Consider offering the material virtually (a DIY – do it yourself), then in group coaching (DWY – done with you) and then a live retreat for people who want the in-person training and community.

VIP Days

These can be very lucrative if you have an area of expertise where you can devote a half or full day to clients and charge a premium. I work with a PR expert, Christina Daves, who does high-ticket VIP days.

Mastermind Groups

These are like group think tanks. Everyone comes with one opportunity and one obstacle and then the group strategizes together.

Certification

If you have a successful business model, you can certify people in the process or methodology. Life Coach Schools provides a certification for those who go through their program. Many of the founders were successful life coaches and then began certifying others in their methodology. Another example is Mike Michalowicz, author of "Profit First: Transform Your Business from a Cash-Eating Monster to a Money-Making Machine." At the end of his book, Michalowicz asks if you want to be a certified *Profit First* Coach. I believe he charges $10k for the certification program. He's certified over 150 people, so he's made $1 million+ certifying others. It's a brilliant strategy, but you must already have a successful business model for this to work.

Many entrepreneurs want to start an online business, but there is a huge learning curve and a lot of predators that promise to help you go from $0 to $100k in 30 days or $0 to $1 million waiting to take your money! Run for your life from these types of offers.

Now that we've talked about profitable online businesses you can start, let's talk about why it's important to invest in yourself.

INVESTING IN YOURSELF AND YOUR DREAMS

In my early 20's, I went on a shopping spree with my best friend Kathy at Macy's one summer afternoon. At that time, we both had bad marriages, we were living paycheck-to-paycheck, and we had a lot of debt. We both had three children and were struggling to make ends meet; shopping was the way we made ourselves feel better. That day, we each found something we absolutely loved and just had to have. Kathy purchased a $250 Gucci watch (this was in the 90's, so that would be equivalent to spending about $1500 these days) and I purchased a $250 purse that was made from snake, lizard and alligator skin. I felt good about the purchase that day, but when the credit card bill came in, I was no longer feeling good.

Debt for luxury items is not a smart investment decision.

It is important to clarify the difference between investing in ourselves wisely and using debt for material things we probably don't need and luxury items.

When investing in ourselves, the implication is we are committing our money, time, and energy to reap a future benefit. Debt is a future obligation, not a future benefit.

The distinction here is there is *good* debt and there is *bad* debt.

Investing in yourself that has a future benefit is good debt.

Spending money on credit for luxury items or material things that is not consistent with your long-term goals and values is bad debt.

While creating your dream life, you are inevitably going to incur some debt along the way. Unless you have an endless supply of money, you are going to come upon situations where there will be a choice to spend money wisely or to walk away.

SMART CHOICES WILL TAKE YOU WHERE YOU WANT TO GO

Get in the habit of making *conscious* choices when it comes to your money. Take the time to step back and think about the consequences *before* you make the choice.

Nicole Williams, co-author of the book, "Earn What You're Worth," says:

"Hating a job that pays well is NEVER a good investment strategy. Not only have I lived this monumental mistake myself, I've seen many of my friends and coworkers struggle in the same trap. I've come to learn that those who hate their well-paying jobs spend a phenomenal amount of money compensating. Food, clothes, vacations – all absolute necessities for someone who hates what they do for a living. I swear, those who hate their jobs actually take home less money."

Having a well-paying job that you hate is a real dilemma. You feel unfulfilled, but you have lots of cash and credit, so to fill the void of being in an unfulfilling job, you spend, spend, spend and the reason you spend, spend, spend is because you hate your job. We can get into an unhealthy pattern of shopping and creating bad debt that keeps us imprisoned in our unfulfilling jobs. We can't leave our job because of our lifestyle, bills and debt.

Spending money on dining out, designer clothes, vacations, upgrades or improvements on your home, new cars, hobbies, is bad debt if you are not living your dreams because it is not advancing you towards your dreams. **Bad debt fills the void that living *without* purpose, passion and satisfaction creates.** Unconscious spending must become a thing of the past or you will continue to delay or never realize your dreams.

Here are four true stories (the names have been changed) and I want you to decide if the person in each story is creating bad debt or good debt (an investment in the future):

Case Study 1

Liz had been out of the corporate world for years and was working as a massage therapist out of her home. She recently paid off a large debt, and she was making just enough money to break even. A course related to her field of study was coming up and she really wanted to take the class. She did not have the money to pay for it in full, however, she could put it on her credit card and pay it off in the next few months. Liz decided this was a great opportunity to learn a new skill and make herself more marketable, so she charged the full amount of the tuition on her credit card – knowing that she would be able to pay it off within the next few months.

Case Study 2

Denise has been employed with the State Government for more than 10 years. Denise liked her job for years, but now she feels burnt out. She is a single parent raising three children with a little help from her ex-husband. He pays the court-ordered child support but not a dime above that for extraordinary expenses. Denise earns what the average American earns, but with three children, her expenses exceed her income. She purchased a house about four years ago, which has increased in value considerably. She constantly cashes in her equity to pay off the credit cards that help her get by. The credit cards were not used solely for necessities like food and household items, but also for expensive jewelry, clothes, vacations, fancy meals out, Christmas presents and household extras. Recently, the jewelry store which she frequents, was having a special show with rare gems. Denise decided she deserved to have nice things and purchased earrings and a necklace for two thousand dollars. She put it on a credit card and will pay for it later.

Case Study 3

Ann left the corporate field over six years ago and has doubled her income in recent years. She has no credit card debt and has a home equity loan that she has used for large purchase items such as vehicles for her teenage children (which they make monthly payments for). Ann lives within her means. Ann uses her American Express card to purchase clothing, jewelry, furniture and some luxury items knowing that she can pay it off in full the next month. It has been years since she has had any credit card debt. Ann works from home; one of the problems she has is she gets distracted from her work with household chores – she loves a clean house! Ann decided to hire a cleaning company so she could focus more on her work instead of the chores. Ann gets lots more work done these days because she knows that every two weeks, the cleaning people will be there to get her house back in order.

Case Study 4

Nicole was in a dull marriage that lacked passion. Nicole had been a stay-at-home mom for several years. Her husband paid all the household expenses so any money she earned was for extra expenses like clothes, dining out, trips, etc. Nicole has a few different side businesses but doesn't focus her energy on any one of them, so she makes a little money here and there, but nothing substantial. Recently, Nicole went on a trip and brought her money to gamble with. The money went pretty quickly with nothing to show for it.

What do you think about Case Study number 1?

It's Good debt – an investment in the future. That's right! Although Liz was just getting by, she lived above her means. She paid all her bills in a timely manner and was trying to improve her business by learning a new skill. Even though she charged the course on a credit card, she was investing in herself and her future. Over time, she was able to pay off the bill without going under.

What about Case Study number 2?

This one is Bad Debt! Denise is unhappy and that unhappiness causes her to shop excessively and purchase things she could do without. It's not that she needs to deprive herself, but she could use that money to invest in another business, a savings account, stocks and bonds, etc. to create more money. Instead, she gets caught up in materialism and the status quo and thinks jewelry and "material things" will make her happy, but they never do. They are a quick fix, but not a lasting fix, which is why Denise has to constantly go out and buy more "stuff." The void of unfulfillment never gets filled with material things.

Case Study Number 3 is actually a story about me.

This is Good Debt! I am the fictitious "Ann" and many years ago I reluctantly hired cleaning people. I knew it was an issue because I am a neat freak, and it was hard for me to concentrate on my business when I knew the house was messy. A good cleaning company is worth it to me because now I have peace of mind, I feel good about it, and I have the money to pay cash for it. It's an investment in the future because it allows me to focus more on my writing and work projects instead of household chores.

Case Study Number 4 – Nicole.

Bad debt for sure! It wasn't that Nicole was spending her bill money on gambling, it's just that Nicole was throwing away money she earned into slot machines. Nicole could have invested that money in one of her businesses, a savings account, stocks and bonds, etc. Consequently, Nicole felt bad for losing money gambling.

FEELINGS AROUND MONEY

Start paying attention to how you *feel* when you spend money. Do you feel good or bad? Do you feel hopeful or hopeless? Do you feel guilty or guilt-free? Do you feel more energized or less energized? Do you feel worried or at peace? Do you feel like your decision was right or wrong?

If you can afford it, you have excess money, and are not in debt, I am all for buying and having nice things. I love luxury cars, quality jewelry, nice vacations, a beautiful home and furnishings, designer clothes, etc. In my opinion, there is absolutely nothing wrong with having or wanting "nice things." The question is first and foremost whether you can afford it, and if not, how you feel when you spend money on these things you know you don't have the money to pay cash for.

Debt is a huge drainer of our energy. If you're tired all the time, you probably have a lot of debt

The bad feelings we get when we spend money on things we really can't afford are red flags shouting to us. **STOP. DON'T DO IT!**

What feeling are you trying to numb when you are shopping beyond your means? Many times when we examine the feeling we're running from, we often find:

- **Boredom**
- **Low self-esteem**
- **Emotional wounds that haven't been processed**
- **Repressed anger**
- **Fear**
- **Pain**

START INVESTING IN YOUR FUTURE

It's funny how we are quick to buy a designer purse or jeans but not so quick to buy a thousand business cards or hire a web designer to create a website for us.

A great way to boost your self-esteem is to stop making choices that make you feel bad and start making choices that make you feel good. I am not saying you should go into a huge amount of debt to start your own business – take small steps -- business cards, an affordable website and logo, etc.

Take actions that tell yourself: "I am important," "I matter," "My future matters." **Invest in yourself and your future**. The by-product is that you will increase your self-esteem and be in a better financial position down the road.

When I made the decision to hire a cleaning company, I said to my best friend, *"I would rather figure out how to make more money to pay for the cleaning company than to NOT have a cleaning company."* Over the years, I have developed a deep trust in myself and:

- **My ability to create and make more money.**
- **My resiliency.**
- **My resourcefulness.**

Now I have a deep trust and knowing that whatever I want or need, I also have the ability to create the money to pay for it. I don't worry about where the money will come from or even *how* it will come. I trust in myself and in the Universe to guide me. I listen to my inner voice and make decisions from that place.

Prince Charming Syndrome

A poor investment strategy many women suffer from is the "Prince Charming Syndrome."

Do you suffer from the Prince Charming Syndrome?

The Prince Charming Syndrome is a deep-seated belief and expectation that another person is going to come rescue you, save you, pay your monthly expenses, lavish you with gifts, and keep you in the lifestyle you desire to be in.

Where did this belief come from, and why do so many women have it?

Many women are taught by their parents and caregivers to look for a man to take care of them, or they watched their own mothers or female caregivers being taken care of by a man, so they learned by example. If you think about it, women have only been allowed to have money and earn money in the last 80+ years that. Prior to that, the man was the sole provider and controlled all the money while the woman traditionally stayed home and took care of the house and the children. So, on some level, we are still operating from this old paradigm even though many things have shifted and changed.

Think about these statistics found in the book "Money, a Memoir: Women Emotions and Cash," by Liz Perle, who says,

"In the 1950's the number of women who out-earned their husbands was so small that the information wasn't even systematically gathered. But fifty years later, almost one in three women do and our numbers rise every year. We control $4 trillion in yearly consumer spending. We make 62 percent of all car purchases. We take 50 percent of all business trips. We control more than 50 percent of all personal wealth in this country. And we do this while shouldering the majority of family responsibilities. We've gotten caught in a time warp where our economic realities have changed faster than our expectations and identities."

What a great point Liz Perle makes – women are in a time warp.

Women are out in the world creating wealth and many times making more money than the men in their lives, but a part of us wants and expects a man to take care of us.

Sometimes we are conscious about wanting Prince Charming to come rescue us, but many times we are unconscious to it. Personally, I have been conflicted with this idea for years. Although I have been very independent since my teenage years, there has always been a hidden part of me that fantasized about a man coming to rescue me so I could "take a break" and let someone else worry about the bills and the future for a change.

Guess what?

Prince Charming never came for me, and he's probably not coming for you either. It's a fantasy, and the quicker you can acknowledge that and move on, the quicker you can take full ownership and responsibility for your finances, your life and your future. Believe me, I understand it's hard to let go of the fantasy; in some ways, it's like giving up on a dream. However, this particular dream has no basis in reality and is simply an illusion.

Here are some great reasons why waiting for Prince Charming is a bad investment:

- **Waiting for Prince Charming is a crutch and an excuse for not taking control of your financial destiny.**
- **It puts you in a subordinate position as well as a dependent position similar to a parent-child relationship. Do you really want to be the child?**
- **Your self-esteem does not have a chance to grow because you do not have positive experiences handling money and lack the ability to take care of yourself.**

We all have a relationship with money whether we know it or not. By ignoring money issues and waiting for Prince Charming to ride up on his white horse and rescue you, you are ignoring your relationship with money. When we ignore any type of relationship, it usually falls apart.

Waiting for Prince Charming to arrive keeps you stagnant; never moving forward. If you're not evolving, you're stuck in the mud. Do you want to be stuck in the mud?

I think that's more than enough reasons for you to let go, once and for all, of the Prince CHARMING fantasy – what do you think?

In addition to the reasons listed above, I have a couple more thoughts on the subject.

Many of the women I know who said they found their "Prince Charming" tell horror stories later about their **"Prince HARMING"** … men who weren't nearly as wealthy as they led the woman to believe; men who came on hot and heavy in the beginning and then turned out to be abusive; and men who stole a woman's heart and her bank account.

My advice (WARNING) to you: If Prince Charming shows up on your doorstep, on your porch, or anywhere on your property, do an in-depth background and credit check on him. Not to be cliché, but if something sounds too good to be true, it's because it is.

Besides, what do we really know about this Prince Charming character anyway?

If we do our due diligence and don't take a stranger's word for it, we often discover Prince Charming didn't own the kingdom outright – he had several mortgages on the property. Oh, and the white horse he rode in on was a rent-a-horse that he picked up on the way to rescuing you and had to be returned by midnight; and the diamonds he brought you turns out they were really cubic zirconia!

In summary, stop investing your time and energy in the illusion that Prince Charming is coming to rescue you – he's not! It's a bad investment of your time and energy.

Instead, take that same time and energy and begin investing in yourself, your dreams, your passions and your life. *Why?* Because you matter, because it's time you started believing in yourself. When we know we matter, our choices and actions reflect that belief, and we spend our time, energy and money investing in ourselves!

NON-FINANCIAL INVESTING

It is important to invest in yourself financially, but not to the exclusion of other areas in your life – mentally, spiritually, physically and emotionally. We must take care of our "whole" selves because if we focus too much in one area and neglect the others, we will suffer.

I know many people who are so obsessed with making money to the exclusion of their physical health. They are severely overweight with many medical problems like high blood pressure, diabetes, high cholesterol, digestive issues, etc. You can make all the money in the world, but if you don't have your health, you have nothing!

We are spiritual beings as well. At the end of our lives, we may have accumulated treasures on earth, but none in heaven. Additionally, if we neglect our mind and our emotions, we won't experience balance and peace of mind.

Take care of your *whole* self. Invest in your whole self. I like what singer Jon Bon Jovi says about his life, "The harder I worked, the luckier I got."

The harder you work at taking the time and energy to invest in yourself and your life, the luckier you will be in life. There is no such thing as pure luck. People that appear lucky have, in reality, worked very hard to get to that place. Hard is a relative word. I work shorter hours than most, and by choice, I have created a life with a great deal of down time.

Remember, you are the creator of your life and you get to decide what hard work means to you. When you work hard and invest in yourself, luck will find you!

Now let's talk about how to take your passions and expertise and turn them into a six-figure business so you have even more time and money freedom...

Chapter 11 – Six Figures Buys More Freedom

"Above all I learned that it's entirely possible for any one of us, with average intelligence, to increase our income without selling our soul."
~Barbara Stanny, author of "Secrets of Six-Figure Women"

You don't have to work 60+ hours to make 6-figures. Many women mistakenly believe this.

I was only working about 20-25 hours per week in my outside sales job when I began making six figures and I had more time and money freedom than I ever had, and I was loving life.

So, what changed? How did I go from making $50k to $100k+ working half the hours?

My mindset, my perspective, and my entire life was changed when I read Barbara Stanny's, "Secrets of Six-Figure Women: Surprising Strategies to Up Your Earnings and Change Your Life." Barbara Stanny is also the author of many other books like "Overcoming Underearning" and one of my favorites, "Sacred Success." Her books have truly changed my life and I highly recommend them.

Barbara has such a fascinating story – her father was the "R" in H&R Block, a large and successful tax firm, and he was the founder of the company. She was raised to let men take care of the finances. Fast forward to when she got older, Barbara married a lousy Prince Charming and he lost a ton of Barbara's trust fund that had been set up for her by her father. After their divorce, she had huge tax bills, three small children, and a "brain incapable of deciphering financial jargon."

Today, Barbara Stanny is a high-income earner. She wrote the book, "Six Figure Women," to learn the characteristics common in women making six figures. She interviewed 150 women, and that's how the book was created.

When you ask women if they want to make six figures, you usually get one of two replies:

1. **Sure, but how do I do that?**

2. **No, because I don't want to give up my soul to do it. I don't want to give up time with my family, friends, etc.**

The good news is you don't have to know the "how" and you don't have to sell your soul to make six figures. The reason I know this is because I've done it.

After leaving the legal field and finding Barbara Stanny's book, I was committed to becoming a six-figure woman. I started my website www.becomea6figurewoman.com when I began making six figures in 2005.

So how did I start making six figures and how long did it take?

I did NOT focus on *how* it would happen. I simply committed myself to making six figures and every day I would write 100 times in my journal *"I am making six figures doing what I love to do."*

We talked in an earlier chapter about the Reticular Activating System which brings relevant information to your attention and programs your subconscious. It's a powerful system that is built into our brains!

Here's how it works:

My goal and written affirmation was,, *"I am making six figures doing what I love to do."* Since I was NOT making six figures doing what I loved at the time, a *structural tension* was created in my brain. The brain always wants to resolve any structural tension. To do that, you will begin to draw to you what is needed to achieve the goal, which will in turn, resolve the structural tension.

Writing your goals down is key! Write them down in present tense as if you've already achieved them. Don't try to do this with ten goals. Just pick one for now. You can even use mine: *"I am making six figures doing what I love to do."*

It's not that you are going to sit back and do nothing, but now your RAS is at work and you will pay closer attention when you see six figure opportunities come your way.

Six Figures in 18 months

I created multiple streams of income doing a variety of jobs. I was reading the employment ads (this was back in the days before online job searching) in the Washington Post and one day I read an ad that said something like:

Make six figures working 20 hours a week selling a fun product. Play Golf. Enjoy Life. Call for more details.

Well, I didn't want to play golf, but I did want to make six figures working 20 hours a week.

I called about the job and found out it was an outside sales job selling hot tubs. I had no outside sales experience (17 years legal) and didn't know a thing about hot tubs. But what I did know was I wanted to make six figures doing what I loved.

I got on a call with one of the managers at the company and said, "Hi my name is Michelle Kulp, and I'm your next top salesperson!"

His reply was, "Do you have any in-home sales experience in a one-call close environment." The funny part was I didn't even know what a one-call close was!

I said something like, "Well not exactly, but I have other sales experience you will be interested in." He told me to fax over my resume and he would be in touch. He was very short with me as I suspected he didn't believe I had the experience they required.

So, I typed up a document called **"Top 10 Reasons Thermospas Should Hire Me,"** and I was very creative with that list.

I then created a new resume' that had every little thing I ever did in my entire life that involved sales; things like working at my dad's clothing store, Bond's Clothing, part-time as a teenager and selling products like Partylite and Christmas Around the World.

I was chosen as one of the 20 top picks by the company out of 200 applicants for an interview. I was the only female chosen (maybe because I was the only one who applied?) Apparently, this was a male-dominated field, and it attracted a lot of experienced sales guys with lots of in-home, one-call close experience.

The interview was via teleconference at an office located in Washington, D.C. (the company was in Connecticut) and I felt pretty intimidated being around all these sales experts. When I walked into that meeting, I felt like I was out of my league; but I was committed to making six figures, so I stuck it out.

When it came my time for the interview, I was so nervous. I don't think I gave the politically correct answers they were looking for during the interview. The final question was: "Why do you think you would make a great in-home salesperson?"

My answer came from my heart: "Because I'm a kind and caring person. People warm up to me right away. I think if I had a quality product, backed by great company, that people would buy from me."

I went home after the interview and told my then boyfriend that I was certain I didn't get the job and that it was a colossal waste of time.

The next day I was surprised to get a call from the company telling me that I was chosen out of the 200 men that applied for the sales position. I was stunned. I said to the manager, "Can I ask you a question…how come out of all those experienced, highly qualified applicants, you decided to pick me?" His answer was "Because you don't have any bad habits."

They felt that people who worked in sales a long time had their own way of doing things and it would be easier to train a novice than to teach an old dog new tricks. Because I knew nothing about outside sales, they felt they could mold and train me how they wanted, and I would do well.

I'm happy to tell you, they were right! Within 18 months, I was making six figures. Was it easy? NO it was NOT. I had to memorize a 42-page script that I had to present in front of the President of the company, attend two weeks of hot tub boot camp in the factory learning all the technical and boring details about hot tubs, and I had to drive hundreds of miles to pre-confirmed appointments in an all-commission job. I can assure you it was not easy at first.

I decided to make it easier on myself and I started learning from the guys that were making six figures. There were a lot of guys struggling and complaining – I didn't hang out or talk to them. I didn't want them to bring me down. Instead, my focus was on the top income earners in the company. I learned everything I could from them.

Within six months of getting that job, there were weeks I wasn't making any money. I decided I was going to quit. So I called my manager and told him I was going to quit and find a *real job*. His reply was, "Michelle, there's about a year learning curve on this job. I promise you after a year, you will be one of our top sales reps."

He believed in me more than I believed in myself at the time. I was way out of my comfort zone, but I knew the potential was there to make six figures, so again, I stuck it out.

I did like driving to new towns, meeting new people and selling a fun product – hot tubs! We were the only company selling hot tubs in-home so we had no competition.

Within 18 months, I was making six figures and my life got so much easier. I had free time to work on my writing, teach classes, spend time with my kids, family and friends. I was also able to buy a house, pay off debt, and breathe.

I want to point out that it wasn't my "Dream" to be a hot tub sales rep, but it was a wonderful FREEDOM JOB that allowed me free time to work on my other dreams. It taught me valuable new sales skills that I could use in the marketplace and I had fun selling hot tubs! That job lasted 10 years until the housing market crashed and the company unfortunately filed bankruptcy.

After that, I had a decision to make. I was running my online business like a hobby with part-time income and I needed to replace my six-figure income. I took other sales jobs, but after eighteen months, I did not find a product or a company I was happy with. I made the decision that I was going to make six figures in my online business.

Of course, it didn't happen right away. As I mentioned, my income increased exponentially when I hired my first business coach, Jason Nyback, who changed my entire business and life. He was a brilliant business strategist, and within three months of working with him, my monthly online income skyrocketed!

In the previous chapter, we discussed investing in yourself – this was a massive investment in myself. I spent $6k to work with him for eight weeks, and then for the next four years I spent $1k per month ($12k per year) working with him. I probably didn't need to stay with him that long, but I loved working with him, and I was always learning so much.

I don't have the exact details about how you can make six figures, but I know that if you commit to making six figures doing what you love and investing in yourself, that it will happen for you.

THE LOWDOWN ON LOW EARNERS

An underearner is anyone who earns below their potential. I am a recovering underearner for sure.

Here's some of the traits of underearners according to Barbara Stanny:

- **Underearners have a high tolerance for low pay** – high earners normally lean towards more lucrative fields. If you don't go where there's a potential to make money, it doesn't matter how hard you work.

- **Underearners underestimate their worth** – They feel that life is unfair, and they are disadvantaged as compared to the "privileged group."

- **Underearners are willing to work for free** – Underearners give away their time, knowledge and skills for nothing.

- **Underearners are lousy negotiators** – Underearners are reluctant to ask for more and let fear control them.

- **Underearners practice reverse snobbery** – They believe that people who have a lot of money are greedy, insensitive and feel superior.

- **Underearners believe in the nobility of poverty** – Many of them take great pride in barely making a living and believe it's more noble to be one of the poor.

- **Underearners are subtle self-saboteurs** – They throw banana peels in their own path in a variety of ways: applying for work they're not qualified for, creating problems with coworkers, procrastinating or leaving projects unfinished, stopping short of reaching their goals. The common thread is their propensity to be scattered, distracted, and/or unfocused.

- **Underearners are unequivocally codependent** – They put other people's dreams ahead of their own and are the sacrificial lamb. They have weak boundaries and put themselves last at the sake of others.

- **Underearners are in financial chao**s – They go from crisis to crisis, constantly moving money from one account to another, borrowing from Peter to pay Paul and heading toward financial disaster.

Do any of these sound familiar? If so, you too are probably an underearner.

CHARACTERISTICS OF AN UNDEREARNER:

- Negative feelings about money.
- Work very long hours or have several jobs to make ends meet.
- Fill your free time with endless chores, tasks, or television.
- Are in debt with little or No savings.
- Have no idea where your money is going.
- Have a family history of debt and/or underearning.
- Put others needs ahead of your own.
- Are in financial pain or stress.
- Give away your knowledge and services for free.
- Undercharge for your services.
- Avoid dealing with money.
- Find it hard to ask for a raise.
- Blame others for your financial situation.
- Are proud of your ability to make do with little.

When I read Barbara Stanny's book, it opened my eyes to the fact that I was a classic underearner. It's taken years of working on these issues, becoming educated and most importantly, implementing what I've learned. Of course, there's still more to improve. It's not a one-and-done event. It's a life-long process.

Self-improvement is ongoing. I believe the purpose of life is to evolve and that the top of one mountain is the bottom of another. I'm always ascending up the ladder.

Don't read this chapter and feel bad about where you are. Knowledge and self-awareness are power.

If you want to quit your job, it's important to take action and make the necessary changes in your financial house so you can live your dreams.

You can make six figures doing what you love. I am living proof of that. You don't have to work 60-80 hours a week as some people inaccurately believe or sell your soul. You can get paid to do what you love. First, figure out what you love and make sure there is a demand for that in the marketplace, and then charge what you're worth.

The more you do what you love, the better you get at it and, the more money you will make. I didn't start out making six figures online, but once I mastered a lot of skills, the value I gave to others kept increasing and so did the money I was earning.

RECOMMENDED RESOURCES:

- Dave Ramsey's Financial Peace University www.daveramsey.com/fpu
- Any of Barbara Stanny's books or classes (she married recently and has changed her name to Barbara Huson) https://www.barbara-huson.com/

Now, it's time for our final chapter on this journey. Taking the leap and planning your exit strategy!

Chapter 12 – Your 6-Step Exit Strategy

"Letting go is death.
People think leaving a job is about leaving a job. It's about
leaving a life, a history, a context, a cubbyhole, the only person
you knew how to be, and the one everybody loved."
~Tama J. Kieves, author of "This Time I Dance! Trusting the
Journey of Creating the Work you Love"

Imagine no more rush hour traffic, no more long commutes, no more deadlines, no more overtime, no more missing family events, dinners, and no more bosses! And more time with your family, money in the bank, and most importantly, more time to enjoy life.

The challenge is to make more money and work less hours so that you can devote your life to pursuing the dreams you have for you and your family.

In order to declare financial independence from wage slavery, you need an EXIT STRATEGY.

6-STEP EXIT STRATEGY FOR QUITTING YOUR JOB

This is a summary of what you've been learning throughout this book. When you put everything together, this is your exit strategy.

STEP 1: PREPARE YOUR FINANCES

Your finances MUST be in order before you quit your job to do work that is meaningful and more fulfilling, even if it's transitioning from full-time to part- time work; or going from a BONDAGE JOB to a FREEDOM JOB; or quitting your job completely in order to do what you love. If you don't get your finances in order, you will have high stress. Ideally, your debt is zero, except for your living expenses, and you have at least one year of expenses in the bank (preferably 18 months if you can swing it). Don't sit back and do nothing and draw on your savings. Have your savings there for peace of mind knowing that if needed, you can survive 12-18 months if everything falls apart.

STEP 2: HAVE A WRITTEN DOWN INCOME PLAN

In the previous chapters, I recommended testing out your dream job, making your first $100 from some of your ideas, and even hiring a consultant at Pivot Planet to get all the details of what that job or business is like. By nature, some businesses are feast or famine. I know because my online business was like that for a long time. When I finally hired my business coach in 2014, I was generating leads by running paid Facebook ads to an automated webinar, but it was expensive.

However, many times when you're starting out, you don't have a huge marketing budget. I don't do any paid advertising now because all of my business comes from referrals. That's because I've spent years developing relationships and I've been doing this work long enough that referrals come in consistently. So, if you're starting your own business, you need to know where you will find your new clients. If you're transitioning from one job to another job, then you know where your income is coming from. I recommend at least two streams of income to start. Remember that done-for-you services are much easier to get your income flowing right away if you're going down the entrepreneurial path. Write down your monthly income goals, your expenses, and your plan for getting leads and clients. Read this plan every day. Even if you're transitioning to a new job, I want you to have a minimum of two streams of income.

STEP 3: PREPARE YOUR BREAK-UP SPEECH

Your boss is most likely going to ask why you're quitting. There's no need to get into specifics or to say things like "Because I hate you, this company, and everyone in it!" Instead, just voice your appreciation for the opportunities the company gave you with something like this: "I am very grateful for having my job for the last ** years, and I've learned so much working here. However, at this point in my career, I'm excited to contribute my skills to another company where I can make an impact on a different level." Or "I am very grateful for having my job for the last ** years and I've learned so much working here. However, at this point in my career, I'm excited to branch out on my own to do something different." Even if you are starting a company similar to the one you're leaving, don't let them know that. Of course, if you have a non-compete agreement with that company, you must consult a lawyer if the business you are starting is the same or similar. But if you're leaving your job to do your own thing in a different field, there is no need to give them details. Unless of course, you think that your boss could give you referrals, then by all means have that conversation.

STEP 4: PREPARE YOURSELF FOR A COUNTEROFFER

It's sad to say, but many times when you try to quit your job, the company will offer you more money, a promotion, better benefits, etc. Of course, that leaves you feeling angry, wondering why they didn't give you that before if they valued you so highly. The truth is, it's not their fault; it's yours for not asking. It doesn't mean they would have given it to you, but many times as underearners we settle for much less than we're worth. Then we make this huge decision and commitment to quit our jobs and the company offers us more money. Very frustrating! Stick to your plan and thank your boss for the offer but tell him or her your mind is made up. It's good to know this is a possibility before you have the break-up conversation, so you don't react impulsively.

STEP 5: SCHEDULE THE BREAK-UP

The day is finally here, and you are going to give the required notice because you don't want to burn any bridges. Also do this in person, not via text or email or social media. Even though you may have fantasies of quitting your job without any notice and making a scene, it's not a good idea. You want good karma as you quit your job. Make sure you ask for a reference if the conversation goes well as it could be useful down the road as you move on to your new life.

STEP 6: PREPARE FOR A MOURNING PERIOD

This last step in your exit strategy is preparing yourself for a period of grieving and mourning. Even if you didn't LOVE your job, there will be period of mourning and the death of your old life. This mourning period can last a few weeks to a few months or even more. My identity for 17+ years was wrapped around the law, being a paralegal, working in the legal environment and the structure my job provided. I wasn't just leaving a job; I was leaving life as I knew it. It's important to mourn the loss of your title, your co-workers, your schedule, your paycheck, your benefits, and who you showed up as in the world. It's also really scary because you now have a blank slate on which to create a new life.

WOBBLING AND UNCERTAINTY ARE GOOD SIGNS

I wrote this book as a "12-month Guide to Being Joyfully Jobless" because I want you to know you can't just snap your figures and be magically transported into a new life. You have to do the work and *the work* takes time. No one can do it for you.

Just know that you will wobble with uncertainty as you take this journey to freedom, but it's better to wobble than to settle for a life of mediocrity.

It helps to have a mindset like a little child who is exploring the world with new eyes for the first time and trying to understand it and figure things out. You will never have all the answers or a fail-proof plan.

You are being called to walk off the beaten path, and I'm here to gently remind you some days you will question your sanity. Just remember that you have an inner guidance system (IGS) that you can access any time when you are feeling overwhelmed or overcome with fear. Your very own IGS will give you all the answers you need when you slow down, get still and listen to it.

When my job at the law firm ended, I had no idea what I was going to do to pay the bills and take care of my three children, but the more I learned to listen to my own inner guidance system, the more I began to find my way, follow my heart and live my dreams.

Uncertainty is the first step to our freedom. Knowing that we don't *know* the way, accepting that fully and having faith that the teachers we need will appear on the path as we begin travelling to unexplored worlds.

You'll never have a magical life that has 100% certainty in it. That's the point. When you have FAITH, then the MAGIC appears.

TRUST.

*****

THE END OF THIS BOOK =
THE BEGINNING OF YOUR NEW LIFE

If you've gotten this far then I know you are serious in your quest to discover and live those dreams of yours. You can connect with me at: **www.becomea6figurewoman.com**

Never, ever give up on Your Dreams!

Michelle Kulp

CAN YOU DO ME A FAVOR

Before you go, I'd like to say thank you for purchasing my book. I really appreciate it!

I'd like to ask a small favor. *Would you take a minute or two to leave a review for this book on Amazon?*

This feedback will help me continue to write the kind of books that help inspire, motivate and educate people to believe in themselves and to find their true purpose in life.

If you enjoyed my book, then please let me know ☺

Michelle Kulp

WORK FROM HOME & MAKE 6-FIGURES

The JOY of Making More in Half the Time

Without the Hassles of a Job, Boss, or Commute

MICHELLE KULP

Imagine working fewer hours, a lot fewer hours.

Imagine working only those hours that fit in with what you really want to do every day – instead of having to force your life around your work schedule.

Imagine being able to work from anywhere you choose – locally, nationally or internationally.

Imagine doubling or tripling your income.

You don't have to imagine it any longer; it can be a reality.

Introduction

I have a confession to make…

I am ambitiously lazy.

Sounds like an oxymoron, right? *Ambitious* and *lazy* in the same sentence?

Let me explain.

When I was a teenager, I loved going to the bookstore and buying "Home-based Business" magazines to research all the different ways to *make money without having a job.*

I imagined one day being my own boss, making my own hours, controlling my money and time…and of course, working from home.

I was born with an entrepreneurial spirit, and over the years, I've had several businesses such as:

- Roommate Matching Service
- Private Process Service
- Personalized Children's Books Publisher
- Public Speaking Facilitator
- Career Coach
- Network marketing companies including PartyLite, Christmas Around the World, and North American Power.
- Cleaning Company
- Crafts
- Babysitting Services
- Resume Writing Service
- And More!

What I realized after having all these businesses is that deep down, what I really wanted was *to make the most amount of money with the least amount of time.*

I think being *ambitiously lazy* is about being smart with your time.

Timothy Ferriss, author of the #1 New York Times Bestseller, "The 4-Hour Workweek," says,

"...the perfect job is the one that takes the least time."

After graduating college in 1983, I had a 17-year traditional 9-to-5 career as a paralegal, and at the end of those 17 years I was working 40+ hours per week making $48,000 per year living paycheck-to-paycheck. The only way I could make more money was to work more hours.

I hated the fact that I had to trade time for money.

After my legal career ended, I began creating multiple streams of income as well as passive income streams. I loved trying out new things to see if I liked them and I also loved not depending on one source of income as I had for so many years.

I was fortunate enough to find a job in outside sales and within eighteen months, I was making six figures working only 20-25 hours per week! I didn't even know making six figures was possible or that I could earn that much and cut my work time in half.

I learned so much working in sales, and I love teaching others that it is possible to make six figures without selling your soul.

I started my first website www.becomea6figurewoman.com in 2005 and I sold online courses for $197. Within my first 30 days, I made $2,500 and I was hooked.

I loved working from home as well as the concept of doing the work once and getting paid over and over!

The online world has changed drastically since 2005 and it's not as easy to make six figures from an online course like I was doing back then without spending a lot of money on paid advertising, copywriting and sales funnels. Plus, there is a lot more competition than there was in 2005.

At the time, I sold mostly to people that were on a small email list which I built from doing live workshops

The 6-week online courses were very simple: no videos, just a PDF and weekly calls.

I really enjoyed developing new programs and teaching them to others.

Over the years, I've made money online in a variety of ways such as:

- Royalties from my books
- Copywriting
- Website Design
- SEO
- Coaching
- Selling Online Courses
- Bestselling Author Program (done-for-you)
- Ghostwriting
- Sales
- Affiliate Income

After my 17-year career in the legal field ended, I worked in outside sales selling hot tubs in-home for 10 years until the company I was working for filed bankruptcy in 2010. I had to make a decision since my cushy 6-figure job was disappearing. At the time, my online business was generating anywhere between $3000 to $5000 per month part-time in a feast or famine rollercoaster mode; I desperately needed to make six figures online or I would have to go back to a dreaded "job."

The thought of going back to a job after being away from one for so long literally made me sick to my stomach. I would do anything to not have to go back to the corporate grind.

This book focuses on exactly what I did to take my side hustle earning $3-$5k per month to $25k+ per month consistently.

I'll also share the mistakes I made along the way, so you can be aware of them and not make the same ones.

I'm going to share with you everything I've done to create an amazing business and lifestyle getting paid to do what I love and having the freedom to work from home.

My online business gives me three reasons to jump out of bed in the morning:

1. Total autonomy

2. Creativity

3. Great work/life balance

I can barely tell the difference between work and pleasure.

If it's your dream to work from home while only working 20-25 hours a week or less, to earn six figures (or multiple six figures) doing what you love so you can have time and money freedom...you're in the right place!

Let's get started!

Chapter 1:
Wealth in a Wheelchair

To trade time is to trade life.

One of my favorite books is "The Millionaire Fastlane" by MJ DeMarco. In his book, he talks about three barriers to wealth:

- Get Rich Slow
- The Slow Lane
- Wealth in a Wheelchair

Many people believe that you "Go to school, get good grades, graduate, get a good job, save 10%, invest in the stock market, max your 401k, slash your credit cards, and clip coupons…then someday, when you are, oh, 65 years old, you will be rich."

Like many others, I followed down this flawed path, but at the end of my 17-year legal career, I was broke, living paycheck-to-paycheck, had less than one year's salary in my 401k, and was struggling financially.

I was on a hamster wheel and I could not see an end in sight.

I did everything I was supposed to do. I graduated from college, got a good job with great benefits, put as much as I could afford to into my 401k, clipped coupons, lived frugally, but as a single mom with three kids living in a high-cost metropolitan area, it was not working.

The message of "Get Rich Slow" is that you have to sacrifice your today, your dreams, and your life for a plan that pays dividends after your life has passed you by.

I don't know about you, but I don't want *wealth in wheel-chair*. I want to enjoy life now.

I've known many people who retire and then pass away a short time after. We don't know how long we have in this life, so why wait until the golden years of retirement to have wealth. The real golden years are when you're younger, more energetic and vibrant.

I'm 56 years old now and when I left my corporate job, I was 37. I didn't have a plan; all I knew was the 9-to-5 grind was not working for me and I needed a change.

As fate would have it, I was given a pink slip from the law firm where I worked and that was the golden ticket to a new life.

I had zero dollars in the bank and three young kids to support.

In my book, "How to Find Your Passion: 23 Questions that Can Change Your Entire Life," I talk about a chance meeting I had with Billy Ray Cyrus. He asked me a question that changed the trajectory of my life: "What are your Dreams?" My reply at the time was, "I don't have any dreams, my life is about survival."

I was living paycheck-to-paycheck and didn't have time to think about things like dreams.

(Billy Ray and me, circa October 23, 1992)

Billy Ray assured me that everyone has a dream and he made me promise that I would look for my dream and never ever give up on my dream once I found it.

I spent a year searching for this elusive dream that Billy Ray talked about. Ironically, I found the answer through another question.

I was at the bookstore browsing the self-help section when "How to Find Your Mission In Life" by Richard Bolles literally fell into my hands. In that book, Bolles asked,

"What do you love to do where you lose all sense of time?"

The only thing I could recall was in my younger years, I loved writing—essays, reports, short stories, poems, and more. I never thought about writing as my passion, but looking back, I realized my favorite part of my job as a paralegal was legal writing and research.

Equipped with the knowledge that *writing* was my passion, I started down the path to becoming a newspaper reporter to gain some writing experience. Then, I started my own blog and wrote blog posts, online courses, website content, and of course, books.

I loved NOT trading my time for money and instead, I focused on different ways to leverage my time.

Having a job is like being on a hamster wheel – you can never get off because they voraciously consume your time.

If you work, you get paid. If you don't work, you don't get paid.

Many people with 9-to-5 jobs talk about 'job security,' but the job market is constantly evolving. Jobs are rapidly disappearing because of new technology. Companies are able to hire contractors globally with no overhead costs. I'm sure you know several people in your life (maybe you) that unexpectedly received a pink slip. Job security is a myth.

A job is a prison that takes away your freedom, your control, forces you to work with people you may not like or respect, forces you to get paid last, and has massive restrictions on your income. You are basically trading five days of life for two days of freedom.

That doesn't sound like a good trade to me.

Tim Ferris talks about the *deferred-life plan* that so many people settle for.

Statistics show that 75-85% of employees are extremely unhappy with their jobs.

Mark Twain once said,

"Whenever you find yourself on the side of the majority,
it is time to pause and reflect."

That time is now.

Don't accept the status quo, and don't waste 10-30 years of your life doing soul-crushing work just because it is the default path.

There is another way.

One year vs. 17 years

Last year, I got a call from one of my youngest clients and authors, Alex, asking if I was still looking for a project manager for my www.bestsellingauthorprogram.com business. "Yes," I replied, "Do you know anyone?"

"Me!"

I was shocked to hear this as Alex had graduated from Virginia Tech with a Bachelor's degree in programming. He took a 6-figure job for a large IT company straight out of college, and from the outside looking in, he was living an amazing life.

Except he wasn't.

He felt trapped in a cubicle.

Alex is a people person who was stuck in a project job, trading time for money.

He did that job for one year and decided he'd had *enough*. He quit his 6-figure job to travel the world, and now he works as my project manager virtually from all over the world.

I look at Alex and wonder why it took me 17 years to break free from job prison when it took Alex only one year? But I was raised in a different generation with a different mindset about jobs and our future.

If you want to read the details of how I broke free from job prison and the step-by-step process in my book "Quit Your Job and Follow Your Dreams."

One of the goals in this book is to help you create wealth fast instead of the default "wealth in wheelchair" approach; it's a simple system to generate cash without consuming time.

Of course, my business does consume some of my time, but my time is much more leveraged than it ever was when I had a job. Most importantly, I choose when I work, where I work, and with whom I work. I'm also able to generate multiple six-figure streams of income which allows me to save six figures per year. We will talk more about that in an upcoming chapter.

Now, let's talk about the *end of jobs* as we know them.

Chapter 2:
The End of Jobs

In the book, "The End of Jobs," by Taylor Pearson, he says:

"Today, a $40 internet connection and a free Skype account gives anyone access to the greatest talent pool in history. Instead of competing against the labor pool of a few hundred thousand or a few million people in your area near you for your job, you're competing against seven billion people around the world."

Ouch! Seven billion people are your competition.

It's tough to get a job, even a low-skill, low-paying job. The competition is fierce.

I remember the days when you could walk into a business, fill out an application and speak to someone about a job on the same day. That face-to-face connection and interaction has been replaced with technology, and it's very impersonal.

Years ago, when I was in outside sales, I watched my manager throw 80% of incoming resumes that were flowing out of the fax machine at about 6-8 pages per minute directly into the trash can.

I couldn't understand how he decided which resumes to keep and which ones to toss with only a 5-second glance, but he said he knew what he was looking for and he could tell immediately if the applicants were qualified or not.

I'm sure some of those resumes were from qualified people, but they were poorly organized and did not accurately reflect the candidate's experience and qualifications.

In fact, my resume was the reason I got called in for an interview. During the interview, my manager said to me, "You had the best resume of anyone I've ever seen in all my years in business." That was a great compliment!

I had copywriting and sales skills and knew how to grab their attention.

But the point is, it's extremely competitive now in the job market, especially for the higher paying jobs, and it's difficult to get a face-to-face interview without doing something extraordinary to stand out.

Plus, you're competing with people around the world who can do many of the jobs available and are willing to do it for a fraction of the cost.

Skill-Stacking is the Next Best Thing

After I left the corporate world, I figured out very quickly that in order to be marketable and sought after, I needed to learn new skills that were in high demand.

I call this *skill-stacking,* and it's the best way to increase your value in the marketplace—especially if you want to work from home and make six figures.

The first skill I decided to focus on when I started my on-line business was copywriting. I remember reading all those "Home-Based Business" magazines and the persuasive writing that made me want to sign up for whatever they were selling.

I was fortunate to connect with a local copywriter legend in my area named Yanik Silver. I was his student for many years and that's where I learned the art of copywriting. I knew that one skill would separate me from the competition.

Joe Vitale, in his book, "Hypnotic Writing: How to Seduce and Persuade Customers with Only Your Words," says,

"There are three keys to the success of any direct marketing campaign, whether it's done online or off:

1. The list

2. The offer

3. The copy"

I knew copywriting was a skill that would pay off so I started as a student and learned everything I could about it until I mastered it.

Robert Collier, one of the most well-known copywriters in the world, said,

"Your problem, then, is to find a point of con-tact with his (the reader's) interests, his desires, some feature that will flag his attention and make your letter stand out from all the others the moment he reads the first line."

Because I was a litigation Paralegal, I knew about the power of persuasion to win legal cases. It made sense to me that you could have a beautiful website, but if you had subpar copywriting, you would probably be broke because you couldn't convert visitors to sales.

Mastering copywriting paid off for me because it gave me the ability to write sales letters, emails, ads, and blog posts to sell courses and programs. Others would pay me for copywriting services, and I started out charging $997 for a long copy sales letter.

I'm sharing this with you because the more skills you can learn and become proficient at, the more options and value you have out in the competitive world.

The second skill I learned was sales, and that has paid off 10x! If you have a business and can't sell, then you'll probably be a broke business owner. So, you'll either need to learn how to make sales or hire someone who is a master at it.

In addition to copywriting and sales, I developed the following skills over the years that pay me dividends still to this day:

- Website Design
- Search Engine Optimization
- Publishing
- Cover Design
- Book Launches
- Writing books

- Sales Calls
- I'm also an expert (self-taught) at a variety of software programs such as Aweber, Hootsuite, Leadpages, Amazon KDP and more

What skills do you have that others would pay you to do, or what skills would you like to learn and then get paid for?

When I see people who are unemployed or stuck in a lower paying job, I know they haven't taken the time to develop new skillsets.

Skills pays the bills!

The more skills you have, the more money you can make.

One of the first ways I made money online was writing and selling online courses. Then, I added coaching to provide more personalized services. I also did website design, SEO, copy-writing, and eventually started publishing and launching books for myself and others. As a result, I now have multiple streams of six-figure income.

I attribute all of this to taking that first step in learning new skills and then stacking those skills to create value in the marketplace.

I've also discovered that sometimes you spend a lot of time learning a new software program and then the market shifts and you have a decision to make. You can stay where you are or shift with the market. If you want to be successful, you have to learn to shift quickly because technology changes at the speed of light.

Consider, for example, Borders Bookstore. They were the top bookstore for many years, but they didn't pivot fast enough with the creation of eBooks and eBook readers like the NOOK and Kindle. They thought they could continue selling physical books in stores and still be successful. That decision resulted in them going out of business.

If you don't change, you'll stay broke.

In his book, "Linchpin: Are you Indispensable" by Seth Godin, he says, a linchpin is "An individual who can walk into chaos and create order, someone who can invent, connect, create and make things happen."

Being an entrepreneur is about connecting, creating and re-inventing yourself over and over and over. I don't see it as a negative, I love it! I was bored with most jobs I had after the first month because they were monotonous and there was very little change. That's why you see so many big brands going out of business – they didn't want to change. Look at Toys R Us, Sears, Kmart, Borders Bookstore, and more.

We have to shift the question from "How do I get a job doing that?" to "How can I create a job doing that?"

When people ask me what I do, I usually answer, "I'm in publishing" because when I try to explain my business, they look at me like I'm crazy.

I've created a business that involves books because I love books, I love creating content, I love teaching, and I love helping authors succeed. I get paid to do what I love, and that happened because I *created* it.

If I went to any job website, I'm positive I could never find a "Job" that involves doing what I do making multiple six figures. It doesn't exist.

So, instead of looking for a job, create the perfect job using skills you already have (or quickly learn new ones) that are in high demand.

Recently, my former business coach sent out an email to his list stating his business was growing by leaps and bounds and he needed a sales enrollment coach to sell his program.

He spends about $1 million per year on Facebook ads and has a highly targeted and successful coaching business. It's so successful that he can't handle all the strategy session applications he receives.

When I saw his email, I reached out to him and he hired me! A one hour call = $1000!

Why?

Because I mastered the skill of selling on a phone call many years ago. Now, I can use that skill to generate another stream of income in my business.

We will talk more about how to generate multiple six-figure streams of income in an upcoming chapter.

This chapter was about skill-stacking to add value to the marketplace. It's a great place to start.

Next up we are going to talk about your expertise…and how to cash in on it!

Chapter 3:
How to Cash In On Your Expertise

In a blog post by author, speaker and teacher, Seth Godin he wrote:

"**Skill vs. Talent**

You're born with talent.

You earn a skill.

I don't think there are many situations where talent is the key driver of success. The biggest exception might be that a drive to acquire skill could be a talent...

Assuming you have even once done the hard work to learn something important, then you have what you need to develop even more skills.

Go do that.

We need generosity and passion. And even more so, we need people who care to develop the skills to deliver on their promises."

There are a few things we need to talk about.

Some people have natural born talents that they cash in on and others learn skills that they cash in on. And some do both.

Either way, you can use your existing skill set to build a lucrative business that earns six figures while working from home or you can take your natural talents, add some new skills, and do the same.

I was born with a natural talent for writing, but I still had to learn different aspects of writing such as copywriting, storytelling, editing, formatting, publishing, and more.

To cash in on your expertise, answer these questions:

- What do people tell me I'm good at? Is there a high demand for this in the marketplace?

- What obstacles and problems have I overcome in my life? Could I help others do the same? Is there a high demand for this in the marketplace?

- What am I an expert at already? Is there a high demand for this in the marketplace?

- What skills can I learn that interest me and is there a high demand for those in the marketplace?

Answering these questions is a good place to start.

We are all experts at many things, and some areas of expertise are very unique. Years ago, I read a story about a couple who paid zero dollars for their groceries because they had an extraordinary coupon clipping talent. They started a blog and charged others to teach them to do the same.

Sounds crazy, right?

I want you to list ten things you are an expert at that you think you might be able to charge for:

1. _____
2. _____
3. _____
4. _____
5. _____
6. _____
7. _____
8. _____
9. _____
10. _____

In my bestselling author program and business, I use all of the skills listed below to make six figures:

- Sales
- Copywriting/Writing
- Editing
- Formatting
- Cover Design
- Project Management
- Amazon Categories and Keywords Research
- Book Launches
- Networking
- Speaking

I developed this skill set over time; it didn't happen overnight.

The more skills you can combine, the more money you will make!

My good friend, Jackie Woodside, was a Licensed Clinical Social Worker for many years. She was very successful, but eventually got burned out in this field. She decided to reinvent herself and became a certified Life Coach.

Jackie loves creating curriculum and eventually created her signature "Life Design" coaching program. She took that business to six figures using her existing skill set and adding new skills to that.

Once her coaching business was successful, she added a training program and certifies coaches on her methodology for her Life Design program. Today, she has a thriving multiple six-figure coaching and training business.

In an upcoming chapter, we will be talking about the 6-figure blueprint I learned from my business coach that turned my business from a side-hustle to a thriving 6-figure business. And we will also be talking about how to create multiple six-figure income streams.

Once your first 6-figure business is up and running, there is usually some aspect of that business that you can turn into another 6-figure stream of income.

Right now you might be asking, "What expertise could I use to create a 6-figure business?"

Let's change the question to this:

*"What expertise do I have right now that
I could use to make my first $1000?"*

This small shift in the question doesn't make it feel so overwhelming.

First, test to see if there is a market for what you are selling. Then, see how you feel about it after you've made your first $1000 doing it. You might discover that you didn't like it that much after all.

After you make your first $1000, you can easily shift gears because you are not that heavily invested in the business.

The mistake I continually see people make is investing thousands of dollars on a website, branding, logos, sales funnels, creating online courses, etc. only to find out it doesn't work, and no one is buying what they're selling. Now, their confidence is down, and they feel stuck because they've spent so much money.

Don't make this mistake!

The foreword of *The 7-Day Startup* by Dan Norris says:

*"Without question, the biggest mistake people make is
obsessing over their idea and not focusing enough on
finding people willing to pay for their product."*

One of my favorite chapters in this book is "You Don't Learn Until You Launch." It's fun to build a website, pick your brand colors and designs, get a logo done, work on the copyrighting, develop a program, talk about your business, etc.

The problem is there's an imbalance - you're spending too much time on an unproven idea. You need to have sales to prove your idea is worth pursuing.

Execution is your ability to present an idea and get customers to pay for that idea and that is all that matters.

Dan Norris wrote this book because he invested 7+ years in a business that failed, and he learned what NOT to do.

Here's what WANNAPRENEURS focus on:

- Building expensive websites
- Optimizing their site
- New life-changing ideas
- Logos
- Branding
- Photoshoots
- Sales Funnels
- Expensive courses
- Reading books
- Listening to podcasts
- Talking endlessly about their idea
- Attending events endlessly

They do everything except get customers!

If you have a natural talent or a skill set and you want to test it out, I highly recommend you do it quickly. Don't spend hundreds or thousands of dollars on the tasks listed above. Instead, create a minimum viable product (MVP) and launch it.

You can launch your MVP without a website or expensive sales funnels.

If you want a roadmap for doing this, then pick up a copy of "The 7-Day Startup" by Dan Norris. It's a great book!

And remember this from Dan Norris:

"It's amazing what you can achieve in 7 days.
You can't deliver on your whole grand vision, but you can
launch something. When you do, you can start talking to people
who are paying you money. This is when you start making
sensible business decisions and avoid assumptions."

I'm telling you this because I made this mistake in 2004 before I launched my first website, Become a 6-Figure Woman. I spent thousands of dollars I didn't have on a website that didn't work, and I wasted an excessive amount of time choosing colors, images, branding, etc.

Looking back, it was my own fear of launching that was causing me to get bogged down in research and I mistakenly felt like I was *busy* working on my business, when, in reality, I was just wasting time.

An MVP is something you can launch in seven days. Sounds crazy, but Dan is right. Don't waste your time on expensive Facebook ads if you don't have any paying customers for that product or service.

When I hired my business coach who turned my business around and tripled my income in 90 days, he told me never to run Facebook ads until you have a proven offer that converts.

Many people think the answer to all their business problems is Facebook ads, but they don't have a proven offer that converts.

You can test ideas and offers with a simple landing page before building a complete website.

I had the ugliest business website for years and I still made six figures year after year. The colors were bad, I had no logo, no style, etc., but at the end of the day, the only thing that mattered was the sales copy, the calls to action, and that my offer converted.

I have a client who is a Master Coach for The Life Coach School and I'm amazed at the types of niche' coaches who have successful businesses:

- Binge Eating Coach
- Real Estate Coach
- Weight Loss Coach
- Autoimmune Coach
- Feminist Confidence Coach
- Money Coach

- Mindfulness Coach
- Menopause Coach
- Running Coach
- The Deep Dive Coach (one of my clients)
- Female Entrepreneur Coach
- Non-Profit Career Coach
- Adoption Coach
- Introvert Coach
- Stop Over-Drinking Coach

So, when people tell me "I'm not an expert"...that's a lie. You are an expert at many things. I'm certain you've overcome problems, and that right there makes you an expert.

Think of it this way. We are all on a path and some people are further ahead of us in different areas and some are behind us. You are an expert to the people who are further behind you on the path.

Right now, some people are making $1000 per month from their online business. I am making $25k+ per month, so I am further along that they are, which means I am an expert, and I can help them.

Have you ever heard "Make your Mess Your Message"? What messes can you turn into a message to help others?

And if you aren't interested in that, then focus on your skills, developing new skills, and using your existing natural talents.

Now that we've talked about how to cash in on your expertise, next we are going to talk about the "sampling" stage.

Chapter 4:
Sample First, Select Second

I hired my business coach in September 2014. He took one look at my website and said "Michelle, what is all this stuff? We need to pick one thing and focus on that one thing."

He was absolutely right. At the time, I was selling a variety of online courses such as:

- Quit Your Job and Follow Your Dreams
- How to Start a Profitable Blog
- Creating Online Courses that Sell
- How to Write a Mission Statement
- 6-Figure Woman

I wasn't making a lot of money from one thing. I was making a little money from a lot of things.

I started my online business in 2005 and it was my part-time side hustle. I had a 6-figure outside sales job from 2004 until 2010, so I had another source of income that paid the bills and wasn't completely reliant on my online business.

Once that 6-figure sales job ended, however, I really needed to turn my side hustle into my 6-figure business, so I hired a business coach.

Even though picking one thing to focus on in my business was brilliant and it catapulted me to six figures, when you're first starting out, it is a good idea to have a *sampling period.*

As we talked about in the previous chapter, you want to create a minimum viable product and launch in a short period of time—ideally 7 days, max-30 days.

Ideas are a dime a dozen. It's the execution that's hard and you don't learn until you execute the idea. So, you won't know if you really like it until you actually do it.

A Cool Way to Sample

There is a website called Pivot Planet (formerly named Vocation Vacations) that allows you to find someone who is doing the job you want to do and consult with them to "test drive your dream job". I love that idea!

Check it out at: https://www.pivotplanet.com/

Enter a description for the type of career or business you want to work in and find an advisor that you can consult with and ask questions about. Here are some featured advisor careers:

- Voiceover Artist
- Blogger
- Filmmaker
- Technology Entrepreneur
- Airbnb host
- Marketing Firm Owner
- Professional Speaker
- Publisher
- Radio Personality
- Web Developer
- Online Course Creator

You can view the full list of advisors at: https://www.pivotplanet.com/browse.

I recommend hiring an advisor so you can see if this is something you really want to do and learn the good, the bad and the ugly about it.

Working from home and making six figures sounds great, but the devil is in the details.

The biggest mistake people make is investing too much time, money and resources before making a dime on their business or idea.

Don't make that mistake. Do your due diligence. Hire an advisor and ask questions. If it's something that still interests you, then create your minimum viable product and make your first $1000. If you still love it after that, then you have the green light to invest more of your money, time and energy into it.

Looking back, it was important for me to "sample" different ways to make money.

I've made money online in dozens of ways, and some of them I liked and some I did not.

Here's an example of something I tried that I did not like:

At the time, I noticed some people were recommending having a year-long program. A year sounded like a long time to me, so I launched a 6-month program instead. Six months to a year is a long time to work with people. I found when there is a shorter amount of time like 6-12 weeks, you get better results with people because there is more motivation to complete tasks when there is a tighter deadline.

I did that 6-month coaching program one time, and it was very lucrative. Six people paid $1000 a month for six months so I made $36,000, but it wasn't really something that I absolutely loved doing so I never offered it again.

You must make money and get your first clients before you will ever know if you really enjoy it.

When my son graduated high school, he told me he wanted to be a massage therapist and the tuition was $10,000 for him to get certified. It sounded like a good idea, but my gut told me he needed to actually *experience* it.

I had a good friend who was a licensed massage therapist working out of her home. I set an appointment for my son to have a one-hour massage and afterwards, he would sit down and talk to her about the business side of things when they were done.

I waited out in the car because I didn't want to influence him. About 90 minutes later, my son came to the car and said, "I could never do that to people. I definitely don't want to be a massage therapist."

Thank God I listened to my intuition because that would have been a $10,000 mistake!

A lot of things sound exciting or sexy or lucrative, but until you know the details involved on the back-end, it might be an illusion and not something you truly enjoy.

In my book, "Quit Your Job and Follow Your Dreams," I include a chapter that shows readers how to do a job autopsy.

Do Your Own Job Autopsy

I suggest going through all of your previous jobs (and current job if you are working) and writing down all the daily tasks you do and then rate those on a scale of 1-10 to see what you love and what you don't.

It's an eye-opening experience because most people who hate their jobs are spending 75% of their time on tasks they hate or dislike and only 25% on tasks they love.

When it comes to creating your own 6-figure business, you want to make sure you're spending 75% of your time on tasks you love and only 25% or less on tasks you don't love.

Of course, you can outsource the tasks you don't love, but it's important to be realistic about what is involved in the type of business you're looking to start.

My online business involves a lot of technology, learning new software, understanding algorithms, research, writing, typing, talking to people, reading manuscripts, managing book projects, etc.

When I first started www.bestsellingauthorprogram.com in 2013, I was doing everything in my business. I was literally a solopreneur. Fast forward now to my business and I worked with a talented team of people:

- Cover Designer
- Editor
- Formatter
- Amazon Ads Expert
- Project Manager
- Proof-reader
- Virtual Assistant

It was hard letting go of the reins, but eventually you have to pick the one or two things you're great at and laser focus on those things.

Go through the list of expert advisors on Pivot Plant and select the top three areas in which you would like to make six figures while working from home.

Go to: https://www.pivotplanet.com/browse

My top three choices for making six figures from home:

1. _____
2. _____
3. _____

Next, talk to at least one successful person who is doing what you want to do and ask them the following ten questions:

1. Does this job have the potential to make six figures?
2. How many hours do you spend on your business per week?
3. What do you love about your business?
4. What do you hate about your business?

5. What have you learned since you started this business that you wish you knew before you started?

6. Do I need any special training to do this and if so, what would you recommend?

7. How many years did it take you to become successful?

8. What advice would you give to someone like me who is just starting out?

9. What were the three biggest mistakes you made in this business?

10. If you could do things over, would you choose this business?

This will give you a good gauge on if this is really something you want to pursue.

If the business involves a lot of sitting at the computer, and you prefer to be outdoors, maybe that's not for you.

> *Performing a job autopsy and talking with an expert*
> *advisor will save you tons of time, money,*
> *and energy going down the wrong path.*

Once you've done this, and you feel good about what you've learned then by all means, get started.

I have a good friend, James, who works in IT and has decided he wants more time and money freedom. He is currently enrolled in the Life Design Coaching training program I mentioned earlier, and he plans to transition to a full-time Life Design Coach in the next year.

James did his due diligence before jumping in and knows what is involved in starting a life coaching business. The great part is James has technology skills which he will need to get his business off the ground.

It does take money to make money.

I recommend keeping your day job and only leaving once you have enough money in the bank to cover one year's expenses, you have no debt, and you've made your first $1000 in your new line of business.

Of course, there are no guarantees. My income was feast or famine for many years which is why I kept my 6-figure outside sales job. I also loved sales and I loved driving to appointments and meeting new people. So that worked for me.

You can also consider going from full-time to part-time work while you build up your new business. Then, when you are financially ready, you can take the leap!

Now that we've talked about sampling and trying things out, next up we are going to talk about going deep and not wide.

Chapter 5:
Go Deep, Not Wide

There are different seasons of a business. When you are starting out, it's important to *sample* things to see what you like. I always recommend making your first $1000 from your selected business model by doing a 7-day or maximum 30-day launch.

After you complete your sampling period, which could be as long as a year, then it's time to go deep, not wide.

I have another confession to make...

I am a recovering 'Shiny New Objects' chaser! It's so much fun in the beginning when you're learning something new with so many exciting possibilities. However, in the beginning you are really looking at whatever "it" is through rose-colored glasses.

This approach worked well when I was in the sampling period, but it doesn't work well in the long term or enable you to build a sustainable six-figure business.

If you're like me, and you like to do a little on a lot of things, it can be difficult to choose one thing.

The Lesson I Learned at Five Years Old

When I was five years old (circa, 1968), my dad took me to the toy store on Christmas Eve to buy presents for me and my three brothers. It was late and the store was closing soon so we had limited time. He took me to the doll aisle and said, "Michelle, you can have any doll you want, just pick one out and I'll be back in a few minutes." He left me on my own to select my "one" doll while he shopped for gifts for my brothers. (Back then, you could leave your child in a store unattended and it was safe. Times have changed!)

When my dad came back to the doll aisle, he found me kneeling on the floor crying with about 10 dolls laid out in front of me. "Michelle, if you don't pick one doll, you're going home with no doll!"

Unfortunately, I couldn't pick one. I wanted them all. And guess what? I went home with NO doll.

The moral of the story is we need to pick one thing and then master that because that's where the big money is. When you become the go-to expert in your field for that "one thing," then the money starts flowing in.

My business coach made me pick one thing to focus on and I thankfully I chose my www.bestsellingauthorprogram.com business because I love books and I love working with authors. It turned my entire business around and within 90 days, I was making six figures! In fact, I had my first $22,000 month because of his advice. And every year my income soars!

I'm not going to lie. It's hard to stay in one lane. I see so many things I want to do, but if I take energy away from my bestselling author program business, then that income will most likely decrease.

I have become a go-to person in this niche' and every year I easily add on new income streams in this business.

Malcolm Gladwell talks about working on something for 10,000 hours to get to the level of mastery. If you want to make six figures from home, then you need to become a master of "one thing" and do it so well that there is no competition.

To Quit or Not to Quit

The reason people start things and then quit is because of what bestselling author Seth Godin calls "the dip." In fact, he wrote an entire book about it called "The Dip: A Little Book That Teaches You When To Quit (And When To Stick)," and in it he quotes Vince Lombardi:

"Quitters never win and winners never quit."
Godin follows with, "Bad advice. Winners quit all the time.
They just quit the right stuff at the right time."

Most people quit. They just don't quit successfully...

Extraordinary benefits accrue to the minority of people who are able to push just a tiny bit longer than most.

Extraordinary benefits also accrue to the tiny majority with the guts to quit early and refocus their efforts on something new.

In both cases, it's about being the best in the world."

So quitting isn't necessarily a bad thing. That's why I suggest sampling different profit paths and then quitting the ones you don't like or are not passionate about.

I've quit a lot of mediocre and passion-less products or services I was selling, and I've even given up on ideas about new products or services that I would like to create. Quitting is a huge part of being successful.

A common problem I see, however, is when we invest heavily in something, it's hard to quit. I know because I've done this myself.

For example, let's say you want to be a Life Coach. So you sign up with the Life Coach School and the tuition is around $18,000. Then, you build an amazing website for $5000. Now you need to create a program to sell, so you spend months creating this amazing program (and you have no idea if it will sell). Then, you build an automated webinar and spend thousands of dollars running Facebook ads to it. Maybe you get some clients, or maybe you don't. Finally, you get a few sign ups and start running the program only to realize you don't really like it. The problem is you've invested so much time, energy and resources, that it's hard to quit.

Here's what you can do in the alternative...

Instead of signing up for an $18,000 Life Coaching School, start selling your expertise or services with a simple website or landing page. You can start a Facebook Group and market to the group. Create a blog and drive traffic that way. Create a simple 6-week coaching program with no content (only coaching) and you make your first $1000. Then decide if this is something you want to move forward with. If it is, then you go deeper on it.

Our culture celebrates superstars and winners. We reward the product, book, song, organization or employee that is #1! In fact, it's common for #1 to get ten times the benefit of #10 and a hundred times the benefit of #100.

That's why you want to go deep, not wide, once you select your business profit path so you can become the best at it.

So why does being #1 matter so much?

Because people are short on time and they don't want to take a lot of risks. They would rather head for the person who's ranked best in the world than waste their time doing research and dealing with a mediocre choice.

Also, there's only room at the top for a few, and that creates scarcity. We pay extra for the best, and the best is often scarce.

Scarcity is a result of most people quitting long before they have created something that makes it to the top.

The reason people quit is because of the dip—the long slog between starting and mastery.

In the beginning, any new venture is fun! You're learning new things, it's interesting and stimulating. Then the dip happens which is the "hard work" phase. The long stretch between beginning and true achievement.

The 80/20 rule applies to everything. 80% of the people will never follow through with things they start or dreams they have.

It may sound fun and appear glamorous to be a CEO, but it's a long, hard road to get there and many CEO's spent decades in the dip before landing their high-paying job.

Seth Godin says, "The Dip creates scarcity; scarcity creates value."

So, if you want to make six figures, after you've had your sampling period, then you will go deep, not wide, and you'll whittle through the dip. And when you come out on the other side, you'll be the best in the world.

The dip really is the secret to success.

It's hard to stay on one path.

One day I emailed my coach and said I needed to speak with him right away. I was feeling tired, overworked and burned out even though my 6-figure online business was going well. I was thinking of switching paths.

Thank God I had an amazing coach who helped me work through a few things:

- I needed to outsource more and build a small team. I was stuck in solopreneur mode doing everything in my business and it was draining me.

- I needed to charge more for my done-for-you services.

- I needed to cut back on what I was including in my packages.

I took his advice and it worked.

It was hard for me to let go of the reins and start outsourcing things, but once I did, I wondered why I hadn't done it sooner. First, I hired an editor for my client's books. Then, I hired a world class book designer. Next, a new virtual assistant to set up book launches, and finally, I hired a project manager to keep the business and projects moving and flowing.

Now, it might sound like I have a huge business, but these are all subcontractors who work virtually. They are not employees. Some work a few hours a month or a few hours a day but having this virtual support team has freed up my time so I can work on my special gifts – writing, coaching, sales, and launch strategies.

When I was going through this tough time, my coach asked me, "Michelle, how much do you need to charge to make you want to get out of bed in the morning?"

I thought that was a funny question, but he was right. I was under-charging for my services, so of course I was getting tons of clients as a result. Then, I had to do all this work by myself and it was stressful and tiring. Because I was under-charging, I wasn't feeling motivated to get out of bed in the morning to complete all the projects I was bringing in.

As a result of our call, I increased my price points and created three new packages for authors.

Lastly, I had to remove some of the done-for-you services I was including in my packages. My coach pointed out that I was trying to give clients everything they could possibly need to build a business around a book.

That wasn't sustainable, and it wasn't what my clients were hiring me to do. I was hired to publish and launch a high-quality book to the bestsellers list that my clients could leverage and use in their business and life. So, I eliminated some of the items included in my packages that were outside the original scope of the project.

Once I made those three changes, things got much better. I've been able to free up my time and add on new 6-figure streams of income as a result.

I'm sharing these stories with you because they are real, and they are part of the mistakes I made as I built my business. I don't want you to make the same ones.

Here's what we've learned:

- Have a sampling period.

- Be a strategic quitter.

- Pick one thing.

- Go Deep, Not Wide (after the sampling period).

- Move through the Dip.

- Be #1 at your one thing.

- Hire a great business coach to help you navigate around your blind spots.

Next up is a chapter about picking high-hanging fruit to create a sustainable six figure business from home.

Chapter 6:
Pick the High-Hanging Fruit

In his book, "The Pumpkin Plan: A Simple Strategy to Grow a Remarkable Business in any Field," Mike Michaelowicz says:

"Ordinary pumpkins are always forgotten. Only the giant pumpkin draws a crowd…The giant pumpkin is legend. And when you've grown one…you will be legend too."

Mike uses the analogy of pumpkin farmers who grow half-ton pumpkins as the secret formula to big time entrepreneurial success: "Plant hearty seeds, identify the most promising pumpkins, *kill off the rest of the vine*, and *nurture only the pumpkins with the biggest potential.*"

This chapter is all about finding your most "promising" business idea, then "killing off" the rest of the vine and nurturing only the ones with the biggest potential.

In his Pumpkin Plan book, Mike shares the story of how he owned a computer technology company for four years. He was working 16-18 hours a day, seven days a week and the grind never let up. Although they were doing a million dollars in revenue, there costs were high, the cash flow was not flowing and there was barely any profit.

Mike hired a business coach who helped him turn around his failing million-dollar business that was burning him out, and the first order of business was to *cut his client list.*

In fact, here was his coach's advice:

"List your clients in order of revenue, then take your top-paying clients and separate them into two categories: great clients and everyone else–from the ho-hum clients to the clients who annoy you so much, you cringe when they call you. Keep the great, top-paying clients and cut the rest. Every single one."

Sounds extreme, right?

It was. But guess what? It turned his business around.

Also it turns out that giant pumpkin growers use the same approach with these seven steps:

"Step One: Plant Promising seeds.

Step Two: Water, water, water.

Step Three: As they grow, they routinely REMOVE all of the diseased or damaged pumpkins.

Step Four: WEED like a mad dog. Not a single green leaf or root permitted if it isn't a pumpkin plant.

Step Five: When they grow larger, identify the stronger, faster-growing pumpkins. Then REMOVE all the less promising pumpkins. Repeat until you have one pumpkin on each vine.

Step Six: FOCUS all of your attention on the BIG PUMPKIN. Nurture it around the clock like a baby and guard it like you would your first Mustang convertible.

Step Seven: Watch it grow. In the last days of the season, this will happen so fast you can actually see it happen."

In the previous chapters, we talked about the sampling period, followed up with choosing one thing. Now, it's time to talk about high-ticket clients vs. low ticket clients.

Put your clients into one of two groups:

- **Group 1**: People with an abundance of time who are short on money.
- **Group 2**: People with a shortage of time who have an abundance of money.

When I started my online business in 2005, I worked with people in Group 1. After years of working with this group, I did not have a six-figure business. I was working hard, but not making much progress.

In 2014, when I hired my amazing business coach, he told me to get rid of all my low-paying courses, programs and services and focus on serving Group 2.

The crazy part was, I was afraid to let go of that income, so this was a great lesson in trust.

I listened to him and shut everything down even though it was scary and hard. At the same time, I was creating what is now my high-level Bestselling Author Program which focuses on Group 2.

The amazing thing about working with people who are short on time, but who have an abundance of money is that they are very low maintenance. They're a pleasure to work with and they have a professional and business mindset.

Unfortunately, most people go after Group 1 – the low hanging fruit.

Why?

Because it's easier to get low hanging fruit than high hanging fruit.

What people don't understand, though, is that the majority of entrepreneurs and business owners are ALL going after the low hanging fruit, so the competition is tough.

Wouldn't you rather go after the 10% of the market that has money and is willing to invest in a high-ticket program to get the results they are seeking?

Getting back to the seven steps I mentioned earlier that Mike got from his business coach, here's what I did in my business to go from a side hustle to six figures:

- Removed all of my low-ticket programs.
- Focused all of my time and energy on one program – the Bestselling Author Program.
- Weeded out "shiny new objects" and stopped chasing them.
- Identified my top-paying clients and removed the rest.
- Focused all of my attention on my top-paying clients.

I know it sounds enticing to create an online course for $997 and sell dozens or hundreds of copies per month, but it isn't quite as easy as it sounds.

Gone are the days of selling from a sales page on your website. People are much savvier these days and they want high-touch engagement that gets results; the people in Group 2 want a VIP experience.

A $997 price point may sound high to you, but it's not. There are coaches and programs that start at $5000 for eight weeks and go up to $10,000 for a done-with-you program. Done-for-you programs (like mine) have an even higher price point ranging from $8,000 to $25,000+.

The beauty of going for the high-hanging fruit is there is a lot less competition, and you need fewer clients to make six figures.

In fact, I only need two to four clients per month to make multiple six figures in my business.

The key here is to focus on getting better clients, not more clients. More isn't necessarily better; better is better.

Consider the following questions when determining if a client is a good fit to work with:

- Can they afford you?
- Do they pay on time?
- Do they refer others to you?

- Do they communicate well, tell you what they want and need and not expect you to read their minds?
- Do they respect your expertise?
- Do they respect your time?

These are the types of clients you want to work with. I don't want to work with people who cannot afford me, aren't good communicators, don't respect my time or expertise and don't value my services.

George Carlin once said,

"Anyone who drives slower than you is an idiot,
and everyone who drives faster is a maniac."

Focus on working with people who are going your speed and you'll be much happier.

Sometimes when we are starting out in business, we are happy to get "any" paying client. I get that. But once you've been in business long enough, you realize you don't want just "any" client, you want to work with the best clients who are going your speed.

I once had a strategy session with a woman who told me she was going to "sell her car" to work with me.

I don't want anyone selling their means of transportation to get a book published and launched.

People at the high levels know they have to pay top dollar to get top service.

If you already have an existing business and you want to grow that business, raise your prices. Maybe even double or triple them.

I've had to do this several times in my business and the quality of people I work with now is phenomenal.

Does a high-maintenance, challenging client ever slip in?

Yes.

But I always deliver on my promises and then I make sure to take a mental note of how that happened and create more barriers to entry to working with me.

Weeding is a constant process, not a one-and-done event.

Also, when you charge premium prices for your services, you can hire other people and preserve your precious time for focusing on your strengths.

Now that we know it's best to go after the top 10% of the market – the high hanging fruit – and to charge premium prices, it's time to talk about hiring out your weaknesses so you can focus on your strengths.

Chapter 7:
Hire Out Your Weaknesses

One of the biggest mistakes I've made in my business is doing everything myself and believing that no one could do things better than I could.

I've learned now that successful entrepreneurs identify problems, discover the opportunities available to solving those problems, and then build systems that *allow other people and other things to get it done*.

In his book, "Virtual Freedom: How to Work With Virtual Staff to Buy More Time, Become More Productive, and Build Your Dream Business," Author Chris Ducker says,

"In late 2009, I found myself burnt out and stressed like never before. I woke up one day and realized something startling: I really didn't have a company. I was the company!"

If you remove "you" from your company and it can't operate without "you," then you really don't have a company.

Also, when you're doing every "thing" in your business, then you're not operating from your strengths; you're operating mostly from your weaknesses.

As my Bestselling Author Program was growing, I was staying up to wee hours of the morning/night editing and formatting books, designing book covers, and managing publishing projects from beginning to end.

Just like Chris Ducker, I was my company.

And guess what? I was working myself into a job. Because unfortunately, I was trading time for money once again.

I finally realized the error of my ways and fired myself from several specific roles that were better suited for other people.

My first hire was a Virtual Assistant to help me with the day-to-day operations of my business, and the second was an amazing editor and formatting assistant. These two hires saved my life and my business.

When you get burned out sometimes you think the only option is to shut things down. I admit, there were dozens of times I wanted to "quit" my business and I'm grateful I stuck with it and got through the "dip" and the hard times.

Deep down I loved books and I loved working with authors, I just didn't love doing ALL the work in my business.

During the time I was working with my business coach, he was NOT a fan of the "done-for-you" business model I had created. Most coaches are not doing done-for-you programs; it's more of a done-*with*-you program.

However, there was something deep inside of me that assured me the people who were my ideal clients (the ones short on time and high on cash) did not want to "learn" how to write, publish and launch a #1 bestselling book; they wanted me (and my team) to do it for them.

I stuck to that belief and today I have a very successful VIP done-for-you business that caters to high-end experts such as coaches, consultants, psychologists, speakers, trainers, doctors, lawyers, educators, and more.

Discover What You Don't Like Doing and Stop Doing It

Aside from the fact that one person cannot perform every role in a business without ending up burned out, stressed out and having a very unleveraged business – sometimes when you start a business you do perform more roles than you'd like to.

The key to long-term success, however, is to outsource your weaknesses as soon as you can afford to do so – and you need to do it sooner rather than later.

My mistake was waiting for years to make this shift.

Being a paralegal for 17 years, I was used to doing a lot of different tasks – some of them I loved and some of them I hated – but I did not have a choice.

I defaulted to this "suck it up" mentality and did everything in my business because it had become the *norm*. Also, I was lazy because I knew it was hard work to find, hire and train others in my business. What I didn't realize was the benefits would far outweigh the costs.

When I hired my publishing assistant to edit and format the books, it was like a weight was lifted off of my shoulders. It freed of more of my time to focus on things I was good at and that I loved like writing, selling and coaching.

Hiring Alex as my project manager was another great decision I made because he had the technology skills I needed to learn several aspects of my business quickly and to take a lot off of my plate.

Alex sets up book launches from start to finish, manages large publishing projects, proofreads books after they've been edited, creates and manages Amazon ads for clients, and sets up media interviews. He's even doing website maintenance for several websites.

He was doing such a phenomenal job, I decided to give him my "problem" clients. It's not that the "client" was a problem per se, it's just that these particular clients hired me months or even years ago, but never gave a manuscript. My program is a 12-week program, so I called these clients my "stragglers." He's completed four of those projects, and I'm so happy he was able to take those off my plate.

I also noticed that every year I hired more people in my business that my income increases. So, my goal became to keep hiring people until I'm only working from my strengths.

According to Gallup research, only 20% of people are in a role where they have a chance to do what they do best every day using their strengths. Often in corporate America, you can't pick and choose your tasks if you want to keep your job.

That means 80% of the time people are not operating from their strengths. No wonder people hate their jobs.

In their book, "First, Break All The Rules: What the World's Greatest Managers Do Differently," authors Marcus Buckingham and Curt Coffman say:

"You would be wise not to ignore your weaknesses. Great managers don't. As soon as they realize that a weakness is causing the poor performance, they switch their approach. They know that there are only three possible routes to helping the person succeed. Devise a support system. Find a complementary partner. Or find an alternative role. Great managers quickly bear down, weigh these options and choose the best route."

When you have your own business, the stakes are even higher. If you're spending time on tasks and activities that are not your strengths, your business will most likely fail, and you may end up broke.

I love the three options that great managers find as solutions for those employees whose weakness is causing poor performance:

1. Get support

2. Find a partner to help

3. Find an alternative role

As I said earlier, I kept firing myself and that is the key to achieving more success. I thought business was about learning and figuring out how to do everything in it, and now I see that the more your business operates without you, the more success your business will have.

In, "Work the System: The Simple Mechanics of Making More and Working Less," by Sam Carpenter, he talks about his failing telecommunications business, Centratel, and says:

"For fifteen years Centratel struggled for survival, always at the brink of disaster. Why did this primary system begin to prosper in year sixteen? Yes, focused attention, terrific staff, targeted marketing, and a consistently high-quality product went a long way, but they were not the cause of the turnaround. Instead, these were by-products of the cause. The reason for the turnaround was the discovery and application of the principle that leadership must focus on improving processes, not on performing the work OR on repeatedly snuffing out brushfires."

My business coach recommended this book to me and it changed my business and my life. It opened my eyes to creating systems.

In "Work the System," Sam Carpenter says:

"Your task is to optimize one system after another, not careen through the day randomly taking care of whatever problems erupt. Your job is not to be a fire killer. Your job is to prevent fires."

When you spend the majority of your time putting out fires, it's hard to change gears. It took some time to set up systems in my business, but now that they are set up, I have more free time.

The catch-22 is it takes time to set up the systems. My mentality had always been "it's quicker for me to just do it." And that's probably true in the short term, but I was doing the same repetitive tasks over and over and over which was not good use of my precious time. Every minute spent on things that weren't my strengths was taking time away from those things that are my strengths.

Sales is one of my core strengths. So when I was spending my time editing manuscripts or designing book covers, I was literally losing business.

It's interesting to me now, looking back, that my business made the same amount every year until I made this shift and then my income doubled and now it has tripled!

I think the best way to determine your strengths is to do the job autopsy I mentioned earlier. I go into great detail about job autopsies in my book "Quit Your Job and Follow Your Dreams: A 12-Month Guide to Being Joyfully Jobless."

The main task of a job autopsy is to look at every job you've had and write down all the tasks involved in that particular job. Then, rate those tasks on a scale of 1-10 with the tasks you enjoyed the most rated the highest. Then, focus on the tasks which you rated 8s, 9s or 10s.

Statistics show that the most successful people create jobs where they spend a disproportionate amount of time doing what they love and it doesn't happen by accident.

In his book, "One Thing You Need to Know: About Great Managing, Great Leading, and Sustained Individual Success," author Marcus Buckingham says:

"Some people will tell you that it doesn't matter if you like your work; you just have to be good at it. Question this advice. You may well be good at some activities you don't enjoy, but your enjoyment is the fuel you require to keep practicing the activity, to keep stretching, investing and pushing yourself to greater levels of mastery. Lacking this enjoyment your performance will like plateau."

Writing is one of my strengths, and it is something I also enjoy and am passionate about. I know that are different schools of thoughts on this – some say just focus on what your good at whether you enjoy it or not – and others (like me and Marcus Buckingham) say that it's important for long-term success to be good at it and to enjoy it.

That's why I keep writing. It's not just because I'm good at it, it's because I truly love it.

What do you love so much that you would do even if you weren't being paid to do it?

Sometimes that's a good question to ask if you're stuck. If you've done the job autopsy exercise, you may have already figured out some of your strengths and things you truly enjoy.

Years ago I was teaching a workshop in Washington, D.C., and I asked the students to raise their hand if they loved sales. Only two people raised their hands out of dozens of people. That made me realize that majority of people hate selling. It's hard to be a successful entrepreneur if you're not good at selling and/or you don't like it.

It's all about self-knowledge and self-awareness. The better you know yourself, the more successful you will become.

Now that we've discussed hiring out your weaknesses, next up is the 6-Figure Blueprint and how you can start using it to create your own 6-figure business.

Chapter 8:
The 6-Figure Blueprint

I recently had a strategy session with a potential client for my Bestselling Author program. She asked me to look at her new website while we were on the call. The colors were vibrant and beautiful, and the design was lovely, but I noticed there were no strong calls to action and I couldn't figure out what she was actually selling. Under the "Services" tab, I found:

- All Services
- Master Course
- Speaking and Seminars
- Soul Adventures
    - Clearing Process
    - The Journey
    - Coaching

There was no clear direction on her website and although she was talented, she wasn't able to convert visitors into paying customers.

As we talked more, I asked her what her main business was and she replied, "Coaching." When I asked her about the Master Course, I found out she spent enormous amounts of time and energy developing a course only to have a couple of people sign up for it.

Remember in an earlier chapter, we talked about launching fast and getting paying customers. Ideas are a dime a dozen. Until you actually have paying customers, you are wasting a lot of time.

This potential client was working on a book to grow her business and I told her to do that she needed to remove everything on her website under "services" and have one signature program. This way, the book and the signature program could work hand in hand.

She is an expert at what she does, highly credible, has a great title and hook for her book, but she was making the same mistake I made before I hired my business coach. She was selling a lot of programs and making a little bit of money on them instead of making a lot of money on fewer programs.

In fact, she was very interested in my program, but when I told her the cost, at first, she told me she couldn't afford it. She ended up moving some things around and did hire me and I'm so happy I can help her with her book and her website.

In this chapter, I'm going to share with you the 5-Step system that transformed my business from making $3-5k per month to making $20k-$50k+ per month.

Is it easy to execute?

No.

Execution is never easy because there is a learning curve and most things that are worthwhile and pay well are rarely easy. The fact is most people will quit in the "dip" – the long slog where it gets really hard before you get to the mastery level.

Hopefully, you'll be one of the 20% of people who take action and implement what I'm about to teach you.

5-Step System:

1. Offer (one that is tested and converts)

2. Facebook Ad

3. Automated Webinar

4. Application

5. Phone Call

The Offer

I want to take you back to when I hired my business coach. I was just like the woman I mentioned above. On my Become a 6-Figure Woman Website, I was offering several online courses as well as coaching, website design, SEO, copywriting services and more. I was all over the place.

My coach told me to pick one thing to focus on while we built this automated system.

I chose the Bestselling Author online program because I already was selling this as a 6-week online course. After students completed the course, they asked me if I could just do it for them, and that's how my done-for-you program was born.

At first, I charged $1000 to get a previously published book to the bestsellers list. I got so many clients (high demand/low supply of my time) that I quickly increased my fee to $2000. I was still getting a lot of clients.

I began noticing that the quality of the books wasn't the best – the covers weren't very professional, the books were not properly edited, the book description was poorly written, and the hook was weak.

My coach said I needed a complete program that covered all of those elements as well as achieving best seller status. He recommended I create a program that took a mediocre book and turned it into a high-quality book that someone could use in their business and that's how my high-ticket done-for-you bestsellers program was created.

He suggested I charge $5000 for a 12-week done-for-you program. I thought he was crazy and said, "No one is going to pay $5000 for this." He said, "We'll see."

He was right and I was wrong.

The first month, I charged $3000 because I was afraid I wouldn't get clients at the $5k price point. That month, I signed up four new clients. My coach said, "Michelle, you just left $8000 ($2000 x 4 new clients) on the table. What could you and your family have done with $8000?"

Darn! He was right. If I had charged $5k like he told me, I would have had an extra $8k in my bank account that month. So, the next month I raised my price to $4k and, again, I had four people sign up. His comment to me this time was, "Michelle, you just left $4000 ($1000 x 4 new clients) on the table. What could you and your family have done with $4000?"

Darn! He was right again. The next month I listened to him and I had my first $20k+ month.

From the outside, I looked like I had one program, but I actually was selling a few different packages, but you couldn't tell that from my website. I learned not to publish packages or prices on your website without a phone call (strategy session).

So, Step 1 of the system is to have a proven offer that converts. I already had that; it was just that I was undercharging.

If you are creating something new, you want to test it out. It must solve a BIG problem in the marketplace that people are willing to pay top dollar for the high value.

I see a lot of life coaches sell generic programs like:

- Live an unstoppable life
- Live your best life
- Improve your life
- Level up your life

These are all very vague offers and most likely will not convert. To be successful, you need a specific offer. You need to tap into problems that keep people up at night, such as:

- My business is failing, and I need help fast
- My relationship is failing, and I need help fast
- My finances are failing, and I need help fast
- My health is failing, and I need help fast

The four big areas people need help with are:

1. money

2. business/career

3. relationships

4. health.

Focus on these.

Dan Kennedy, master copywriter and author of many books on direct marketing and sales, said in this book, "NO B.S. Direct Marketing:"

> *"Offer Services People WANT, Not What They Need."*

Sell people what they want (or think they want) and then give them what they need once they are a client.

For example, in my publishing business, my clients want to become a bestselling author. That's the result they want so that's what I sell them. I'm not selling them "self-publishing" or "how to write a book."

When I work with my clients, however, I give them so much more. I give them a high-quality book and coach them on how they can leverage this bestselling book to achieve their goals. It's a 12-week done for you program.

If you have a program or service that is working and is proven, you can transform it into a high-level program.

Sometimes, you need to add some done-for-you elements, but you should never charge for your services by the hour. That's just making a job for yourself and this book is about getting out of the corporate grind and creating a 6-figure income working the least amount of time.

"Charge what the market will bear."

I was undercharging when I started out, and my prices have increased every year along with the quality and level of service I offer.

The minimum you should charge for a program that gets people the result they want in a specific period of time, ideally 8-12 weeks, should be $3000. Of course, when you're just starting out you can run a "BETA" program and offer it at a discount while you finalize the details.

My done-for-you program was originally offered at $1000. Once I saw how popular that service was, I developed it into the program I have now and increased the prices over time.

Remember, launch and learn quickly.

Don't make the mistake of not charging enough because then you will start attracting Group 1 – those with an abundance of time, but no money. This group of people can be very draining and burdensome. They are typically the shiny object chasers who don't want to do the hard work and follow things to execution. Make sure you're charging enough to attract the VIP people in Group 2.

People pay top dollar for transformation, not information.

Your offer should provide a transformation, not only information.

Here are some examples of very specific offers:

- Scale your business in 90 days

- Discover a traffic system that can turn $1 into $3, $4, $5 or more on an ongoing basis

- How to Build a Business That Gives You a Freedom Lifestyle in two years or Less

- Break up Coaching: Survive Your soul-crushing breakup. Bounce back with understanding, insight and self-worth.

- Become an Irresistible Catch to an Irreplaceable Partner of the Opposite Sex

Facebook Ads

I started running Facebook ads in 2015 and stopped running them at the end of 2017 because I had more business than I could handle! Now, I get all of my business from referrals. I pay a commission to anyone who refers business to me.

I am by no means an expert at Facebook ads. Facebook ads is NOT an easy platform for beginners, and you may need support which I'll talk about more later.

This section provides an overview of the ads that I ran for my business during this time which grew my business exponentially and were an important piece of my 6-figure success.

There are other types of paid advertising that works well such as YouTube ads, LinkedIn ads, and more. My coach once told me, "If you don't have paid traffic getting you clients, you don't have a business." Remember that.

History of My Facebook Ads

Before I created my automated webinar in 2017, I ran an ad that directed Facebook traffic to my "Case Studies Page" on my website.

My First Ad

(That was me before my hair turned white! lol)

I call this my "beginners ad." It wasn't terrible, and it did get me strategy sessions, but in today's savvy social media world, I don't think this ad would work very well. But everyone has to start somewhere, and this is where I started.

Clicking on the "Learn More" button on the ad above took visitors to my website where I presented six case studies.

This beginner ad worked for a while as I was busy developing my program, increasing my package prices, and creating my automated webinar.

It was not easy getting my webinar finalized. The biggest obstacle I faced was that I was "over-teaching" in my webinar. Thankfully, my coach kept correcting me, and then I would redo the webinar. It took several months to get it right.

We will talk below about the content of the webinar, but the rule of thumb is "Teach them the what, but not the how."

A webinar is a sales tool, not a training session detailing everything you know about a topic. I'm a natural teacher, so I would try to teach way too much on each slide. The webinar was too long and probably would not get me strategy sessions.

It's a tough line to follow – to just tell people about your topic and not how to solve their problem.

Okay, getting back to the Facebook ads...

My Second Ad

 6 Figure Woman
Sponsored ·

Want to Become a #1 Bestselling Author and Boost Your Brand, Business and Visibility? There's a secret "Backwards Book Launch" method that allows you to increase your profits.

Free Training Reveals my Proven "Backwards Book Launch" Formula for Becoming a #1 Bestselling Author
Discover the 3 Reasons Why You Absolutely Must Become a #1 Bestselling Author with my secret "Backwards Book Launch" method and how to make bigger...
ONLINEMEETINGNOW.COM

 Like   Comment   Share   Buffer

On Facebook, it's important to test each of the following parts of your ad to create a "winning ad."

- Images
- Headline
- Call To Action

When you put all the winning parts together, then you have a winning ad!

I tested three images to get the winner.

Below are the other two images that did NOT convert:

I have to tell you I got very attached to images I found that I thought would work. My coach kept saying, "It doesn't matter whether you love or hate the image, the data will tell us what works."

Data outweighs your opinion.

What matters is what appeals to prospects and what image they click on, not what you like. So keep that in mind as you choose images – don't get too attached!

Always test three images.

My first Facebook ad included a photo of myself, but I would not recommend doing that unless you are famous. People are not on Facebook to see ads; they are there for social reasons. If they see your photo with ad copy around it, they will *know* it's an ad and most likely will ignore it.

Select vibrant photos that make people HAPPY. Beach pictures do well and interestingly, sunflowers, always do well.

At the time, the ad above with the starfish was the winning ad because we tested the image, the headline, and the call to action. Then, we ran this ad for a few months to three different target groups.

*Detailed targeting is a feature available with Facebook ads that allows you target very specific demographics such as age, gender, income, marital status, interests, and more.

My Targeting for This Ad

1. Writers/Authors as follows: Writer's Digest, Association of Writers & Writing Programs, The Writer's Circle, Kindle Direct Publishing, AuthorHouse, Amazon or IBooks Author, Field of study: Creative Writing, Job title: Published Author or Penulis; **REACH – 300,000** (I named this **campaign "Writers"**)

2. Business Coaches, Career Coaches, Certified Health Coaches, Certified Trainers, Executive Coaches, Executive Consultant, Health and Wellness Coach, Health Coach, Health Consultant, Health/Wellness Consultant, Life Coach, Life Coaching, Life Skills Coach, Motivational Speaker, Nutritionist, Performance Coach, Personal Coach, Personal Development Mentor, Personal Wellness Coach, Public Speaking, Sales Coach, Speaker, Success Coach, Trainer/ Coach, Wellness Advocate/Consultant, Wellness Coach (I named these *Coaches*); **REACH – 21,000 ;**

3. Ali Brown, Bill Barne, Fabienne Fredrickson, Frank Kern, Lisa Sasevich, Female Entrepreneur Association, Kevin Nations, Marie Forleo, Mike Koenigs (I called this *Gurus*); **REACH – 390,000**

NOTE: In September 2017, Facebook made an update that no longer allows you to target "job titles." So, the ads I previously had that targeted anyone who had "writer or author or coach" in their title would no longer be allowed. To work around this limitation, find associations in which a specific job title belongs and use those in your ads.

For example, if I want to target my ads to writers, then I can use the Non-Fiction Writer's Association (or any other writer's groups) in my ad. This will require you to do some research when setting up your ads.

Okay, getting back to the ads I was running…

My detailed targeting included:

- Homeowners
- Age 30-60
- Both men and women
- English language only
- US only
- Income ranges:
    o $75,000-99,000
    o $100,000 to 124,999
    o $125,000 - 149,000
    o $150,000 – 249,000
    o $350,000 – 499,999
    o over $500,000
- Desktop and mobile.
- Feeds
- Traffic destination: website
- I ran for Link Clicks and did Automatic bidding.
- $10 per day spending on these ads.
- Buying type: Auction

The starfish ad "fatigued" after a while and the price per click increased. So, we paused that ad. I copied the text and added a new image and ran this new ad:

This image above had the best conversions and I know that because we tested it! I loved this image so much, when I designed my new website, I used it on the home page:

www.bestsellingauthorprogram.com

For this ad, I increased the budget to $22.00 per day and ran it to the GURU's Group:

Ali Brown, Bill Barne, Fabienne Fredrickson, Female Entrepreneur Association, Frank Kern, Kevin Nations, Lisa Sasevich, Marie Forleo, Mike Koenigs

As I mentioned, we tested three images before we came up with the one in this ad.

Below is another image that did **NOT** convert:

 **6 Figure Woman** Like Page
Sponsored · 🌐

Want to Become a #1 Bestselling Author and Boost Your Brand,
Business and Visibility? There's a secret "Backwards Book Launch"
method that allows you to increase your profits.

Free Training Reveals my Proven "Backwards Book
Launch" Formula for Becoming a #1 Bestselling Author

Discover the 3 Reasons Why You Absolutely Must Become a #1 Bestselling Author
with my secret "Backwards Book Launch" method and how to make bigger profits...

ONLINEMEETINGNOW.COM

👍 Like   💬 Comment   ↪ Share   ⧉ Buffer

The winning ad that was working fatigued after a while, so we
copied it and tested new ad copy (using the same image with three
different ad copies) and ran it to the same gurus group at $22 per
day split up between the three ads:

Ad #1:

6 Figure Woman
Sponsored · 🌐

Want to Become a #1 Bestselling Author and Boost Your Brand,
Business and Visibility? There's a secret "Backwards Book Launch"
method that allows you to increase your profits.

Like Page

Free Training Reveals my Proven "Backwards Book
Launch" Formula for Becoming a #1 Bestselling Author

Discover the 3 Reasons Why You Absolutely Must Become a #1 Bestselling Author
with my secret "Backwards Book Launch" method and how to make bigger profits...

ONLINEMEETINGNOW.COM

Ad #2:

 6 Figure Woman
Sponsored ·

👍 Like Page

Do you dream of becoming a #1 Bestselling Author? Here's the secret formula that has gotten 60 authors to the Amazon Best Seller List.

Free Training Reveals my Proven "Backwards Book Launch" Formula for Becoming a #1 Bestselling Author

This is the exact formula that virtually nobody uses or knows about that I've used to help 60 authors skyrocket their books to the Amazon Best Seller List.

ONLINEMEETINGNOW.COM

1 Like 1 Comment 1 Share

 Like   Comment    Share   Buffer

Ad #3 – The Winner!

 6 Figure Woman
Sponsored · 🌐   👍 Like Page

Imagine becoming a #1 Bestselling Author in the next 30-60 days.

What would your business look like if you were the go-to expert in your niche' and people were lining up to be your client?

Being a #1 bestselling author immediately turns YOU into an expert in your market.

Free Training: How to Become a #1 Bestselling Author Using The Secret "Backwards Book Launch" Formula.

Discover how to write a bestselling book that can double and triple your income and the #1 reason why must become a #1 bestselling author now.

ONLINEMEETINGNOW.COM

So, Facebook ads is all about TESTING! And to TEST, you have to spend money.

I recommend a minimum of $10 a day to start and then increase your budget when you have a winning ad. Run the ad for about 4-7 days to see which one is the winner.

Track the following numbers to select the winner:

- Click through rate of 1% or higher (how many people are clicking on your ad)
- Relevancy score of 3 or higher (how relevant your ad is to the audience)
- Frequency rate under 2 (how often FB shows the ad)

Get Started Running Facebook Ads and Automated Webinar Funnel:

The System:

1. The first step in this "process" is to bring cold traffic in through the top of your funnel (your webinar). It's very important to start this process by split testing at least 3-5 different audiences. When I began, I tested audiences of "writers/authors," "coaches," and "gurus" – and the winner was "gurus."

2. Your ad spend during this testing phase should be no less than $10 per day per audience.

3. Drive these audiences to a landing page where they can register for your webinar. I used Leadpages for my landing page.

NOTE: A healthy cost per registration is about $2.50, however, this is only one piece of the puzzle. Depending on the market it can be $5-$10 per registration, BUT as long as you are getting a high ROI on your ad spend, and converting them into sales, that's okay. My average cost per click is between $3 and $4 typically; my average cost per registration was about $14.)

The Tools

- I used Stealth to run my automated webinar because they will set everything up for you. There is a $97 setup fee and then $67 per month after that. Here is the link to connect with them: http://www.stealthseminar.com/

Using an automated webinar platform has *huge* benefits. The system is designed to nurture your registrants with reminder emails and follow up emails which makes the process super easy for you...and that is what we want, *right?*

Evergreen Webinars

An Evergreen Webinar is a webinar you can run over and over and over.

The goal of the webinar funnel is to drive COLD traffic through Facebook ads so people can register for your automated webinar.

What are most people doing in these webinar trainings?

These webinars provide a ton of value and end with a sales pitch for their product, service, course or event.

I wasn't selling anything, but instead I offered a strategy session with me at the end of my webinar.

TIPS:

- Most people know that you're going to pitch your product at the end of your webinar, so they leave before it's over. Offer a FREE gift at the conclusion of the webinar for those who stay until the end (of course, you want to mention this at the beginning of your webinar).

- Some prospects who were potentially interested will not stay for the entire webinar.

- Others will register but not show up.

None of the above circumstances necessarily means the people who registered for your webinar aren't the right prospects; it just means that life happened, and they may need some time to convert, or it will take a different path to convert.

Ideally, you want people to sign up and convert on the spot, but it doesn't always happen right away.

It's great to get multiple webinar registrations, but the majority of conversions happen through retargeting.

The Retargeting Process

As soon as a lead registers for the event/webinar/training, they are immediately put into a website traffic custom audience funnel based on which confirmation page they were on when registering for the webinar.

To successfully organize your leads, you must have your pixel set up properly on your website. Stealth will put your custom conversion pixel on the thank you or confirmation page for you.

Once the segments are properly set up, and leads register for the event, I can send out specific ads to just those people.

Now, you're probably wondering, what type of ads do I send them?

I'm glad you asked.

I immediately send them ads that directly pitch the offer I talk about on the webinar itself.

This is such a powerful and useful tool to bring in sales or strategy sessions over and over.

Remember, these were cold leads which means more time is often needed to convert. Because they weren't quite ready during the webinar, doesn't mean they are not your ideal audience and that they're not going to buy at some point.

In conclusion, this simple but incredibly powerful Facebook Ads Funnel consists of:

- Testing images, headlines and calls to action
- Split testing 3-5 audiences to find your best audience.
- Filling your value-packed webinar using traffic from Facebook Ads that target cold traffic
- Making the offer on the webinar itself (strategy or discovery session)
- Retargeting those registrants with ads promoting your offer

All you need is two ad campaigns — one to grab the cold leads for the funnel, and one to retarget with them with your offer once they've registered.

This is truly one of the simplest yet most effective funnels out there.

Questions to answer when creating your ads and campaign:

1. What are three things your clients struggle with? For example, in my market, clients are struggling with how to become a #1 bestselling author, how to make money from their book, and how to become the go-to expert in their market with a book. Write the three struggles your clients are having below.

_____

_____

_____

_____

_____

_____

*You are going to turn these struggles into a pain point statement or question that leads into your Facebook ad. For example, in one of my ads I say, "Imagine becoming a #1 Bestselling Author in the next 30-60 days; What would your business look like if you were the go-to expert in your niche' and people were lining up to be your client; Being a

#1 bestselling author immediately turns YOU into an expert in your market." OR I could have said, "Struggling to become a #1 bestselling Author?"

2. Take your ideas above and turn them into a statement or a question below:

    _____

    _____

    _____

    _____

    _____

    _____

    List three benefits that anyone who purchases your program or service will receive:

    _____

    _____

    _____

    _____

    _____

    _____

3. What images represent your offer? I use water and beach scenes and they seem to work well. Other people use graphics made with Canva or Picmonkey. What images would work well in your niche'?

    _____

    _____

    _____

    _____

    _____

    _____

4. It's very important to do this research before you set up your ad. Who does your ideal client "follow" and "like" that are similar to you? List 10 pages, groups or people here:

_____

_____

_____

_____

_____

_____

5. What is the BIG goal you have for your Facebook ad–to grow your list, create brand awareness, schedule strategy sessions, or sell a product?

_____

_____

_____

_____

_____

_____

Answer the questions above and then design your ad using this template:

Text (words above the image): Want to Become a #1 Bestselling Author and Boost Your Brand, Business and Visibility? There's a secret "Backwards Book Launch" method that allows you to increase your profits. **THINK: What result is the potential client is looking for or what pain point are they having?**

Headline (directly below the image): Free Training Reveals my Guaranteed and Proven "Backwards Book Launch" Formula for Becoming a #1 Bestselling Author. **EXAMPLE: FREE Training,**

FREE ebook, or FREE Masterclass about some topic or twist on a topic they haven't heard of before.

Description (below the image): "Discover the 3 Reasons Why You Absolutely Must Become a #1 Bestselling Author with my secret *Backwards Book Launch* method and how to make bigger profits from your book. **THINK: What will they discover by clicking on your offer and what will be the BIG benefit?**

6 Figure Woman
Sponsored ·

Want to Become a #1 Bestselling Author and Boost Your Brand, Business and Visibility? There's a secret "Backwards Book Launch" method that allows you to increase your profits.

Free Training Reveals my Proven "Backwards Book Launch" Formula for Becoming a #1 Bestselling Author

Discover the 3 Reasons Why You Absolutely Must Become a #1 Bestselling Author with my secret "Backwards Book Launch" method and how to make bigger...

ONLINEMEETINGNOW.COM

 25　　　　　　　　　　　　　1 Comment　11 Shares　

 Like　　 Comment　　Share　　 Buffer

Once your ad is designed, you need to do the following:

1. Put the pixel on your website

2. If doing the webinar funnel, put a custom conversion pixel on the confirmation page of the webinar

3. Create a campaign (Purpose of the ad)

4. Create the ad set (who you want your ad shown to and how)

5. Create three ads and test them.

6. Run the winning ad for a week or so and check the stats every day or every other day.

7. Continue running that ad as long as the numbers are good.

8. Pause the ad at any time the numbers aren't ideal.

9. Once the ad fatigues, create a new ad.

10. I recommend getting Facebook Ads training or hiring a Facebook Ads Coach or Company to set this up properly.

I worked with my coach for a year before we had this funnel set up, but remember, I already had an offer that was and proven and that converted which was my bestselling author program.

Do NOT run Facebook ads unless you have the same.

How to get automated webinar up and running:

1. Create Webinar slides in PowerPoint or Keynote.

2. Record the webinar (45-60 minutes max); I recorded mine using a free/low-cost program called screen-cast-o-matic.

   a. Upload to Stealth via their Webinar Encoder

3. Record a 3½ minute **Confirmation Page Video** that attendees will be redirected to once they sign up for your webinar (this increases the show up rate exponentially and is highly recommended).

4. Upload the Confirmation Video to **YouTube**.

    a. Copy the link because you will need that for Stealth.

5. Create your Webinar Registration Page in Lead Pages

    a. Stealth will duplicate this page so don't worry about the Integration settings. Copy the link to send to Stealth.

6. Create your **Strategy Session Application** page using Gravity Forms

    a. Note: If you already have a strategy session application on your website and navigation bar, do not use that one. Create a new page with no navigation bar – only the form – to be used by people who register for the webinar that come from Facebook ads. *I bought the domain www.bestsellerchat.com and I use this to redirect leads from the automated webinar via Facebook ads to the strategy session application. So, bestsellerchat.com redirects to: http://bestsellingauthorprogram.com/coaching

7. Create a new list in Aweber or have Stealth create it.

    a. Call the list "Webinar Leads" or something similar

    b. Send that list to Stealth so they can have webinar registrants added to your list

8. **Write Symptom-Based Emails** and put them in your Webinar Leads Autoresponder series. Start with a few and add to them. Schedule one email to go out daily, but do not send out until day 2 or 3 because they are already getting follow-up messages from Stealth with the replay. *** Please note that Stealth will set up their own webinar follow-up email reminders to people that register for the webinar, so you don't have to do that. *A Symptom-Based email addresses the pain points your prospective clients have.*

9. **Submit a support ticket to Stealth** to have your webinar set up. Stealth will provide a link you can use to submit everything needed to them, including

   a. The name of the Webinar you want to use (in case you have more than one).

   b. A link to the confirmation page YouTube video.

   c. The Leadpages registration page link for the webinar.

   d. The link to the Strategy Session Application.

   e. The Aweber account details and list (or whatever email system you use).

10. The **Button** you want to use for your **CALL TO ACTION**. Watch your webinar and make note of when you start talking about signing up for a strategy session. For example, if your webinar is 50 minutes long, and you land on the final page where you share the link to sign up for a call with you at the 40-minute mark, then you need to tell Stealth to insert your Call to Action Button at the 40-minute mark.

Notes About Stealth

- Use the "Just In Time" Top of the hour setting for your webinar to play. My webinar played from 9 a.m. EST to 9 p.m. EST *This does cause a problem for other countries, but currently I am only running the ads to the US market.

- Disable chat replay

This summarizes the Offer to Facebook Ads to an automated Webinar to the Application Page and finally to a Strategy Session.

Now, I want to talk about the Automated Webinar content, the Strategy Session Application and the Strategy Session itself.

Automated Webinar *Content*

As I mentioned, I struggled creating the content and slides for my webinar because I was over-teaching. I think this is a common problem that creators have because we have so much knowledge we want to share with the world. When you over-teach, you make it hard for people to follow because they are going to be on information overload.

Two ways to overcome this common problem.

First, teach the "Top 5 Mistakes" or whatever number you can come up with. So, I could do my webinar on "The Top 5 Mistakes Authors Make When Publishing a Book." That's a great title and it is curiosity-driven which is what you want. If you're an aspiring author, then you would want to know what those mistakes are, right?

Think about your niche' and the mistakes you've made or the people you've worked with have made. Make those mistakes the topic of your automated webinar. It's very powerful and this will prevent you from over-teaching on your topic.

Another method that works well is to "Teach the What, but NOT the How." In my bestselling author program, I created a webinar titled: "3 Steps to Becoming a Bestselling Author" and on it, I taught the what, but not the how.

For example one of the steps to becoming a bestselling author is selecting the right categories and keywords for your book. I explain that this is a part of the process and why it's important, but I don't go into the details on "how" to select the categories and keywords.

My webinar would be 6 hours long if I taught all the details on this topic! You cannot teach everything you know, and you should not try to.

Remember, the webinar is a tool designed to get you strategy sessions so you can sell your program. It's not for you to teach everything you know or to prove how smart you are. You will not be teaching on the strategy session call either. The purpose of the strategy call is to find out if your solution is the best option for the problems your prospect is having.

The length of your webinar should be based on the type of clients you are trying to attract. If you're going for high-ticket clients, the webinar should be 20-40 minutes long as they are short on time and high on cash. If you are trying to attract lower-ticket clients, your webinar can be 60 minutes or longer. For reference, a high-ticket client will spend $3000 or more and a low-ticket will spend less than $2000.

Create PowerPoint or Keynote slides for your webinar so you can follow along and not leave anything out. You don't want to sound rehearsed; you want to be yourself. You can have notes for each slide when you're recording your webinar that attendees don't see.

I really struggled with designing the slides. I let that slow me down a lot as I spent an inordinate amount of time selecting the images and writing the copy for each slide. I don't recommend doing what I did.

To make it simple, you could have a white background with some black font and no colors or images and still make six figures. I see it done all the time.

I often included too much copy on the slides and then had to remove the majority of it. People don't want to read slides with multiple lines of text. List the major talking points on the slide (think headlines), but do not write everything you are going to say word for word.

I'm an introvert, so I think a lot of my procrastination was a result of my fear of being seen. I don't really like doing videos. I prefer the written word; however, I knew that a webinar would be a great way to get new clients, so I stepped out of my comfort zone and did it.

Next up is the application page.

APPLICATION

At the end of your webinar, you are not selling anything. What you are offering is an opportunity to set up a strategy call with you. It's brilliant really. No hard sell, let's just get on a call and have a chat.

Take a look at my strategy session application at:

http://bestsellingauthorprogram.com/coaching/

Of course you want to collect the basic information about the person like name, email, phone, website address, country. Then, ask questions like:

- What is the biggest obstacle holding you back regarding _____ (your topic)?
- What is your goal regarding (this topic)?
- Why have you reached out to me at this time?
- What are you struggling with right now?
- What is your target income?

Ask any other questions that will give you more insight into their problems, obstacles, struggles, desired goals, and reasons why they are reaching out to you.

To weed out leads that are not qualified, ask a question similar to this one at the end of it:

"Are you looking for an experienced mentor to ensure your book is done right and to help you achieve your dreams of becoming a #1 Amazon Bestselling author?

- **Yes - I invest in myself often and get massive returns on my investments.**
- **Maybe - I haven't done this before but I am committed to being a #1 Amazon Bestselling Author!**

- **No - I am not able to invest in myself right now, but please send me any free information you have."**

Don't schedule a call with anyone who answers No. Review the answers from anyone who says maybe and send them an email with additional follow-up questions before scheduling a call.

Strategy Session (Phone Call)

Selling from a sales page on a website is hard. It is much easier to sell on a phone call (as long as you don't fear asking for what you're worth). I've found that a personal phone call is the best way to get new clients. On a strategy session, listen to the prospect talk about some of their challenges and problems, then share a personal story or two. If it's a good fit, invite them to join your program.

When you invite them to join, don't go over all the details of your program, such as:

- I have 24 video tutorials
- I have 100 PDFs, and assessments and quizzes
- I have workbooks or manuals

Don't sell the details of what the program contains, just sell the solution – which is YOU!

Also remember, the point of the call is not to "teach, train or coach." You want to determine what this person is struggling with to see if you can help them.

I use an automated scheduling software to book my calls, so the process goes like this:

- They land on my strategy session application either through a google search or an automated webinar and they fill it out.

- Once they hit submit, they are redirected to my scheduling software. I use **OnceHub**.

- If an appointment comes through that is not qualified, I cancel it and email the lead. Otherwise, I do the call on the scheduled day.

- I sign up 50-75% of people I talk to once they are qualified. I have a unique program that offers high value and high engagement which is what people are looking for.

Next up is an important topic about overcoming under-earning and charging what you're worth!

Chapter 9:
Overcoming Underearning

In her book, "Money, A Memoir: Women, Emotions and Cash," author Liz Perle says:

"Whether we want to admit it or not, each of us has a relationship to money that goes beyond the getting and spending. Money is never just money; it's our proxy for identity and love and hope and promises made and perhaps never fulfilled. It's our social sorter. It's the ticket to our dreams."

Whether we want to admit it or not, we need money to achieve our big dreams and goals.

Unfortunately, women are chronic underearners and one of the challenges is that we often were raised and taught to be kind, nurturing, cooperative and collaborative. Therefore, our roles revolve more around relationships, than money.

Men, on the other hand, use money as a differentiator and society sizes them up by how much they earn. Men rank their self-esteem by their productivity in the world as well as how successful they are because they are raised this way.

Don't misunderstand the term "underearners." They are often NOT lazy people in any way. In fact, they are almost always the hardest working people usually having multiple jobs, working long hours, and volunteering at non-profits, etc.

Karen McCall, author of *Financial Recovery: Developing a Healthy Relationship With Money*, describes an underearner as:

"Underearners compromise their financial circumstances by accepting less for their work than it is worth, and often less than they need to live the way they want and deserve to. They commonly have difficulty setting limits, saying no, or asking for what they need and deserve..."

So where does this underearning come from?

Not from a lack of intelligence or hard work, it comes from something much deeper – a profound sense of deprivation and shame.

Deprivation comes from our unmet needs, and in order to fill those needs we have to be honest about them. When you live in a state of deprivation, you are living in a state of emptiness and longing. This often happens when our physical, emotional, social or spiritual needs are not met early in life.

Deprivation often turns into self-neglect, overindulgence, addictions, helplessness, compulsions, and taking care of others at the expense of our own wellbeing.

The first step to healing these emotional wounds is acknowledging that you have them which helps you become more aware about them.

The next step is learning how to meet your needs and eliminating that deprivation mentality.

In the book, "Earn What You Deserve," by Jerold Mudis, he defines underearning this way:

> *"...to repeatedly gain less income than you need,*
> *or than would be beneficial, usually for no apparent*
> *reason and despite your desire to do otherwise."*

So, if you are an underearner, you are probably bringing in much less than you could be and have a lot of excuses as to why that is happening.

Author, Barbara Stanny, who has written numerous books on money, women, and power, writes in her book "Secrets of Six-Figure Women" about the 9 Traits of Underearners which are:

1. *Underearners have a high tolerance for low pay.*

2. *Underearners underestimate their worth.*

3. *Underearners are willing to work for free.*

4. *Underearners are lousy negotiators.*

5. *Underearners practice reverse snobbery.*

6. *Underearners believe in the nobility of poverty.*

7. *Underearners are subtle self-saboteurs.*

8. *Underearners are unequivocally codependent.*

9. *Underearners live in financial chaos.*

I included this chapter to make you aware that although you might say you want to make six figures, if you are an underearner, you are probably going to self-sabotage yourself, undercharge, and not achieve your income goals.

If you continually find yourself in financial crisis, you probably are an underearner.

For many years, I was an underearner and I had to do a lot of therapy, read many books on the subject, and work on myself-worth to overcome being an underearner.

The crazy part is you could actually be making six figures and still be an underearner. Either you are capable of making much more, or you are still living in financial chaos.

Therefore, it's not about the income level you are at, but about the nine traits mentioned above.

I would recommend reading any of Barbara Stanny's books on this topic. I also love Karen McCall's book as well as a book by Deborah Price titled "Money Magic" in which she says:

> *"Money is a tool meant to help transform your life in more meaningful ways."*

I love that!

You absolutely have the power within you to manifest everything that you desire and the power to evolve and make a difference in the world. To do that, we have to step away from the anxiety, fears, and shame we feel about money.

I want you to have everything you desire and to step into your power around money.

When I first started making six figures in 2004, I felt somewhat guilty that I was making more money than my parents and most of my friends. Eventually, I realized my faulty thinking and now I see that money helps me provide for myself and my family, have fun experiences, go to cool places, enjoy life, and share my gifts with the world.

If I was still stuck in my 9-to-5 job living paycheck to paycheck, I would not be writing this book or living in my beautiful house on the water or working only 20-25 hours per week earning multiple six figures.

When you grow and evolve, so does your income. If you're stagnant in your financial life, you're probably stagnant in other areas.

If you want to take a money assessment test and find out what kind of money archetype you resonate with, go to Deborah Prices website at:

www.moneycoachinginstitute.com/money-type-quiz/

The eight money types are:

1. The Innocent
2. The Victim
3. The Warrior
4. The Martyr
5. The Fool
6. Creator/Artist
7. The Tyrant
8. The Magician

I am a money magician and proud of it! Magicians know how to transform and manifest their own financial reality and claim their power.

It's been a long road to get here, and I want the same for you.

It may take a little work, but you deserve financial prosperity, wealth, and to enjoy your life with all the desires of your heart.

Next we are going to talk about the art of making multiple six figures.

Chapter 10:
Creating Multiple 6-Figures

The goal is to generate the most amount of money in the least amount of time. *More* money buys you *more* freedom and *more* options.

Mike Michaelowicz, author of "Profit First: Transform Your Business from a Cash-Eating Monster to a Money-Making Machine," says:

"Without enough money, we cannot fully realize our authentic selves. Money amplifies who we are. There isn't a single ounce of doubt in my mind that there is something BIG you are intended to do on this planet. You wear the cape of what I believe is the greatest of all superheroes: the Entrepreneur. But your superhero powers can only yield as much power as your energy source provides. Money. You need money, superhero."

Just imagine the BIG things you could do with a multiple six-figure income and the impact you could make changing the world and leaving a legacy.

You don't have to create a huge company with hundreds of employees. I believe the perfect size for your business will happen naturally.

Earning six figures is a great and worthy goal to achieve; and once you get there, the next goal, if it feels right, should be multiple six figures.

Once you've made your first six figures, you can usually find new income streams that complement your main business.

The best part of making multiple six figures is that it allows me to be very selective with whom I work with in my business. I don't have to take on the wrong clients or projects that are out of my wheelhouse just to generate income.

Below are some case studies of entrepreneurs who have taken successful 6-figure businesses to multiple six and seven figures.

CASE STUDY #1:

Brooke Castille, Founder of The Life Coach School, went from making six figures to multiple six figures, and now she is making multi-millions.

She started her business doing individual coaching, then added group coaching. Once she had a successful six-figure business, she began certifying others in her coaching methodology because she was getting more clients than she could help.

CASE STUDY #2

Mike Michaelowicz, author of "Profit First," also has a certification program that allows others to become a "Profit First Professional" certified coach.

Instead of thinking small and only working with clients that come to him from his bestselling book, instead, Mike created a certification program and certifies accountants, bookkeepers, financial planners, business coaches and more in his methodology. He generates seven figures from his certification business!

CASE STUDY #3

Me! For years I made six figures and last year I added another 6-figure stream of income related to my main business.

I am now able to get client's books to the Wall Street Journal and USA Today Bestsellers lists in addition to the Amazon bestsellers list.

It happened by accident, but when I saw the opportunity, I knew it would be transformative for my business and for my clients.

My core business is helping clients publish high-quality books that have an important message and then launching those books to #1 on the Amazon bestsellers list.

In 2018, I had a multi-millionaire client that wanted to be a Wall Street Journal and USA Today bestselling author. At the time, I had no idea how those lists worked. I did some research, found the criteria required to hit those lists, and partnered with a successful author whose business books have all hit those lists.

We put together a high-ticket program and with just three clients, I now have an additional 6-figure stream of income!

I've learned there will always be clients who want the next level higher than what you are offering. If what you are offering is already high-ticket, then they want high-high-ticket!

Some ways to create additional streams of income:

- If your core program is an 8-12-week program, consider adding a recurring monthly coaching program for $1k-$3k per month.
- Add on an exclusive in-person training or event
- License your materials
- Create a certification program
- Write a book

I think writing a book is one of the best investments you can make because a book can attract new clients. So, if you have a $5k or $10k+ program, just a few clients per month from your book can generate thousands of dollars in income.

You can make money on the backend of your book, like many speakers, coaches, and consultants. You can also earn royalties from sales of your book.

Is it easy to write a book a month?

No it's not easy. But if you have a system and are consistent, you can go from zero to $3100+ in monthly passive income like I did.

I've created an entire community and course on writing a book a month that you can learn about here:

https://bestsellerbizacademy.thinkific.com/courses/28-books-to-100k

Also, you can join the Facebook community of authors who are writing a book a month at

https://www.facebook.com/groups/28BooksTo100K.

If you're just starting out, keep all of this information in the back of your mind. I promise you opportunities will present themselves once you make your first six figures.

And now for my Closing Thoughts....

Closing Thoughts

When you have more money than you need, that's WEALTH. When you use your money to make a difference in the world, that's POWER.

Money is power. Money is influence. Money is freedom. Money is options. Money is impact. Money is flow. Money is opportunity.

Once you become financially secure from making six figures, you can use your money to make your mark. Look for opportunities and ways to gain more influence, have an impact, and to give back to others.

Don't let obstacles stand in the way of your dreams.

In his book, "The Obstacle is the Way: The Timeless Art of Turning Trials into Triumph," author Ryan Holiday says:

"The struggle against an obstacle inevitably propels the fighter to a new level of functioning. The extent of the struggle determines the extent of the growth. The obstacles is an advantage, not adversity. The enemy is any perception that prevents us from seeing this."

Wherever you are on this path, you are going to face obstacles. Embedded in these obstacles are jewels of wisdom and benefits that are only for you.

Adversity is always waiting to be transformed into an advantage.

When I was fired from my job at the law firm, with no money in the bank and three young children to support, I had no idea what I was going to do.

Getting fired was the best thing that ever happened to me. It led me down a new path, one where I was able to create my own freedom and generate a 6-figure income without a boss, commute, or job.

Don't allow the obstacles on your path right now stop you from achieving your dreams.

The book "A Course in Miracles" reminds us: "You do not ask too much of life but far too little."

Stuart Wilde, one of my favorite authors, talks about how money is just energy in motion.

In his book, "The Trick to Money Is Having Some," he says:

"The reason why money is such a JOY is that it allows you to grow spiritually, to understand the finer subtleties of life and to come to grips with many aspects of yourself."

Money will empower you, empower others, set you free, and make the world a better place.

I want you to DREAM BIG and never, ever give up on your dreams. Understand that the obstacles are the way to everything you desire.

I want to leave you with this affirmation which you can repeat to yourself daily:

"I am always in the right place at the right time. Abundance is simple and natural to me; all of my needs are constantly met."

Would you do me a favor?

Reviews are so important on Amazon. If you loved this book and found it helped you, will you share your thoughts in a review on Amazon?

Thank you so much for reading, I truly appreciate it!

With much Love and Gratitude,

Michelle Kulp

MAKE MONEY WHILE YOU SLEEP

*Use the Knowledge You Already Have to
CREATE PASSIVE INCOME FREEDOM
(Go From Idea to Income in Only 30
Days)*

MICHELLE KULP

IF YOU DON'T FIND A WAY TO MAKE MONEY WHILE YOU SLEEP YOU WILL WORK UNTIL YOU DIE

Introduction

Imagine waking up each day with more money in your bank account than when you went to bed. In 30 days, this can be your reality if you capitalize on your existing experience, knowledge, and wisdom to help others.

Every morning I get to experience this because my books sell on Amazon on autopilot. I am currently averaging $100 to $200 per day in book sales. Additionally, I sell an online course that goes along with one of my top selling books, 28 Books to $100K and that course is generating money while I sleep! I made over $4000 in 30 days from that course and I had not even started promoting it.

My goal is for you to have the same success and peace of mind. When your passive income pays your bills, you choose how to live your life and spend your most precious commodity – time!

By the way, this book is NOT about generating royalties from writing books. I wrote an entire book on that subject — "28 Books to $100K."

This book is about generating passive income by creating an online training course using your unique knowledge and selling it to others who need your help.

In 2005, I started my first online business with my website www.becomea6figurewoman.com. I sold my first online course, "Quit Your Job and Follow Your Dreams," and made $2,500 in 30 days. I was hooked! I turned that course into an Amazon bestselling book that makes money from royalties while I sleep.

After working as a paralegal for 17 years and trading time for money, earning passive income is exciting and exhilarating! If you're used to working a 9-5 job, I know you'll love making passive income. And, if you're like me, you'll LOVE not having to be in an office.

Transforming your unique knowledge into a signature online program that you can sell repeatedly is the apex of working smart, not hard!

In, this book, I'm going to share everything I've learned while creating multiple streams of passive income — including what's working now and what's not working.

I currently have a multi-6-figure business, www.bestselling-authorprogram.com, where I sell a high-ticket done-for-you program; I also sell low-ticket DIY online courses. My online training program for my bestselling author program is not advertised on my website, as it is my "secret" down sell for those who aren't a good fit for my high-ticket program.

"Make Money While You Sleep" is a step-by-step blueprint that will show you exactly how to use your real-world knowledge, wisdom, and experience (your Intellectual Property) to create a profitable online course that makes money 24/7. Yes, even while you sleep!

Creating an online course gives you a BUSINESS ASSET that will continually generate money for you and your family.

There are many different paths and philosophies on creating and selling online courses – sell high-ticket, sell low-ticket; add coaching, don't add coaching; create it first and then sell it; sell it first and then build it. It can be confusing and overwhelming.

The goal of this book is to teach you my Lean Launch Method (LLM), so you can create your first online course in 30 days or less with easy-to-use online tools.

I know people who spent months, and sometimes years, working on their online program to find out people weren't willing to pay money for it. You can avoid that by "validating before you create," which I'll explain in this book.

Creating an online program is perfect for anyone with a desire and deep commitment to share their valuable expertise and wisdom with others while making large profits.

My Courses (past and present)

- Quit Your Job and Follow Your Dreams
- How to Create a Mission Statement
- How to Start a Profitable Blog
- How to Make Your First $1000 Online
- Creating and Selling Information Products
- Getting in the 6-Figure Game
- Bestseller Biz Academy (present)
- 28 Books to $100K (present)

When you create a **BUSINESS ASSET**, you will have so much more impact, independence and income in your life.

Over the past 15+ years, I've earned income in a variety of ways, such as:

- Selling Digital Online Courses
- 1:1 Private coaching
- Group Coaching
- Website Design
- SEO (Search Engine Optimization)
- Copywriting Services
- Ghostwriting Services
- Earning Royalties
- Done-For-You Services
- Book Launches
- And more

And here's what I've learned…

Earning passive income from digital online course sales is the fastest way to leverage your time and create more freedom in your life, especially if:

- You have a full or part-time job
- You are a busy mom or dad
- You are a busy speaker, coach, consultant, or business owner
- You have a full life

According to Forbes[1], the eLearning market is climbing, and could reach $235 billion by 2025. With the lockdowns and social distancing rules due to the COVID-19 pandemic, online learning is where the world is headed, and it's time for YOU to get on board the money train.

Wouldn't you love to tap into and profit from this multi-billion-dollar industry?

You absolutely can, but *first*, I must share with you the four biggest mistakes I see people make when trying to make money selling online courses:

1. **OVER-COMPLICATING.** Spending months or years on activities that don't get money into the bank account, such as creating logos, selecting colors, branding, business plans, unnecessary certifications, endless research, and expensive websites that don't convert. Instead, focus on a few profitable activities to keep it simple. Here's a secret… if you want to *multiply* your income, *simplify* your business. I'm going to teach you the **Lean Launch Method (LLM)** to quickly get cash into your bank account, even without an email list or website.

2. **GOING TOO BROAD.** Making a program too broad, believing *everyone* can benefit from what's being taught. You can't reach everyone. If you want your target market to hear, you have to call out to them. You either *niche and grow rich*

---

[1] https://www.forbes.com/sites/tjmccue/2018/07/31/e-learning-climbing-to-325-billion-by-2025-uf-canvas-absorb-schoology-moodle/#45b4eef13b39

OR *go broad and go broke!* Your online course is NOT for everyone, and I am going to help you become crystal clear about who is NOT a target customer for your course.

3. **BELIEVING MORE IS BETTER.** We have an *unconscious addiction* to making things complicated. Don't try to sell a BIG course with dozens of training modules, videos, checklists, and add-ons because, in reality, LESS IS MORE. An online course that contains easily digestible content allows students to take action and implement quickly. I once signed up for a $1700 online course that I never finished because the videos were so long (and boring). It would have taken 4-6 months to go through everything. I recommend creating an online course on a niche subject you have validated that can be completed within 6-8 weeks. Remember, you can always create additional courses for related topics or establish different levels of your signature course once you have your first online course up and running.

4. **USING THE WRONG PLATFORM TO HOST YOUR COURSE.** Not having a way to distribute content prohibits many from turning their knowledge, expertise, and passions into profitable businesses. I suffered from "paralysis by analysis" and spent more than a year researching online course platforms instead of creating and selling my course. Don't let technology stand in the way of your dreams. I will show you exactly how to create your online course so you can make money fast!

If you DREAM about creating an online course, I'm here to tell you your dream can become a reality faster than you think. I am living proof that you can have a successful 6-figure online business that supports your family and allows you to have true time and money freedom.

Once you create a BUSINESS ASSET, you can repurpose the content to create more streams of income. You will become a *Money*

Magician once you learn how to multiply and generate your own income streams.

The #1 block to creating an online course is identifying a topic and niche.

I get it.

It's not easy to figure it out by yourself, and you're probably procrastinating because you can't get clear on your topic.

Either you have too many ideas or not enough, and you're *stuck*.

From my experience creating and selling online courses and helping my clients do the same, I know exactly how to select an in-demand and profitable topic that you are passionate about for an online course. I will teach you my 3-pillar method that will jog your memory to find the perfect topic so you can get started.

An online course is merely a means to transfer your knowledge to someone else to help them solve a problem and achieve TRANS-FORMATIONAL RESULTS.

You might be thinking, "Michelle, this sounds great, but I hate sales."

Usually, someone says they don't like sales because they are afraid of self-promotion or have had a bad experience with a pushy or obnoxious salesperson.

Here's a new way for you to look at "sales"...

If you have information that can help someone else, you're doing a disservice by withholding it from others. Any money that exchanges hands represents the value you are providing to your customer.

Also, sales are a transference of conviction, so you must pick a topic that you are passionate and enthusiastic about which will make selling it so much easier.

It sounds simple because it is!

Remember, your brain wants you to over-complicate things, so you DON'T TAKE ACTION. If you listen to your "lizard brain" that wants you to keep living in the status quo, you'll never make money online.

Once we select a topic for your online course, we will move on to things like:

- Low-tech platforms to create and host online courses (I've researched many platforms, and I'll show you what I use)
- The Validate and Create method
- Creating a sales page that converts
- Free discovery calls that sell
- Creating Urgency
- Finding your Most Valuable Payers (MVPs)
- Lean Launch 30-Day Blueprint
- And more!

My passion is helping people who feel stuck in a job or career they hate and want to create time and money freedom in their lives by earning passive income.

After reading this book, you will know how to make money while you sleep (and while you're awake).

I've invested more than $100,000 in my education to build my 6-figure online business, and it has paid off in so many ways.

I can't wait to help you create your profitable online course and *MAKE MONEY WHILE YOU SLEEP!*

Let's get started…

Chapter 1 –
The Profitable
Online Course Trifecta

We each have a unique and extraordinary wisdom that we can share with others to transform their lives. Remember this: People are desperate for transformation, not just information.

A successful digital online course trifecta has these three elements:

1. Your unique wisdom

2. Your tribe (who you want to work with)

3. What your tribe needs that they are willing to pay you for

Trifecta

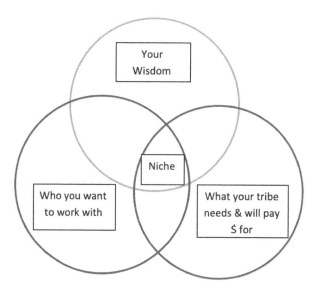

I'm sure you have a lot of ideas about what you want to teach, and that's great.

Or maybe you have ZERO ideas, that's okay too.

In Chapter 2, I share my "Memory Joggers," where I outline my 3-Pillar method to help you get clear on selecting a topic for your online course. I'll also share the mistakes I've made along the way (and have seen others make) so you can avoid making them.

The biggest mistake I see most often is course creators providing what they think customers *need* instead of *want*.

It's important to give your audience what they want and NOT what you think they need.

For example, in my www.BestsellingAuthorProgram.com, I give clients what they want — to become a #1 bestselling author. To do that, they *need*:

- A great title and subtitle for their book
- A unique hook for their book
- An edited and formatted manuscript for their eBook and print book
- A magnetic book description that sells the book
- The right keywords and categories
- A book launch strategy
- A great cover
- Amazon Ads
- Media Interviews

I don't discuss every single detail when I'm signing up a new client; instead, I sell them what they want — #1 bestseller status. Then I give them the components they need to be successful.

Let's look at a few successful online courses in some interesting niches to get your juices flowing:

CASE STUDY #1 – The Social Brand School with Julie and Samantha, who turned $2k in ad spend to $60k with an online course:

Julie and Samantha work with business owners who need help building their brand and offer their students a six-week course for $497 that includes:

- Turning Your Instagram followers into cash flow
- Getting a huge following before you make your first sale
- Getting crystal clear on your brand

Social-Brand-School.Teachable.com/p/SocialBrandSchool

CASE STUDY #2 – The T-Shirt Profit Academy, whose creator made $20k in four months with his online course:

He offers different courses at $179, $279, and $997, and teaches beginners with no design experience:

- How to make six figures selling t-shirts
- How he sold over 34,000 t-shirts
- How to get the same results as he did

TshirtProfitAcademy.com/course/

CASE STUDY #3 - The Virtual Savvy: VA Bootcamp with Abbey Ashley made $41k on her first launch:

Abbey teaches people who want to earn money as a Virtual Assistant to go from start-up to sold out in an at-home business. She often has a waitlist to get into her course.

Abbey teaches newbies how to:

- Work on their terms
- Create a 6-figure at-home business
- Have more freedom
- Get clients
- Package services
- And more

TheVirtualSavvySchool.Teachable.com/p/VA-Bootcamp

CASE STUDY #4 – Lindsay Weirich teaches watercolor painting and launched her first course at $79 and had 246 sales. That's almost $20k!

Lindsey teaches essential tools and techniques for watercolor painting to people who want to learn the art. Some of her topics are:

- Foundations and building blocks
- Tools and supplies
- Techniques
- Painting tutorials

LindsayWeirich.Teachable.com/p/Essential-Tools-and-Techniques-for-Watercolor-Painting

These course creators have one thing in common—the Trifecta.

When designing your online course, include these three Trifecta elements to ensure you are successful:

1. Your unique wisdom
2. Your tribe (who you want to work)
3. What your tribe needs that they are willing to pay you for

Next, in Chapter 2, we will use my 3-pillar method to explore some ideas for topics to teach in your online course.

Chapter 2 –
The 3-Pillar Method
to Tackle Your Topic

Deciding on a topic for your online course can be challenging. Over the years, I've created more than a dozen online courses, and I either have too many ideas or not enough.

Sound familiar?

Don't worry; I've come up with three pillars that will help you gain clarity about what to teach in your online course. We'll use these three pillars to help jog your memory while exploring potential topics for your online course.

PILLAR ONE: SCARY TIMES SKILLS – Life challenges, struggles, and obstacles that you have overcome can make an excellent topic for your online course.

PILLAR TWO: JOB AUTOPSY – Your skills, talents, and expertise that you enjoy and/or others say you are good at are perfect for an online program.

PILLAR THREE: THE CURIOSITY MAP – Identifying your curiosities and following the bread crumb trail can lead to a great topic for an online course. You are probably an expert at many things, but you just don't realize it!

Don't be concerned that there is too much competition in the area you want to teach. There may be online courses similar to your course, but that usually means there is a high demand for your topic.

Adding your unique story and messaging to a course will distinguish your program from other programs.

Stories are compelling, and if you can tell your story in an authentic, engaging, and persuasive manner, people will connect with you and sign up for your course because they will know you are the real deal. *Your* story, *your* personality and *your* style will make *your* product, program, or service **unique**.

When you love what you teach, others will feel that enthusiasm and excitement and be wildly attracted to you.

Let's do some investigative work that will help you TACKLE YOUR TOPIC for your online course.

PILLAR # 1: SCARY TIMES SKILLS: CHALLENGES, STRUGGLES, AND OBSTACLES

Let's take a deep dive into those scary times in your life and identify what you learned and see how you came out on the other side of these challenges, struggles, and obstacles.

I love having a coach who has overcome a challenge that I am struggling with because they can teach me what they learned while going through that experience.

Life brings us many unique "lessons"; some we label "good" and others we would rather forget. Our hardest lessons can provide an opportunity to teach others what we have learned.

A great example is Chris Wark (www.chrisbeatcancer.com), who was diagnosed with stage 3 colon cancer at age 26 and decided to forgo traditional medical treatment and take a natural and holistic path. He now teaches others to do the same. Chris has a book, online course, podcast, and a passion for helping others diagnosed with cancer. I love what he stands for and what he teaches!

Ask the right questions and you'll get the right answers.

I have some questions to help you remember how you overcame obstacles in your life.

For example, I overcame fears and learned many lessons by leaving a dead-end corporate job that was sucking the life out of me. I worried I would not be able to support my three kids and that I would be broke and struggling. The unknown terrified me. Now that I've left the corporate world and have a successful 6-figure online business, I share what I learned with others and teach them how to start their own successful online business.

I did it, and so can you!

Find a quiet place where you can be alone to contemplate, reflect, and answer the questions below to see if there might be an idea for an online course lurking here.

MEMORY JOGGER #1

What challenges, struggles, or obstacles have you overcome in your life that might position you to help others in a similar situation?

Don't over-complicate this exercise. Just think about PIVOTAL MOMENTS in your life that you could possibly teach others.

Examples: Have you overcome a financial situation, a health crisis, a relationship problem, a spiritual awakening, a career shift, a family challenge, an affair, an abusive relationship, etc.?

Below, list any significant obstacles that you have successfully navigated through and come out on the other side.

_____

_____

_____

_____

_____

_____

_____

_____

_____

_____

_____

_____

_____

_____

_____

_____

_____

_____

_____

_____

_____

MEMORY JOGGER #2

Write 1-10 sentences describing how you overcame these challenges, struggles, or obstacles. What results did you achieve by working through the challenges?

_____

_____

_____

_____

_____

_____

_____

_____

_____

_____

_____

_____

_____

_____

_____

_____

_____

_____

_____

_____

_____

_____

_____

_____

_____

_____

MEMORY JOGGER #3

When you think about a difficult situation, what help or resources do you wish you had to more easily work through the process?

_____

_____

_____

_____

_____

_____

_____

_____

_____

_____

_____

_____

_____

_____

_____

_____

_____

_____

_____

_____

_____

_____

_____

_____

_____

_____

_____

_____

_____

MEMORY JOGGER #4

Describe the pain you felt about the situation. Give as many details and use as many feeling words as you can. Be honest about how bad you felt and your pain level at the time.

_____

_____

_____

_____

_____

_____

_____

_____

_____

_____

_____

_____

_____

_____

_____

_____

_____

_____

_____

_____

_____

_____

_____

_____

_____

_____

_____

_____

_____

_____

MEMORY JOGGER #5

When you reflect on the amount of pain, how much would you
have paid to resolve it?

_____
_____
_____
_____
_____
_____
_____
_____
_____
_____
_____
_____
_____
_____
_____
_____
_____
_____
_____
_____
_____
_____
_____
_____
_____
_____
_____
_____
_____
_____
_____

MEMORY JOGGER #6

What skills and knowledge did you acquire during this challenging time?

_____

_____

_____

_____

_____

_____

_____

_____

_____

_____

_____

_____

_____

_____

_____

_____

_____

_____

_____

_____

_____

_____

_____

_____

_____

_____

_____

_____

_____

_____

MEMORY JOGGER #7

How can you use what you learned to help others in a similar situation?

_____

_____

_____

_____

_____

_____

_____

_____

_____

_____

_____

_____

_____

_____

_____

_____

_____

_____

_____

_____

_____

_____

_____

_____

MY ANSWERS

1. What challenges, struggles, or obstacles have you overcome in your life that might position you to help others in a similar situation? **After a 17-year career in the legal field, I was burnt out, drained, and despised my job. I was a single mom with three young children to support and didn't know what else I could do to earn money. I was living paycheck-to-paycheck and desperately wanted to get out of that job.**

2. Write 1-10 sentences describing how you overcame these challenges, struggles, or obstacles. What results did you achieve by working through the challenges? **I was let go from my job which was a blessing in disguise. Consequently, I created multiple streams of income to support myself while I figured things out. After a short time, I took an outside sales job, and, within 18 months, was making six figures working half the time of my corporate job. This gave me the freedom to pursue my passions, which were writing, speaking, and teaching. I started my website and began making money online.**

3. When you think about a difficult situation, what help or resources do you wish you had to more easily work through the process? **I wish I had a mentor to help me figure out what to do after being let go from the law firm. I felt lost and confused most of the time. I would have loved to work with someone who had been where I was and came out the other side being joyfully jobless (and not broke!)**

4. Describe the pain you felt about the situation. Give as many details and use as many feeling words as you can. Be honest about how bad you felt and your pain level at the time. **I felt drained every day I had to go to work. I complained about my job and called in sick so often that I thought I would**

eventually get fired. I felt spiritually and creatively numb and stuck in a place I didn't want to be —JOB PRISON.

5. When you reflect on the amount of pain, how much would you have paid to resolve it? I would have paid thousands of dollars to someone to wave a magic wand and help me navigate leaving a job I hated and creating a life I loved.

6. What skills and knowledge did you acquire during this challenging time? I learned to think outside the career box I had been in for 17 years, and I discovered new and fun ways to make money. I created multiple streams of income and made enough to pay the bills. Then I landed my part-time 6-figure, outside sales job, which gave me even more freedom.

7. How can you take what you learned and help others in a similar situation? I created an online course for people who want to change career paths, discover their passion, and make six figures from home.

PILLAR 2: JOB AUTOPSY

Next, it's time to dig deep into your past work experience by doing a job autopsy. This will allow you to discover the skills, talents, wisdom, and experience you can use to create a successful online course.

Provide the following information for your last 3-5 jobs:

MEMORY JOGGER #1

- Job Title
- Job Tasks
- Task rating on a scale of 1-10. (1 – Hated to 10 – Loved)

Example

Job Title: Paralegal

Tasks:

1. Writing pleadings – 10
2. Legal Research – 10
3. Editing documents – 3
4. Filing – 1
5. Answering the telephone – 1
6. Making copies – 1
7. Interviewing Clients – 10
8. Typing on the computer – 8
9. Going to Court – 10

The goal is to see which tasks you find joy in and then potentially create an online course around this high-passion skillset you have. If you excelled at a specific skill but found no pleasure doing it, you would not want to create a course based on that task.

If you've been working long enough, you have skills that others are willing to pay you to learn.

A great example of someone who took her skills to pay her bills is Lynda Weinman. Lynda was the co-founder of www.lynda.com, which was sold to LinkedIn for $1.5 billion dollars! Lynda Weinman taught different business courses at an affordable price. Check out some of the courses at

www.lynda.com/business-training-tutorials/29-0.html.

Now it's time to explore the jobs you've had. For each job, list the job title, job tasks, and rate each task.

JOB 1

Job Title: _____

List all the tasks you performed in this job and rate each one from 1-10 (1 – HATED to 10 – LOVED).

1. _____
2. _____
3. _____
4. _____
5. _____
6. _____
7. _____
8. _____
9. _____
10. _____

JOB 2

Job Title: _____

List all the tasks you performed in this job and rate each one from 1-10 (1 – HATED to 10 – LOVED).

1. _____
2. _____
3. _____
4. _____
5. _____
6. _____
7. _____
8. _____
9. _____
10. _____

JOB 3

Job Title: _____

List all the tasks you performed in this job and rate each one from
1-10 (1 – HATED to 10 – LOVED).

1. _____
2. _____
3. _____
4. _____
5. _____
6. _____
7. _____
8. _____
9. _____
10. _____

JOB 4

Job Title: _____

List all the tasks you performed in this job and rate each one from
1-10 (1 – HATED to 10 – LOVED).

1. _____
2. _____
3. _____
4. _____
5. _____
6. _____
7. _____
8. _____
9. _____
10. _____

JOB 5

Job Title: _____

List all the tasks you performed in this job and rate each one from 1-10 (1 – HATED to 10 – LOVED).

1. _____

2. _____

3. _____

4. _____

5. _____

6. _____

7. _____

8. _____

9. _____

10. _____

NOTE: If you have your own business and don't have a "job," think about what you are asked you to do. If you are successful in your business, others will ask you for help doing the same; this is how many of my online courses and programs were born.

www.BestsellingAuthorProgram.com was created after others saw me publish and launch books on the #1 bestsellers list, and they wanted help doing it for their books.

What aspects of your business do people ask you for help doing?

_____

_____

_____

_____

_____

_____

_____

MEMORY JOGGER #2

Using the information from the job autopsy above, list the tasks you gave a 7 or higher rating. How could you use your current or past work experience to create an online course using these skills?

_____

_____

_____

_____

_____

_____

_____

_____

_____

_____

_____

_____

PILLAR 3: THE CURIOSITY MAP

Next up is another method to help you find a topic for your online course using a breadcrumb trail of your curiosities. Here's what we'll be exploring:

- Podcasts you listen to
- Books you read
- YouTube videos you watch
- Webinars you enjoy
- Magazines you read
- What you talk about in your spare time
- Your hobbies
- Your certifications and extracurricular activities

MEMORY JOGGER #1

Name the last 5-10 books that got you excited. Next to each title, explain why you love it.

_____

_____

_____

_____

_____

_____

_____

_____

_____

_____

_____

MEMORY JOGGER #2

Name the last 5-10 podcasts that got you excited. Next to each one, explain why you love it.

_____

_____

_____

_____

_____

_____

_____

_____

_____

_____

_____

MEMORY JOGGER #3

Name the last 5-10 magazines that got you excited. Next to each one, explain why you love it.

_____

_____

_____

_____

_____

_____

_____

_____

_____

_____

_____

MEMORY JOGGER #4

Do you have an obsession or something you talk about regularly? If so, describe it below:

_____

_____

_____

_____

_____

_____

_____

_____

_____

_____

_____

MEMORY JOGGER #5

Name your favorite 5-10 hobbies and explain why you love it.

_____
_____
_____
_____
_____
_____
_____
_____
_____
_____
_____
_____

MEMORY JOGGER #6

List any certifications you have or extracurricular activities you enjoy.

_____
_____
_____
_____
_____
_____
_____
_____
_____
_____
_____
_____

Great job exploring your life! Now it's time to PUT ALL THE PUZ-ZLE PIECES TOGETHER

Consider your answers from the 3 Pillars above. For each Pillar, select one topic that gets your juices flowing:

PILLAR #1 TOPIC (Obstacles and Struggles)

_____

PILLAR #2 TOPIC (Job Autopsy)

_____

PILLAR #3 TOPIC (Curiosities)

_____

EXTRA:

(If you have a business, what things do others ask you to help them with?)

_____

It's important to find something you are passionate about and, of course, helps others. Please take a few moments to answer the following questions:

1. What topic from the three choices above do you feel most strongly could help others?

   _____

2. In what areas do you feel you are a true expert?

   _____

3. What type of person would benefit the most from working with you? Where are they in their life (probably somewhere you have been in your past)?

   _____

After completing these exercises, you should have some great ideas for potential online course topics. This is huge! Be proud of yourself for exploring, documenting, and observing where your energy and passion flows.

Next, we'll niche down this topic even further to create a magnetic title for your online course.

Sleep on it, meditate on it, or pray about it if you like, and then go with the one you have the most energy around. Of course, we will need to validate your idea before you create it to ensure it's in demand.

The #1 topic for my online course is

_____

Chapter 3 –
Niche & Grow Rich
or Go Broad & Go Broke

Most people have what I call "niche aversion." They don't want to pick one audience or group of people to work with, and instead, try to sell to everyone!

Niche averse people have a Fear Of Missing Out (FOMO) and believe money is being left on the table if they exclude anyone from their offer.

GO BROAD & GO BROKE

Before I started my online business, I taught live in-person classes and workshops at adult education centers, community colleges, and my church. I wanted to reach everyone.

I remember teaching a class where 80% of the attendees were women, and 20% were men. When I used analogies or gave them exercises to do, the men often said, "I don't get it." There seemed to be a disconnect.

I realized then that my ideal audience was women, and that's how www.becomea6figurewoman.com was born!

Women spoke the same language as I did (i.e., Men are from Mars, Women are from Venus), and I wasn't "efforting" to get my message across.

Some might say I reduced my audience size by half since I was only focusing on women. When I looked at the statistics for self-help readers and the type of courses I was teaching, I discovered that most readers and customers for my topics were women. That's when I decided to niche down and selected women as my target audience.

It's natural to want to reach as many people as possible with our knowledge, wisdom, and, ultimately, our online courses. In our unfocused minds, we want to reach the masses and make millions.

Know that if you go broad, you will probably go broke.

You are much better off trying to reach a small, targeted group of people than trying to reach the whole world.

When you create your message, you must be able to speak to one specific person about their problems. Your online course should be created to provide a solution for that one specific person.

PICK ONE THING

When I hired my first high-ticket business coach, he looked at my website and said, "Michelle, what are you teaching? You have so many different programs."

I admit I was all over the place selling a little of everything.

My coach helped me choose one area to focus on — my Bestselling Author program. Within 90 days, I went from making $3K to $5K per month to my first $22K month!

I picked a niche because of my absolute love for books, and my tribe, of course, was "authors!" I also discovered there was a need in the marketplace for my done-for-you services. It worked well because I am a writer and a published author, so I was teaching others to do what I was doing.

If you want to make money with your online course, you must pick a niche. You can create more courses on various related topics in the future, but for right now, I want you to select a specific audience to reach.

FROM GENERALIST TO SPECIALIST

Author, Speaker and Course Creator, Steve Scott has written 40+ books and makes $20k+ per month in passive income. When he was struggling to make money online, he promoted several affiliate programs.

In 2012, he started writing and self-publishing books on Amazon in the "make money online" space. He did not have much success at first.

Once he niched down and focused on habits, his income grew exponentially. He started his website, DevelopGoodHabits.com and multiplied his audience size and income.

Be fully aware that your brain will NOT want to niche down. It's going to tell you to help everyone. Don't listen!

PICKING YOUR NICHE

Let's start picking your niche based on your answers to the questions in Chapter 2.

When considering your online course topic, choose from one of the five big areas listed below:

1. Finances

2. Relationships/Dating

3. Career/Business

4. Health

5. Spirituality

Note: some areas have audiences that have money and are willing to spend it; others – not so much.

When I told my coach I wanted to start teaching in the spiritual space, he said, "Great, I hope you like being broke."

My coach was a broke pastor for many years before starting his online business teaching Facebook ads for coaches, eventually earning seven figures.

Keep in mind when you are selecting your topic that the bigger your potential client's pain, the more money they will pay to solve it.

Which of the five areas above would you like to focus on for your online course? (Make sure the audience you are targeting has money to spend).

Some other things to consider as we go through this process:

1. What do people say you are good at that you also love doing?

2. What are your top three core values? (Examples: truth, self-worth, safety, integrity, dignity, relationships, honesty, respect, kindness, freedom, inner peace, service, trust, love, equality, faith, positive attitude, excellence, justice, hope, nobility, joy, wholeness, humility, honor, charity, simplicity, etc.)

3. What group or tribe do you want to serve, inspire, and impact? (Example: women, men, children, the elderly, animals, people with disabilities, health-challenged people, CEO's, Leaders, Introverts, Extroverts, singles, couples, divorced, Authors, Speakers, etc.)

4. What do you most want to teach and represent in this world?

Now that you've done the work and have more clarity, it's time to pick a working title for your course.

Here are some fill in the blank templates you can use:

- How to get [desired outcome] without [usual problem]
- [Number] Simple Steps to [desired outcome] without [usual problem]
- How to get [desired outcome] in [a short time/without usual problem]

Write the working title of your course below:

_____

Tip: Use www.surveymonkey.com to create a survey and test multiple title ideas.

Below are some example course titles to help you select a name for your course.

- How to Make Money While You Sleep
- How to Write a Sales Page
- How to Hire a Virtual Assistant
- How to License your Program
- How to Become a 6-Figure Ghostwriter
- How to Overcome a Bad Divorce
- How to Heal from an Abusive Relationship
- How to Ask for a Raise and Get Paid What You're Worth
- How to Become a Full-Time Writer
- How to be Happily Single

Getting More Clarity

My course _____ (1. Working title) helps _____ (2. Tribe; group you most want to impact and work with) learn how to _____ (3. What you are going to teach specifically) so they can _____ (4. The result they will get; what they will be, do or have after taking your course).

Example

My course, *Make Money While You Sleep*, helps *People with Unique Knowledge and Wisdom* learn how to *Earn passive income from home by creating a signature online course (business asset)*, so they can *have MORE time and money freedom and not be trapped in a job.*

People buy programs to get the RESULTS you are promising.

What is the BIG PROMISE to students who buy your online course?

In my bestselling author program, I promise clients that they will become a #1 bestselling author or their money back guaranteed!

Name your BIG promise here:

_____

Your brain is a trickster; don't listen to it.

As soon as you select one thing to focus on, your brain will come up with a gazillion different ideas for new topics. I believe it's a form of procrastination and self-sabotage.

If you want to be successful, pick a niche, and stick with it. Trust your intuition and take into consideration all the exercises and work you've done.

Let's summarize:

- What group/tribe do you most want to influence and impact?
- What are you going to teach this group, and what result will they get?
- What is the working title of your course?
- What is your **BIG PROMISE**?

If you can teach your material in a specified time frame, consider including that in the title to niche down even further. Adding this additional layer will attract people interested in learning that topic but are short on time.

Include the time frame in your working title:

- How to Make Money While You Sleep *in 30 Days or Less*
- How to Write a Sales Page *in 48 hours*
- How to Hire a Virtual Assistant *in the next 7 days*
- How to License your Program *in 90 days*
- How to Become a 6-figure Ghostwriter *in 12 months or less*

Title Tips

- Use a short (2-3 word) title and add a subtitle (7-10 words) that clarifies and adds context to your title, including the student's transformation, results, and desired future state.

- Add a time frame if it makes sense.

- Limit the title and subtitle to two lines max.

- Research other titles in your genre that you like and create something similar. For example, for teaching others how to create online courses, I found titles like "Courses from Scratch," "Courses that Sell," "Launch Academy," "Scale with Success®." These are short and catchy. What can you come up with?

- Create at least five course titles and do a survey if you can't decide which one to use.

If you want to read a great article on finding titles, check this out www.Psychotactics.com/Create-Book-Names.

Define Your Avatar

Now that we have a working title for your course, let's define your avatar and write a letter to your perfect prospect.

Interview someone who is a good candidate for your course or think about someone you know who would be a good fit and answer the following questions:

- Gender
- Age
- Income
- Education Level
- Family Status
- Experience level with your topic (newbie, intermediate, advanced)

- What type of work do they do?
- Hobbies?
- What kind of books do they read?
- Do they have a spiritual practice?
- Where are they feeling most challenged in their lives right now?
- What keeps them awake at night (related to your topic)?
- What is most important to them right now?
- What are their hopes, dreams, and aspirations?

When you interview someone who would benefit from your course, you will get the exact information you need for your message that you can also use on your sales page and in follow-up email sequences (autoresponders).

Another great exercise to obtain even more clarity is to write a letter to your ideal client.

Exercise: Write a Letter to Your Ideal Client

In the letter, acknowledge the client's problems, pain, and fears, and tell them what solutions your course provides. Speak from the heart and explain why you created your course.

Remember, your course is not meant for everyone.

If you still think everyone can benefit from your course, you need to further narrow your niche.

Think about who would NOT be a good fit for your course.

For example, in my bestselling author program, I do not work with authors who write children's books, romance novels, fiction, or science fiction.

Caitlin Bacher, creator of "Scale with Success®," clearly states on her website who her program is designed to help, and who it is not.

THIS **IS** FOR:	THIS IS **NOT** FOR:
✔ Course creators who want to generate an extra $15k-$40k per month from their online course	• People who have NO CLUE what their course will be about.
✔ Course creators who are tired of living launch to launch and want to create consistent, scalable revenue	• People who secretly like being stuck in business so they can make everyone feel sorry for them.
✔ Course creators who are decisive and ready to take action right NOW to scale their business with success	• People who want to join Scale with Success® just to hang out and chit chat, but have no interest in actually doing the work.
✔ Course creators who actually CARE about their students and love to watch them win	

Now, it's your turn…Three types of people my course is **NOT** for:

1. _____
2. _____
3. _____

Now that you've dug deep, selected your course topic, defined your avatar, written a letter to your ideal prospect, and determined who your course is NOT for…it's time to validate your course idea.

VALIDATE BEFORE YOU CREATE

Validate your idea so you don't waste precious time like so many wanna-preneurs do. Here are four methods to validate your ideas, and I recommend you do each one.

METHOD 1: Find courses similar to what you want to create. Check online platforms like: udemy.com, masterclass.com, Lynda.com, or Google your topic with the words "online course." Write down the title, the length of the course, the cost, and list the main benefits. This is your market research.

METHOD 2: Send an email to your list to share that you have a brand new "BETA" program coming out soon called [Working Title of Course]. Include a link to a landing page where they can sign up to receive more information (more about landing pages below). I use Aweber to collect email addresses for my business (you can use ActiveCampaign, Mailchimp, etc.). You don't need thousands of people to sign up — 25-100 people indicates there is good initial interest.

METHOD 3: Send people from your social media platforms to a landing page to sign up and receive more information about your upcoming program.

METHOD 4: Come up with 4-8 titles around the same topic or niche and create a survey using surveymonkey.com so people can vote on the title. I discovered people loved the title: *"Make Money While You Sleep"* by conducting a survey. I had other good titles, but that got the most votes! Below are the other titles I included in the survey:

1. From Zero to 6 Figures

2. Your First $5k Day

3. 6 Figures in 90 Days

4. Big Money Coach

5. Your First $10k Day

6. Quit Your Job and Create Work You Love

7. Make Money While You Sleep (MMWYS)

Always look to the market (real people) for real answers. Don't try to guess or speculate about what people want. I could have gone in a lot of different directions for this book title, but I asked my audience (my email list), and they gave me the answer I needed.

Make sure the people taking the survey are your ideal clients. One way to do this is to start a private Facebook group about your course topic, and once you have 100-250+ members, survey the group.

Create a landing page so anyone interested in your course topic can sign up to receive more information about your upcoming program. Ideally, you want 25-100+ people to sign up. Fewer sign-ups indicate you may not have a good message/offer/title, or there is not enough interest.

Remember, you must share your BIG PROMISE with your audience when you are validating.

Example

> Hello,
>
> I'm creating a new program called "Make Money While You Sleep," which shows experts how to create and launch an online course in 30 days or less and go from zero to $1000+ using my Lean Launch Method. If you are interested in receiving more information about my new program, click the link below to sign up: [LINK]
>
> Thanks so much!
>
> Michelle Kulp

Great job! Don't skip the validation step. You don't want to waste time creating a program that has zero interest.

Landing Page Resources

Most email marketing services like Leadpages, ConvertKit, Aweber, ActiveCampaign, Mailchimp, or GetResponse, include features to create landing pages. Here are a few resources:

- ConvertKit.com/features/landing-pages
- Aweber.com/landing-page-builder.htm
- Mailchimp.com/features/landing-pages/
- GetResponse.com/features/landing-page-creator

I use Aweber for my mailing list and I've used Leadpages for landing pages. Most email services include landing pages so you probably won't need a separate provider.

ClickFunnels is perfect since the entire funnel is set up using their software.

Now that we have a working title for your course, an avatar, a personal letter to your ideal customer, you've identified your course audience, and have validated it, let's start creating the course content.

WARNING: Do not start creating a course until you validate the topic!

In the next chapter, we'll create a course outline and list the main points.

Let's get started...

Chapter 4 –
Online Course
Fill-in-the-Blank Template

"Never try to sell something you're not sold on."
~Dan Sullivan

To me, creating an online course is a lot like writing a book. Over the years, I've developed some great systems and processes for content creation. I learned a lot about this when I decided to write a book a month for all of 2020.

Here are the six steps I use:

Step 1: Decide on my topic/niche

Step 2: Select my Working Title/Subtitle

Step 3: Mind Dump (write everything related to the topic that you want to teach on using Post-it notes)

Step 4: Group the Post-it notes logically

Step 5: Create an outline using the fill-in-the-blank template

Step 6: Use my Rapid Writing Secrets to add more content

We completed Steps 1 and 2 in the previous chapters. Step 3, the Mind Dump, is a great way to start writing the content for your course. I've tried a lot of different methods, and this one works really well.

Mind Dump

Get a large poster board or a white board, a pack of Post-it notes, and a pen. Start thinking of everything you want to teach on your selected topic.

Here's an example using a new project I'm working on: "Secret Strategies of Six-Figure Women":

Usually I have 20-30 Post-it notes – which seems overwhelming at first until you understand the process.

Group your Post-it notes together by topic on your poster board or whiteboard. These will become your Modules and Lessons.

Note: I frequently refer to "modules" and "lessons." A "module" is like a chapter heading in a book. "Lessons" under each module are like the subheadings under each chapter.

Here is how I grouped the topics for "Secret Strategies of Six-Figure Women":

Review the notes in each group, remove any that are redundant, and reword any that might be unclear. Once you're happy with your groupings, then you will transfer the information to the fill-in-the-blank template shown below.

*TITLE: _____

*WHO YOUR COURSE HELPS: _____

MODULE TITLE	LESSONS	HANDOUTS
MODULE 1:	* * * *	
MODULE 2:	* * * *	
MODULE 3:	* * * *	
MODULE 4:	* * * *	
MODULE 5:	* * * *	
MODULE 6:	* * * *	

Create an Outline Using the Fill-in-the-Blank Template

- Module Name – Theme of that Module Topic
- Lessons – Topics around this theme that you will teach in this module
- Video – Indicate if you will have a video tutorial for this module/lesson
- PDF – Indicate if you will you have PDF handouts for this module/lesson

Outlining the content first makes it easier to create an online course. I've written books without doing an outline first, and I can tell you from experience, it takes twice as long to get done. So save yourself time and do the pre-work.

The Post-it notes from the Mind Dump have been transferred to the course outline template for my new project:

*TITLE: Secret Strategies of Six Figure Women

*WHO YOUR COURSE HELPS: Women Who Want to Make More and Work Less

MODULE TITLE	LESSONS	HANDOUTS
MODULE 1: FREEDOM AWAITS	1. Get Off the Financial Ledge 2. Hustle till You Don't Have To 3. The Keys to Break Free From Job Prison 4. Survive, then Thrive 5. Creation vs. Consumption	
MODULE 2: MAKE MONEY AT HOME	1. Virtual Money Machine 2. Pick Your Path 3. Duplicate & Originate 4. Combine to Shine 5. Learn and Teach	

MODULE TITLE	LESSONS	HANDOUTS
MODULE 3: FAST MONEY VS. SLOW MONEY	1. No Free Rides 2. Money Mentor Accelerator 3. The Power of One 4. Find BIG Pain Points 5. High Ticket = High Transformation	
MODULE 4: MAKE MONEY WHILE YOU SLEEP	1. Multiply Your Money 2. All Paths Lead to You 3. Buy Your Income 4. Double Your Money 5. Prepare to Execute	
MODULE 5: SIX FIGURE WOMEN CASE STUDIES	1. Lisa 2. Marisa 3. Jackie 4. Bev	

I made revisions to the lesson names as I entered them into the template.

Now you have a working outline for your course that will save you so much time!

Sell, Then Create

You don't have to create the entire course before you sell it.

In the past, I created one or two lessons then signed people up for my program. I released one lesson every week and created the content as I went along.

Some course creators will make all of the content available at once, but it's not required. "Dripping" the content is a great way to pace your students so they are not overwhelmed.

Others will sell their program and then do live weekly webinars. The webinars are recorded and included in the course for anyone unable to attend live or joined the course after the initial launch. In other words, they don't have any content created when they are making sales.

I signed up for a year-long online course last year, and I'm happy to tell you that I finished it. I believe I was successful because I received a weekly email with a link to a new lesson. I would watch the video and read the handouts right away. I didn't feel overwhelmed since I was digesting bite-sized content weekly instead of consuming the entire course at once (like binge-watching Netflix).

If you create all the content before you sell it, that can work as long as you validated your idea before you created the course. Once my bestselling author done-for-you program was validated, I created an online course for those who were not a good fit for the high-ticket program or could not afford it.

The Lean Launch Method enables you to create and sell your course in the least amount of time. If creating all the content will slow you down, create one or two lessons and focus on sales. Don't get hung up trying to create everything before you sell it. You already have your outline, and once you start making sales, you will be motivated to get the weekly lessons done.

Create your course so it can be completed in 6-8 weeks to avoid customers losing interest.

When creating an online course from a book with more than 6-8 chapters, combine a couple of chapters into one module.

Keep your videos short. People love content they can get through in 10 minutes or less. I see more people consuming my shorter videos than longer content.

RAPID WRITING SECRETS

The last step in creating an online course is to create the lessons. Using PowerPoint or Keynote, list each lesson on one slide with bullet points for the main talking points. Create downloadable PDFs for any templates or worksheets that reinforce the lessons.

Use the template I gave you to provide a quick outline for each module, including the main topic, lessons, and any additional resources such as videos and PDFs. Not every lesson will require videos and PDFs, but you should include some in your course where it makes sense.

Write a short script for each lesson so you stay focused when you're teaching and recording your videos.

Below are some of the *Rapid Writing Secrets* I created for the authors in my Bestselling Author program to write their books that can also be used to create an online course. The goal of the Rapid Writing Secrets is to get the knowledge out of your head and onto the paper.

SPEAK YOUR COURSE

Record the lesson and have the recording transcribed. Download the "Rev" app to your smartphone and after recording, you can instantly send it to be transcribed. Also, if you include videos in your courses, you can provide the transcripts as a download.

WRITE THE MODULE SUMMARY FIRST

Many courses write themselves once you start writing, so begin with a module summary to help get the ideas out of your head and on to the paper.

GET OUT OF THE HOUSE AND INTO A FRESH ENVIRONMENT

I always get more writing done when I am away from my house. It's easy to get distracted at home doing chores or talking on the phone. Go to a coffee shop, your local bookstore, or just sit outside; anywhere that you won't be distracted from getting your writing done.

KEEP AN IDEA/BRAINSTORM JOURNAL

As ideas come to you, write them in a journal (let your subconscious write your course for you). Once you decide on the course topic, you'll start getting ideas when you're out walking, showering, drinking a cup of coffee or tea, eating a meal, etc. Usually when we aren't trying to chase ideas, they will come to us effortlessly.

TEXT YOUR LESSONS TO YOURSELF OR USE THE NOTES APP

When we text others, we get right to the point. Text your lessons via the "notes" feature on your smartphone so you're not sitting at the computer staring at a blank document. Sometimes, we have to trick our brain to get things done.

WRITE YOUR COURSE WITH BLOCK TIME

We do our best work when we are in a "FLOW" state—when a person is completely absorbed in the activity at hand; also referred to as being "in the zone." Do your highest value work first, early in the day. Set this time aside as your block time, and don't do any activities that can distract you beforehand (email, news, social media, etc.).

****

Now it's time for you to select your favorite Rapid Writing Secrets and start writing your content.

Next, we'll talk about the low-tech set up for your online course.

Chapter 5 –
Low-Tech Set Up

When I started my online business in 2005, there weren't many platforms available to host online courses. Today, there are so many it isn't easy to select one to use.

If you ask 10 different people which platform to use, you'll get 10 different answers. I've researched all the popular platforms and have used several different ones over the years.

I've found that Thinkific is easiest to use. I set up my first online course on Thinkific in seven days. I pay $49 per month to host my course on their platform, and they don't take a percentage of the sales like other platforms do.

I've also hosted courses on my WordPress site using the Wishlist plugin. Websites aren't *set it and forget it* and require a lot of maintenance, updates, etc. So, I prefer using a paid platform that is already set up and is regularly updated and maintained.

Thinkific's monthly fee is minimal for what you're getting. Nothing is FREE, and if you are trying to start or run a business using only free tools, you're not going to be very successful. Invest in yourself and your business to provide a high-quality platform for your students.

I got a lot of complaints from students when I was using Wishlist on my site. Now that I'm using Thinkific, I get a lot of compliments – not just about the course content, but also the ease of use of the platform.

Thinkific is a drag and drop platform that allows you to upload your videos, PDFs, and presentations into your modules and lessons.

You can use any platform that gets the job done in the next 30 days. Pick one platform and stick with it.

THE 3 COMPONENTS OF CREATING AN ONLINE COURSE

1. PowerPoint or Keynote slides

2. Video recordings where you teach the details of each lesson

3. Handouts (optional)

Below is the step-by-step process I used to set up a course in seven days that I sold the very next week.

Step 1: Create PowerPoint or Keynote slides for each Module/Lesson using the course outline you created earlier. My slides were set up as shown below:

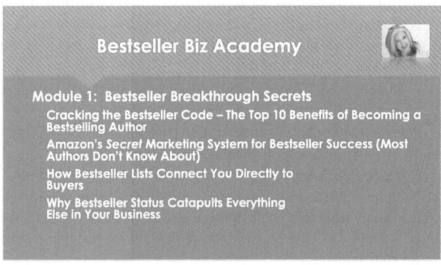

Step 2: Add speaker notes to the bottom of the slides to reference while you are recording your training videos.

Step 3: Pull up the slide for each Module/Lesson and record your video. I use Loom, which is a free service. I've also created videos using Screencast-o-matic and paid services like Zoom, but found Loom to be the easiest to use. I record my screen and then save the .mp4 on my computer. I create a file for each video and keep them in one folder.

Step 4: Set up your course in Thinkific. Add the course name and any course graphics. Then add the Module and Lesson headings.

Step 5: Open each Module/Lesson and drag and drop the corresponding video. If you created a PDF or other handout, drag and drop that file as well.

Step 6: If you have course graphics, you can change the thumbnail for each video so it looks consistent and professional.

Here's what a video thumbnail looks like in Thinkific:

When recording videos, your options are:

1. A screenshare

2. A partial screenshare where you are live in the corner of the video

3. No screenshare. Video recording of you speaking to the camera only

I usually record my videos with option 1 or 2. I use option 3 for my course Welcome video.

NOTE: Thinkific allows you to customize the course settings. Also, the percentage completed is shown to students in the upper left corner of the screen as they move through the course.

I provide a lot of handouts for my students. I create them in Word, insert my course graphic, save it as a PDF, and upload to Thinkific. Below is an example of a handout I created.

Bestseller Checklist
The Foundation of a Great Book!

This goal isn't just to write and publish a fast (mediocre) book; the goal is to put out a high-quality book that will be launched to the bestsellers list and that will stay a bestseller for a long time. With that goal in mind, I have created a Bestseller Checklist for you.

Make sure you have all of these checked off and your book will not only be a bestseller, but will stay a bestseller!

1. START WITH THE END

Pick Your Profit Path Strategy First - The 4 Biggest Authority Profit Engines from a Bestselling Book are: 1) Speaking Engagements; 2) High-Ticket Coaching; 3) Digital Courses; and 4) Live Events. Many Authors are making 6-7 figures on the back-end of their books. Think beyond the book. Your book is just the beginning. It's often the first introduction people have of you and it warms up a cold lead and turns them into a warm lead effortlessly. Once a person reads your book, they often need your help with implementing your material and that's your opportunity to help them as well as to increase your profits from your book. Win/Win!

Thinkific can't make it any easier. If I had my videos and handouts ready, I could set up my entire online course in one day and sell it the next day.

However you set up your course, keep it simple. Don't choose a platform, software, or plugin that requires weeks or months of set up; especially if you can't do it yourself. Pay the $49 a month, and get it set up in less than a week.

Remember, the goal of the Lean Launch Method is to get your course up and running in 30 days. Many people get stuck in the *perpetual planning mode* believing they are making progress, but they're not. They have a "failure to launch" problem, just like the movie. Some planning time is required, but you need to spend most of your time on the execution or stay broke.

When I was researching platforms to host my online course, I spent weeks watching YouTube videos comparing platform A to platform B, and platform B to platform C, and so on. I became more confused with each option I researched.

Deep inside, we all have either a fear of failure or a fear of success, which keeps us doing everything EXCEPT selling our course. We spend too much time planning and perfecting instead of selling and succeeding.

Don't make this mistake. Allow yourself 30 days to get your course set up, and that's it. The good news is I have the 30-day blueprint all laid out for you at the end of this book!

In the next chapter, we will discuss how to set up a high converting sales page.

I don't have a sales page for my bestselling author course because it is actually a "secret downsell" from my high-ticket done-for-you program. I'll talk more about this later.

My process may be different than yours. I run Facebook ads to an on-demand webinar, and then to a strategy session with me. That's my entire sales funnel and process.

When I get on a call with a prospect, I either sell them into my high-ticket done-for-you program or offer them access to my DIY training course.

I once told my business coach that I wanted to sell my online course directly from Facebook ads. He said "Sure, if you want to go broke, go ahead and do that."

Some people do sell their courses this way, but it's expensive to run Facebook ads, and there is a lot of trial and error involved. Once you get a good ad going, it's challenging to turn cold traffic into a $997 or higher sale. It works better, at least in my experience, to not sell from the webinar but instead to offer a free "strategy session" or "discovery call." This method works really well selling high-ticket since that requires trust, which can be established on the strategy session call.

If you're selling a DIY online course, you need a sales page with a video to create a connection between you and the prospect. You can include a payment button on the sales page or send them to another page to schedule a strategy session with you before purchasing.

I know there are many other ways this can be done; I'm just sharing what has worked for me.

If you have a sales page, make sure you understand copywriting and you have a high-converting sales page, which is the topic of the next chapter.

Chapter 6 –
Ready-To-Go Sales Page

Writing good copy that sells and persuades is both an art and science. If you're an experienced copywriter, you can write the copy for your online course; if not, you can use the fill-in-the-blank sales page below.

Would you like to _____ (state what you are teaching them/benefit) without _____ (problem/what don't they want)?

Answer "Yes," and you'll never have to worry about _____ (problem they have) or _____ (another problem they have) ...

Instead, you will _____ (what the outcome will be that they want; the BIG results) and never have to _____ (pain they are in).

You can _____ (paint the picture of what their life will look like when they have achieved the BIG result).

[INSERT YOUR PHOTO or preferably, VIDEO – PEOPLE WANT TO CONNECT WITH A LIVE PERSON]

Dear Friend:

Let's be honest, _____ (what the goal is they want to achieve) is very tough! It's not something can happen overnight, but I can assure you there are some shortcuts. Of course you want _____ (big benefit), but you've tried so many things/products/etc., and they just haven't worked. You just want _____ to stop more than anything else in the world...and you should!

That's where I come in. My name is _____ and my specialty/background is in _____.

Let me ask you a few questions:

Are you _____? (Negative feelings #1 they are experiencing because of this problem).

Do you feel like _____? (Negative feeling #2 they are experiencing because of this problem).

Is it hard to _____? (Negative feeling #3 they are experiencing because of this problem).

Are you tired of _____? (Negative feeling #4 they are experiencing because of this problem).

I know how you feel, because I _____

_____

_____

_____

_____

[THIS IS KEY...YOU MUST ADD YOUR PERSONAL STORY HERE EXPLAINING WHY YOU ARE THE PERSON THAT CAN HELP THEM OVERCOME THEIR PROBLEM. THIS GIVES THEM A PERSONAL CONNECTION WITH YOU AND HELPS THEM UNDERSTAND WHY YOU ARE THE RIGHT PERSON TO HELP THEM].

Now imagine

_____

_____

_____

_____

_____

_____

(Describe in detail here what their life would be like if the problems you listed were solved and no longer existed; create a very detailed picture of how great life will be once they learn what you are going to teach them.)

Sounds too good to be true?

Well, it isn't if you have the right _____ (tools, resources, mentor guiding you, etc.).

That's why I have created _____ (Put the name and/or title of your course, c.), to help people just like you _____ (overcome the problem).

This _____(course) can take years off your trying to learn this on your own!

At Last! A _____ (describe program in detail that you have created).

Here's what my amazing, one-of-a-kind program covers (and/or will help you achieve):

BENEFIT # 1

BENEFIT #2

BENEFIT #3

BENEFIT #4

BENEFIT #5

BENEFIT #6

BENEFIT #7

BENEFIT #8

BENEFIT #9

BENEFIT #10

Sounds great, doesn't it? Well, don't take my word for it, here's what my customers (clients/students) from all over the world (country) are saying about my _____ (program/system/course, etc.):

INSERT TESTIMONIAL HERE. USE PHOTOS IF POSSIBLE AND FULL NAMES. ALSO IF THE PERSON HAS A WEBSITE, INCLUDE THE LINK. (**If you don't have any testimonials yet, offer your eBook or course or product free to three friends or business acquaintances and have them write a testimonial after they've completed it.)

TESTIMONIAL #1 GOES HERE!

TESTIMONIAL #2 GOES HERE!

TESTIMONIAL #3 GOES HERE!

AND IT CAN WORK FOR YOU TOO…
BUT ONLY IF YOU TAKE ACTION!

So, tell me which of these powerful benefits
could help you in your life right now:

Powerful benefit #1
Powerful benefit #2
Powerful benefit #3
Powerful benefit #4

Listen, this may sound like an old cliché,
but if you keep doing the same thing over and over,
you are going to get the same results.

My program (course) is for people who are beyond tired of
_____ (describe problem again) and are
serious about _____ (solution)!

Here are the (3/4/5/6) Biggest Myths about
_____ (the problem/situation)
that will NEVER get you the results you want:

(you must make them believe everything out there and everything they've tried is not going to ever work)

MYTH #1

MYTH #2

MYTH #3

This is why you need to try something different…NOW!

PROOF POSITIVE

Take a Tiny Glimpse at my Amazing Track Record:

Proof #1 of how this has worked for you or how you've helped others with this problem.

Proof #2 of how this has worked for you or how you've helped others with this problem.

Proof #3 of how this has worked for you or how you've helped others with this problem.

**INCLUDE PHOTOS IF APPROPRIATE.

So you're probably wondering what the cost is for this incredible resource (product/system, etc.)?

Well, to be honest I know that I could easily sell my product for _____ (High amount of $/ hundreds or thousands of dollars). I know without a doubt my _____ (product) has that much value.

But I'm not going to charge you anywhere near that amount because I want this program to be affordable to people everywhere because I know it has the power to change lives!

So your investment for _____ is only $_____. Think of it this way...you really can't afford not to "invest" in my program.

In addition to making my product affordable for you, when you purchase my Course NOW, you will receive these 3 Free Bonuses!

FREE _____

FREE _____

FREE _____

Whether you buy my program or not, I can tell you things I know for sure:

The world is not going to change and give you what you want...

People will not change and start handing you what you want...

Your circumstances will not change on their own and start providing what you want...

If you're ready to discover the exact strategies I used (or helped others use) to _____ (describe how this worked for you), and create your own strategy to _____ (describe what they will achieve), then I urge you to (grab your copy of _____) (SECURE YOUR PLACE NOW!)

Click here to reserve your copy NOW!

Sincerely,

***Your name and photo again here.

P.S. Just think...once you complete my program, you'll never suffer through the pain of _____ again!

OPTIONAL GUARANTEES IF ANY

The secret to writing a sales page that converts is using powerful words that are proven to sell.

You can learn more words from the amazing book, "Words that Sell," by Richard Bayan, and I've listed some powerful words for to use on your sales page.

Powerful Words That Help "Sell" on a Sales Page

PLEASING

1. Satisfying
2. Memorable
3. Unforgettable
4. Special
5. Perfect
6. Entertaining
7. Inviting
8. Appealing
9. Engaging
10. Wonderful

GENUINE

1. Authentic
2. Accept no substitute
3. Pure
4. True
5. True to Life
6. The Real Thing
7. Stood the test of time
8. The one and only
9. Actual
10. Proven/Tested

EASY/CONVENIENT

1. Fast, easy access
2. Accessible
3. Versatile
4. Handy
5. Within your reach
6. Never again will you need to...
7. Eliminates the need for...
8. All in one place
9. Facilitates
10. Simplified

SIMPLE

1. Straight-forward
2. Instant
3. User-Friendly
4. Fast
5. Within minutes (hours/days, etc.)
6. It's that simple...
7. Easy to follow
8. Amazingly Simple
9. Step-by-Step
10. Uncomplicated

EXPERTISE/EXPERIENCED

1. We invented...

2. We developed...

3. Ingenious/ingenuity

4. Trained/Gifted/Seasoned

5. Professional

6. Talented/Talent for

7. Qualified

8. Accomplished

9. Well versed in...

10. Masters at...

HONESTY

1. Truthful

2. Straight talk about...

3. Reliable

4. Factual Information

5. We uncover/unmask/offer proof

6. Sincere/Open/Direct

7. Uninhibited

8. Candid

9. Straight forward

10. Genuine

INSTRUCTIVE

1. Educational
2. Enlightening
3. Unlocks the secrets of...
4. Expands your knowledge/mind...
5. Eye-opening/Mind-opening
6. Illuminating
7. Unique learning experience
8. Answers the questions you've always wanted to know...
9. Keeps you informed...
10. Stirs your imagination...

MONEY-GENERATING

1. Pays off
2. Cash in on...
3. Profit from...
4. Build your Nest Egg...
5. Profitable/Easy Profits
6. Watch your Money Grow
7. Make a bundle on...
8. ____ your way to riches!
9. Double your money...
10. The fast track to wealth...

A BARGAIN

1. Money-Saving Ideas/Opportunity

2. Pays for itself

3. Tremendous Savings

4. Low Cost

5. Fits your Budget

6. The best deal in town

7. Finally, a _____ you can afford.

8. You get more for your dollar.

9. Affordable/Surprisingly Affordable

10. Our loss is your gain.

FAMOUS

1. Favorite/All-time Favorite

2. Acclaimed

3. Celebrated

4. Legendary

5. Endorsed by.../Approved by.../Recommended by...

6. Famed/Famous

7. Always in Demand

8. The People's Choice

9. Known far and wide

10. Phenomenally Successful

ADVANCED

1. Innovative
2. The latest
3. Sophisticated
4. Revolutionary
5. Groundbreaking
6. High-tech
7. Futuristic
8. Unprecedented...
9. A revolution in...
10. A radical approach in...

POWERFUL

1. Mighty/Dynamic/Potent
2. Overwhelming
3. Explosive/Electrifying
4. Mesmerizing
5. Riveting
6. Commanding/Compelling
7. Shocking/Stunning
8. High Voltage
9. Mind Blowing
10. Forceful

PERFORMANCE/RESULTS

1. Fast results/Instant results/Remarkable results/Proven results

2. Increases/Boosts

3. Acts/Performs

4. Works Wonders

5. Works Immediately

6. Gets the job done/Does the trick

7. Raises/Restores/Revitalizes

8. Fixes

9. Pays off

10. Produces/Delivers/Improves

RELIABLE

1. Trusted.

2. Solid/Sound/Valid

3. Proven techniques

4. Carefully tested

5. High performance

6. High standards

7. Top credentials

8. Functional

9. Will never let you down.

10. The quality you've come to expect.

PEACE OF MIND

1. For your protection...
2. Total security/privacy
3. Relax!
4. Takes care of itself
5. You can rely on...
6. Protects your...
7. We're always there when you need us...
8. Your guarantee of...
9. Your assurance of...
10. Safe

SERVICE

1. Guides you every step of the way
2. We do it all for you
3. The solution to your...
4. Solves/assists/performs
5. Prompt Service
6. Helps you...
7. Permits you to...
8. Sound advice on....
9. The answer to all your needs on...
10. We make it easier for you to....

BETTER

1. First-class

2. First-rate

3. Brilliant/Excellent/Elite

4. Unsurpassed

5. Top of the line

6. Unparalleled

7. Nobody beats...

8. Matchless

9. Incomparable

10. Paramount

UNIQUE

1. Rare/Remarkable

2. One of a kind

3. A fresh approach to...

4. Refreshingly different and unique...

5. Out of the ordinary

6. There's nothing quite like it.

7. No other _____ comes close.

8. Off the beaten track

9. Original

10. Hard to find.

FLATTERY TO THE READER

1. We know that you...

2. For people with high standards...

3. You're very selective when it comes to...

4. You're the kind of person who...

5. For special people of your caliber...

6. For those with discerning taste...

7. For those who strive for excellence...

8. You demand the best.

9. For leaders/achievers/doers

10. For those who appreciate only the finest...

ORDERING INFORMATION

1. To grab your copy now just...

2. Your order will be filled promptly.

3. Rush me...

4. Yes, I want to learn about...

5. Yes, I want to enjoy...

6. Yes, please enroll me...

7. Yes, I'm ready to...

8. To sign up and get instant free access, just click here...

9. Don't hesitate...order now!

10. Order now!

DISCOUNT

1. Substantial Savings

2. Price Break

3. Extra Savings

4. For a limited time only!

5. Now only _____.

6. Check the Savings.

7. A steal at these prices.

8. New low price.

9. Take an extra __% off...

10. Don't pay more.

MAKING A DECISION

1. It's a winning decision

2. See for yourself

3. Act Now!

4. Don't Delay!

5. Don't miss this opportunity!/Don't miss out!

6. Now is the best time...

7. Do it today!

8. Put our ideas to work!

9. Order now while there's still time

10. Take this important first step...

THE ART OF PERSUADING

1. This is a once in a lifetime opportunity...
2. The opportunity you've been waiting for.
3. We're ready to prove everything we claim.
4. You won't be disappointed.
5. You can't lose.
6. Why settle for ___, when you can have _____.
7. What have you got to lose?
8. You'll be glad you did.
9. Remember, time is running out.
10. You'll wonder how you ever managed without...

TIME

1. It's finally here.
2. Just in time for...
3. Isn't it time...
4. Long-needed
5. Long overdue
6. Long awaited
7. Just when you need it most
8. It was only a matter of time
9. There's never been a better time.
10. There's no time like the present.

IMPROVEMENT

1. Awakens your creativity

2. Awakens your spirit

3. Your chance to...

4. We'll stretch your mind.

5. Live your dreams.

6. You've dreamed about it, now you can...

7. A golden opportunity.

8. You owe it to yourself to...

9. Gives you the competitive edge.

10. Keeps you ahead of the game.

I can't make it any easier for you than giving you a fill-in-the-blank sales page and power words that you can add to it.

Once you are clear on the benefits your course provides and the problem you solve for others, you will have no problem writing a sales page that sells.

Of course, you could hire a copywriter, but good copywriters aren't cheap. Using the template above is a great way to get started.

Adding a personal video to the sales page is also another great idea. If you are available to do calls and answer questions from your sales page, you will probably sell more courses.

In the next chapter, we will discuss how to determine a price for your online course.

Chapter 7 –
Selling High-Ticket
vs. Low-Ticket

Your goal is to make money. My goal is to show you the pros and cons of selling high vs. selling low so you can choose which path to take. Let's get started.

High-Ticket Pros

- Selling a "course" with weekly Q&A calls has a higher perceived value than selling a DIY course, so you can charge $3k-$10k+.

- You only need 1-3 customers per month to make six figures, depending on your price point.

- You can quickly convert cold traffic from Facebook ads into high-ticket clients with an automated webinar funnel.

- You don't need quantity, just quality.

High-Ticket Cons

- You cannot sell from a sales page.

- You must have a proven offer that gets big results or it won't work.

- You must be good at sales and selling over the phone.

- You must have paid traffic or a very engaged email list and/or social media following.

- It is harder to sell high-ticket only because not everyone can afford the price point.

- Technically, you can't make high-ticket sales while you sleep since you must speak directly with potential clients. Also, one-on-one coaching will require more of your time.

Low-Ticket Pros

- You can sell from a sales page.

- Customers won't have to "think about it" at a lower price point.

- You can make money while you sleep since sales can come in anytime, day or night.

- You can sell from a Facebook group without running ads.

Low-Ticket Cons

- You need a lot of paid traffic to get to six figures.

- You need good SEO on your website to get organic traffic.

- It's hard to sell a course from cold traffic with Facebook ads, and it's very expensive.

- It's harder to make six figures with only one low-ticket course.

I'm not going to tell you to do high-ticket or low-ticket because I don't know where you are on your *make money online journey*. Perhaps you already have a high-ticket coaching program and want more passive income. Maybe you are a newbie and don't have a website, an email list, or a large social media following. You may have made some money online selling services but want more passive income.

When I started my online business in 2005, I didn't know what I was doing, and I took the path of least resistance, which was to sell low-ticket courses. The first month, I made $2500 selling a $197 course to an email list I built doing live workshops. However, I never made six figures from selling low-ticket courses only.

I've also offered copywriting, ghostwriting, website design, and other services, which are all very labor-intensive ways to make money.

I like to tell people that I am ambitiously lazy. I don't want to work *that* hard, especially the older I get.

I think we can learn something about pricing strategies from Elon Musk. I want to share with you the Tesla 10-year plan and why Elon Musk chose high-ticket first...

In 1996, Elon Musk was making the first "Master Plan" for his business.

Step 1 – create a low-volume, high-ticket car.

Step 2 – use the money made in Step 1 to develop a medium-volume car at a lower price point.

Step 3 – create the highest volume car at the lowest price point.

He did this to make the most amount of money with the lowest volume in Step 1 to fund Step 2 and Step 3.

So, Elon Musk chose to do high-ticket first to fund low-ticket later. You can read the full article here:

https://www.tesla.com/blog/master-plan-part-deux

To me, this makes sense. It's hard to build a 6- or 7-figure business with a $97 or $197 product, especially if you are a newbie and don't understand how to generate traffic and convert it into sales.

If your goal is to make six figures right away, use this 5-step automated selling process:

1. Facebook Ad (Instagram Ad/ Linked In Ad) to Cold Traffic goes to Opt-In (Landing Page)

2. Automated Webinar Training (Stealth or ClickFunnels)

3. Call Booking Page > Scheduler

4. Indoctrination Page

5. Sales Enrollment Call

My business coach and I used this 5-step automated selling system for my bestselling author program. Once my offer was converting, we started running Facebook ads, which involved testing the image, the copy above the image, and the call to action (CTA) below the image.

Below are more details about using this strategy.

Success with Facebook ads is all about data and testing. We sselected the winning ad once we tested the image, headline, and CTA for 3-5 days at $10 a day.

We were looking for a:

- Click-through rate of 1% of more
- Relevancy Score – 3 or more
- Frequency – Under 2

Anyone who clicked on an ad was redirected to a Landing Page:

Exclusive Webinar On How to Be a #1 Bestselling Author

"THE GUARANTEED STRATEGY FOR BECOMING A *#1 BESTSELLING AUTHOR* IN 30 DAYS OR LESS USING MY SECRET BACKWARDS BOOK LAUNCH FORMULA"

Claim My Spot Now!

Monday
September 11th
at 6:00 AM Pacific, 9:00 AM Eastern

Presented by
MICHELLE KULP

Time left until webinar starts...

0	11	22	56
DAYS	HOURS	MINUTES	SECONDS

YOU'RE GOING TO DISCOVER:

- ✔ The #1 Biggest Mistake 99% of Authors Make that Virtually No One Knows About Until It Is Too Late
- ✔ The Proven System that Works 100% of the Time (even if you don't have your book written yet)
- ✔ My Secret "Backwards Book Launch" Formula that shows you how to make massive profits from your book
- ✔ The 3 Reasons WHY you must be on the Amazon Bestsellers List (most authors don't know the *real* reason why)

If you don't have an automated webinar, you can use a lead magnet and run ads. I did this for a year before my webinar was set up.

Lead Magnet with Ads instead of Webinar

I didn't sell a product on the webinar; I sold a FREE strategy session with me. Prospects were required to complete a strategy session application to book a call with me.

You can view my application at: www.bestsellerchat.com or http://bestsellingauthorprogram.com/coaching/

Apply NOW For Your Bestseller Strategy Session with me and
let's talk about it!

Fill out the questionnaire below and after you hit submit, you'll be redirected to my
scheduling software where you can book your FREE Call with me!

***NOTE: My expertise and focus is on Non Fiction Books. I do NOT take Fiction, Children's, Poetry
or Erotica.*

Name *

First   Last

Email *

Phone *

Please write what country you are from: *

Business Website - If you don't have one, please type "No Site" *

Is your book published? If so, please provide a link below to your book. If your book is NOT
published, please provide the working title for your book, the idea behind it and why you
want to write this book. *

Please check which one most resembles where you are with your book: *

○ I have an idea for a book, but I need help with mapping it out

○ I know I need a book to help my business, but I'm not sure what book to write

○ My book is written and I need help with publishing and marketing it

○ My book is written and published, I need help with marketing and promotion

○ I have an idea for a book and need a ghostwriter to write it for me and also help
with marketing and promoting it

Briefly describe your current business: Who do you serve; What do you sell; What's the
price point? *

Why do you want to be a #1 Bestselling Author (Impact, Legacy, Leads, Income, Media,
Credibility, etc.): *

I use Once Hub for Scheduling

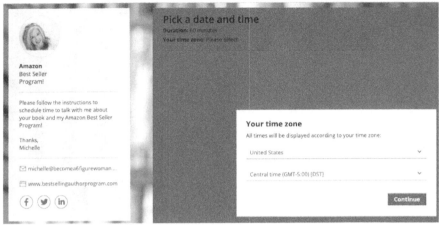

https://go.oncehub.com/BestsellerProgram

*Setting Up Your Indoctrination Page

Your potential client will be redirected to an Indoctrination page AFTER booking a call with you. This page should be designed to create a bond with customers who have booked a call and create a relationship with them.

Record a 15-minute video that tells your story! Don't talk about how awesome you are... NO ONE cares about your awesomeness at this point. If they booked a call, they already are confident that you are good at what you do, and they believe you can help them.

In your video, tell your story like you are having a conversation with someone you want to get to know. Highlight the challenges you have overcome that relate to what you help your clients overcome.

Include things like testimonials (if you have them) and extra training you think will influence your potential client to work with you.

If you don't have any testimonials, don't worry. The primary goal of this page is to create a bond with visitors.

I built my 6-figure business using this model. My business requires a lot of my time, and that's why I've been focusing on creating business assets, like online courses, that generate passive income to free up my time.

Three ways I am currently earning passive income:

1. Royalties from my books – Currently, I earn $3,150 per month in passive income from my books; the numbers are growing each day, which is exciting.

2. Secret down sell – When I do strategy sessions for my best-selling author program, if the prospect isn't a good fit, or they can't afford the high-ticket program, I sell them my online course at a lower price point.

3. 28 Books to $100K – I created a Facebook group and sell an online course that includes add-ons like group coaching.

I plan to add more passive income streams, so I am earning multiple six figures just from passive income alone.

So, whatever path you choose, commit to it and go all in.

If you do low-ticket to start, that's fine, because making money with a side-hustle is a great way to get your feet wet and to gain experience.

To do high-ticket, you must already have a proven offer that converts. Never run Facebook ads until you have made money with your offer, or you are just throwing money away.

Next up, we are going to look at how to find your MVP's — Most Valuable PAYERS!

Chapter 8 –
Finding Your MVPs
– Most Valuable Payers

In the previous chapter, I gave you the five steps to run paid ads to enroll clients in a high-ticket program. If you are selling low-ticket, or don't have a big budget for marketing, there are ten ways to get organic traffic.

10 Ways to Get Clients Now Through Organic Traffic

1. **Create a lead magnet** related to your new course that can be consumed in five minutes or less.

2. **Optimize all of your social media profiles** (Facebook, LinkedIn, Instagram, etc.) – Have a public group related to your new program/opportunity.

   a. Create a free Facebook group – use Canva to create a group banner

   b. Post on your personal profile and in your free group

   c. Purchase a domain name on godaddy.com and redirect it to your free Facebook group (it's easier to share and the URLs are typically shorter)

   d. Intro – ADD your domain here (limited space). I help _____ with _____ without _____ by _____.

   e. Fill in Bio information and add your domain to "work and education" add social handles, etc. If you have a Facebook business page, add it to your bio; add photos for your "featured" photos, including some professional photos.

   f. Balance personal and business

3. **Social Media Posts in Other Groups – Hidden Carrot -**Give really specific advice and mention the overall results you have achieved while being humble. *Make sure you reply to comments and keep open loops going. Take a stand. Get people's attention, but don't ask members to DM you. If they like what you say, they will seek you out.

4. **Social Media Post – Polarity Post (outside and your audience)** – works the best. Think of a hot topic that people will argue about if you mention it. The goal is to initiate intelligent dialogue on a topic* and tie it to your business. Ask others what their thoughts are and monitor engagement. (*NOT religion or politics.)

5. **Social Media Post — New Member Bait.** Once a week, create a post and tag all NEW members. Welcome them to the group, encourage them to introduce themselves, and ask them what they hope to learn or what problems they are having. Finally, remind them to get your FREE Resource (lead magnet) if they haven't already and drop a link to your webinar. (Welcome New Member Script: GROUP NAME is a community of WHO where NICHE learn how to DESIRE. In this group, you'll learn from YOUR NAME, who has achieved INSERT ACHIEVEMENT. **RULES: Do Participate. Do not share promo posts or be rude to other members. If you haven't yet, grab our FREE Cheat Sheet on NICHE by clicking here: LINK. Finally, please introduce yourself and share what you are struggling with so we can create more content just for you.**

6. **Social Media Post— Test your concepts.** Write an outline for your webinar, new opportunity, concepts, epiphany story, etc. Make an announcement in your group that tomorrow at ** a.m./p.m., you will be going LIVE to cover _____. Go live the next day, and ask for feedback. Try to overcome objections during the live call and see the response. Doing

this helps you clarify your message and concepts. Goal: See if your concept resonates with your audience

7. **Social Media Post— Live Q&A.** Schedule a Live Q&A. Prepare stories and responses for possible questions and objections. Watch the live replay and jot down the questions that you covered.

8. **Social Media Post— Post Testimonials.** Screenshot posts from students in your private group OR ask students who had success to record a short video (1-3 minutes) to share their recent success. Ask them to post their success in your private student Facebook group so you can take a screenshot and post it on your personal profile, biz page, IG, etc. Respond to questions and comments. DM directly to take conversation to private messaging. Invite them to a call/ strategy session with you.

9. **Social Media Post—Hook/Story/Offer or Hook/Value/ Offer.** Grab audience attention (pattern interrupt/hook), then tell your personal story or a piece of your story. Make an offer. Book a call. Explore working together in your program. Give a CTA. Link in comments.

10. **Offer your new webinar to your email list and social media groups as well as to others email lists and social media groups. Incentivize them.**

I signed up clients for my low-ticket online courses years ago by doing live workshops and writing targeted blog posts using key-words. This is known as SEO – search engine optimization.

This is a slower path, but it's FREE! Don't underestimate the power of blogging. I still get clients for my high-ticket programs who found me from blog posts I wrote a long time ago. If you use SEO and know which keywords people are searching for to find a pro-gram like the one you offer, it's a great way to generate free traffic.

Many experts encourage selling only high-ticket, but this isn't a one size fits all business.

Customize it to what works for you. How much time you can devote to this endeavor and how much money you want to invest to make it happen will be the two factors that influence your decision.

When I first set up Facebook ads to my automated webinar, some of the costs I incurred were:

1. Automated Webinar software/platform – $67 per month (Stealth)

2. Leadpages – $50 per month ("opt in" to sign up for the webinar)

3. Online training portal hosting – $49 per month (course content delivery)

4. Facebook ads – $700 to $1000 per month *I know experts who spend much more than this. My program doesn't need quantity; I only need 3-4 quality clients per month.

Once you get your Facebook ads running, you can retarget people and customize audiences.

I'm in the process of creating a new webinar and plan to use ClickFunnels to deliver it "on-demand." It will cost me $97 per month but having an on-demand webinar allows those who sign up to view it right away.

Facebook ads are not easy, and I recommend you engage a coach or an expert to help you. Do not hire an "agency" to do your ads because most of them are either too expensive or won't get you the results they promise and will take your money anyway.

If you are going to do Facebook ads with an automated webinar funnel, learn how to do this yourself first. You must understand the process before you try to outsource it.

I believe I've been successful online because I never outsource anything until I fully understand how to do it myself. I invested a lot of time and energy learning many platforms, and it has paid off.

How can you outsource Facebook ads if you don't understand the platform, the terminology, and how it works? You will likely get ripped off. Trust me, I know. I hired an agency once, and they failed big time. Luckily for me, there was a money-back guarantee if a certain click-through rate wasn't achieved. I got my money back, but only after a big fight. They thought I didn't understand the numbers, but they were wrong. Someone without the knowledge and experience from running their own ads would have lost thousands of dollars. Always learn the platforms before you consider outsourcing!

When deciding whether to do low-ticket or high-ticket, here's my recommendation:

If you need to leverage your time, you need income from sources that don't require your time, which can be accomplished through low-ticket DIY online courses.

If you need to generate money quickly and you are trying to earn a full-time income online, start with high-ticket sales and then add DIY online courses down the road.

Next up is how to get sales and create urgency.

Chapter 9 –
Getting Sales and
Creating Urgency

There are multiple ways to get sales for your course. Think about driving somewhere for a vacation. If you use a driving app, you will be given multiple routes to drive to your destination. The same is true for getting sales for your course – you want to have multiple paths that lead to your course.

Once your course is set up, there are multiple ways you can sell it:

- Do a 5-day free challenge in a Facebook group; then offer it with a discount.

- Offer FREE tools or FREE access to a module or lesson. A percentage of people who take the free module will sign up for the paid course.

- Do a live webinar about your topic and offer a discount to anyone who signs up while on the call.

- Blog about your topic using targeted keywords and promote your blog posts to all of your social media platforms and your email list.

- Speak about your topic on virtual summits or workshops and offer a special promotion to anyone who signs up by a certain date.

- Do daily Facebook live trainings and invite viewers into your program during the training.

- Find an affiliate with a big email list and social media following and offer them a share of the sales to promote your webinar.

- Create a BETA course and offer the first "x" amount of customers a discount for founding members.

I want to share a case study from one of my very successful clients who built a multiple six-figure business around her book by selling online courses and coaching programs.

CASE STUDY

Lisa Phillips teaches beginning real estate investors how to invest in $30-$50k properties in working class neighborhoods. She offers a free mini-course on Thinkific. This is a good strategy because prospects who go to her Thinkific site also see her other available programs at different price points:

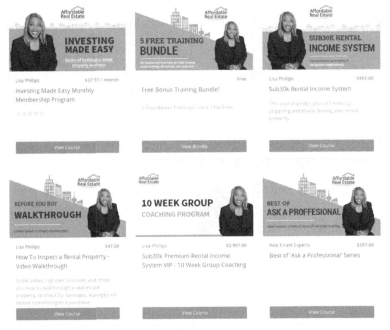

Check out Lisa's free course at https://lisa-phillips.thinkific.com/

In addition to giving away free modules/lessons, Thinkific also allows you to drip feed content so you can offer payment plans and only release content once the payment is received.

Lisa's a brilliant marketer who has mastered combining low-ticket and high-ticket to create a multiple six-figure business!

Next up is my client, Daniel Rondberg...

CASE STUDY

Daniel signed up for my high-ticket bestselling author program to get his book written and launched to the #1 bestsellers list. Five days after we launched his book, he sold a $997 online course and made $23,000 in a one-hour "live" webinar.

How did he do this?

Using someone else's platform and email list!

If you are starting from scratch – you have no list or only a small email list and social media following – this is a good strategy.

Find someone who complements what you teach (not the same as what you teach) and offer them a share of your sales in exchange for promoting your live or automated webinar to their list.

In this case, Daniel knew the author who had a big following, so he offered him 20% of the sales to promote his webinar.

I advised Daniel to sell the course for $997 (he was going to do it for less) and offer a discount to anyone who bought while they were on the webinar. He also added some pretty big bonuses to incentivize the attendees.

Over 500 people signed up for the webinar, and 70 people attended live. Daniel made $23,000 and his partner made $4,600 from offering it to his list and social media followers.

Don't think because you are just beginning that you can't make money fast. Daniel made $23,000 within 30 days of creating his online course. I coached Daniel on how to set up a course, and gave him the webinar slides template, but he took massive action and made it happen.

Be an action taker like Daniel!

When you offer a BETA program, frame it as you are looking for "Founding Members" to join and give you feedback. For example, you can list the price of the program at $1997, but then offer a substantial discount to the founding members.

When I started selling online courses in 2005, it was easier to sell from a sales page and much less competitive than it is now.

I have had the most success selling high-ticket with my 5-step automated selling system, and then offering a secret down sell to my stand-alone online training.

You may be looking to make a few hundred or a thousand dollars per month from a side hustle and selling a DIY course is a great way to do that.

People will pay high-ticket prices when they want coaching and accountability.

Danielle Leslie is a very successful online course creator. She sells a $1997 course with group coaching and has taken her business to $10 million using that model. She has mastered Facebook ads, the automated webinar and selling system, as well as follow-up emails and retargeting.

You can check her out at: https://www.danielleleslie.com/

Sign up for her email list and see what she's doing.

Obviously, she didn't do this overnight, and I'm certain she had a great business coach or mentor to help her achieve this massive success. She also spends thousands of dollars per months on paid ads.

Don't compare yourself to Daniel, Danielle, me, or anyone else. Everyone has to start where they are and learn how to be a course creator, online marketer, and entrepreneur.

I promise when your first sale comes in, you'll be hooked and will gain loads of confidence knowing that all your work and effort is finally paying off.

Let's talk about some ways to create more urgency to get people to sign up for your program.

Add value and sell your course by offering bonuses, such as:

- A coaching call with you AFTER completing the course, which encourages the client to complete the course to talk with you. In Thinkific, you can see if a student completes all the content.

- Office Hours that you offer for Q&A to students. You want your students to be successful, and they will have a higher chance of success with your help. Obviously, you don't want this to be a big time suck, so you can offer office hours anywhere from once a week to once a month, or even bi-monthly. Include this a bonus when they sign up and have time blocked on your schedule to allow customers to sign up for a meeting during your office hours. You can set it up on Zoom as a recurring meeting.

- If you have written a book or you have other printed support material, give a FREE copy to anyone that signs up for your course.

Bonuses move people to take action. Offer something with real value, but don't give too many bonuses where they feel overwhelmed. Create urgency by only offering the bonus for a short period of time.

In the next chapter, I share the 30-day blueprint I created so you can get your online course up and running as fast as possible.

Through the process of writing a book a month in 2020, I learned that having timelines, deadlines, and accountability allows you to get a lot done in a short period of time.

If you want to be successful, commit to getting your course done and making your first sale in the next 30 days.

Let's get started with your 30-day plan now…

Chapter 10 –
The 30-Day Lean
Launch Blueprint

I can write and publish a 100-125 page book every 30 days, so I know you can create and launch an online course in 30 days or less using my Lean Launch method.

Warning: Your lizard brain will give you 101 reasons why you can't and shouldn't do this.

My top 10 reasons why you should create and sell your online course in the next 30 days

1. You don't learn until you launch.

2. You can sell an online course *before* you create the content.

3. A minimum viable product is better than NO product.

4. "People don't know what they want until you show it to them." – Steve Jobs

5. Execution matters more than ideas; ideas are a dime a dozen.

6. You won't waste time (weeks, months, years) getting ready to launch or researching your topic; you will spend all of your time on execution and selling your program.

7. When you have a clear end date, it drives you forward.

8. It forces you to focus on paying customers instead of on the myriad of distractions that entrepreneurs typically focus.

9. The technology available today allows you to create and launch quickly.

10. A good plan executed poorly now is better than a perfect plan never executed.

There is no reason you can't create and sell an online course in 30 days. If you don't get paying customers, you may be a wanna-preneur and not an entrepreneur.

Execution is all that matters.

30-Day Blueprint to Create, Validate and Sell Your Signature Online Course

Day 1: Choose your topic for your online course using the 3 pillars: Scary Time Skills; Job Autopsy and the Curiosity Map.

Day 2: Select one of the 5 Big Areas to focus on: Finances; Relationships, Career/Business, Health, Spirituality. Make sure your target audience has money to spend.

Day 3: Answer these 4 questions: 1) What do people say you are good at that you also love doing? 2) What are your top three core values? 3) What group or tribe do you most want to serve, inspire, and impact? 4) What do you most want to teach and represent in this world?

Day 4: Fill in the blank to create a working title for your course: How to _____ **[get desired outcome]** without _____ **[the usual problem].**

Day 5: Run a 1-2 day survey using social media or your email list on surveymonkey.com. Provide at least five course title choices.

Day 6: Fill in the blanks for more clarity: My course _____ _____ **[1. Working title of course]** helps _____ **[2. Tribe or group you most want to impact and work with]** learn how to _____ [3. what you are going to teach specifically] so they can _____ [4. the result they will get; what they will be, do, or have after completing your course].

Day 7: What is your BIG promise for students who purchase your online course?

Day 8: Define your avatar by answering some of these questions (interview someone or think of a real person you know who would be your ideal client): Gender; Age; Income Status; Education Status; Family Status; Experience level about your topic (newbie, intermediate, advanced); What type of work do they do?; Hobbies?; What kind of books do they read?; Do they have a spiritual practice?; Where are they feeling most challenged in their lives right now?; What keeps them awake at night (related to your topic)?; What is most important to them right now?; What are their hopes, dreams and aspirations?

Day 9: Write a letter to your ideal client acknowledging their problems, pain, and fears, and explain how your course is the solution to their problems and why you created it. Speak from the heart.

Day 10: Write down three types of people your course is NOT for.

Days 11-14: Validate before you create using these four methods:

METHOD 1: Find courses similar to what you want to create. Check online platforms like: udemy.com, masterclass.com, Lynda.com, or Google your topic with the words "online course." Write down the title, the length of the course, the cost, and list the main benefits. This is your market research.

METHOD 2: Send an email to your list to share that you have a brand new "BETA" program coming out soon called [Working Title of Course]. Include a link to a landing page where they can sign up to receive more information (more about landing pages below). I use Aweber to collect email addresses for my business (you can use ActiveCampaign, Mailchimp, etc.). You don't need thousands of people to sign up — 25-100 people indicates there is good initial interest.

METHOD 3: Send people from your social media platforms to a landing page to sign up and receive more information about your upcoming program.

METHOD 4: Come up with 4-8 titles around the same topic or niche and create a survey using surveymonkey.com so people can vote on the title. I discovered people loved the title: *"Make Money While You Sleep"* by conducting a survey. I had other good titles, but that got the most votes!

Day 15: Once your course is validated and you've selected your working title, create a course outline using the Mind Dump method. Get a poster board or whiteboard, a pack of Post-it Notes, and a pen. Start thinking of everything you want to teach on your selected topic. Write down one idea/topic on each Post-It Note. Then, arrange similar notes into groups that will become your Module/Lesson topics. Review the notes and remove anything that seems redundant. Reword if needed. Once you're happy with your groupings, transfer them to the course template (see Chapter 4).

Day 16: Using your course outline, create PowerPoint or Keynote slides for each module/lesson.

Day 17: Review the Rapid Writing Secrets and use those when creating course content. Most courses are videos with some handouts. You can write the content on the speaker notes section at the bottom of your slides so you can follow as you record.

Days 18-21: Sign up for Thinkific (you can start with the free program) and create at least two Modules with Lessons for your course. Use your slides to record your content. Create handouts if you like, but don't get stuck on that yet.

Day 22: Have graphics made for your course on fiverr or somewhere with fast turn-around. You can create graphics in Canva if you are proficient in that program. Use the graphics for your Facebook group (public) banner and for the thumbnail on your video lessons. Invite people to join your new Facebook group.

Day 23: Decide on low-ticket or high-ticket. Review Chapter 7 for pros and cons of each. Low-ticket is a DIY course that doesn't require much, if any, of your time. High-ticket requires you to sell from a strategy session/call.

Day 24: Write a sales page for your course using the template in Chapter 6 if you are selling low-ticket. If you are selling high-ticket, you don't need a sales page. Prospects will apply for your program, and you'll do strategy calls to enroll them. You can read my book **Work from Home & Make 6-Figures** which goes over high ticket selling in great detail.

Day 25: Decide which three bonuses you will offer to people who sign up for your course by a certain date.

Day 26: Start finding your MVP's – Most Valuable Payers using the 10 Organic Ways to Get Clients in Chapter 8. Post on multiple platforms daily. If you have an email list, market your BETA program to your email list.

Day 27: Start Selling Your Course using your email list and/or social media platforms.

Day 28-30: Implement at least three ways to sell your course: 5-day free challenge in your Facebook group; Facebook live trainings on your topic where you invite members into your program during the training; offer free tools via a free module with lessons that are part of your full online course on Thinkific as a teaser to get them interested; speak about your topic at virtual summits; use another person's email list and social media to promote your course to and offer a share of the profits.

Please use this blueprint and treat it like it is GOLD!

I wish I had this blueprint when I created my first online course. That was a long time ago, and we didn't have the technology we have today to quickly create, set up, and launch a course.

You purchased this book not to just be *inspired*, but to create a long-term business asset that can make you money and give you more FREEDOM.

If you already have a high-ticket program, a service-based business, or you're just starting out, creating a signature online course will leverage your time and multiply your profits.

Go forth and multiply!

Closing Thoughts

You have a wealth of knowledge to share with the world.

I know it is scary to put yourself out there for fear others will criticize you. Those people usually aren't the ones out there doing the work.

I've always loved this quote by Theodore Roosevelt, and I think it will inspire you as well:

"It is not the critic who counts; not the man who points out how the strong man stumbles, or where the doer of deeds could have done them better. The credit belongs to the man who is actually in the arena, whose face is marred by dust and sweat and blood; who strives valiantly; who errs, who comes short again and again, because there is no effort without error and shortcoming; but who does actually strive to do the deeds; who knows great enthusiasms, the great devotions; who spends himself in a worthy cause; who at the best knows in the end the triumph of high achievement, and who at the worst, if he fails, at least fails while daring greatly, so that his place shall never be with those cold and timid souls who neither know victory nor defeat."

I encourage you to read this quote every day for the next 30 days while you create your online course.

Don't let the fear of criticism or the addiction to approval stop you from living your dreams.

I have failed many times with different programs and books, but that hasn't stopped me. I'm living my dreams now because I've developed a thick skin to the naysayers who give me non-constructive criticism. Over the years, I've learned that it's easier to sit on the sidelines and criticize than to get in the arena and create something.

I love reading books and often read two books per week. There are some books that I just don't connect with, but I would never

512 · MICHELLE KULP

consider writing a bad review online about the book or the author. I appreciate all the "creators" who strive to do the deeds.

You have what it takes to be a creator. Take the years of knowledge, wisdom, experience and the mistakes you've made, and teach others.

Go forth and create!

About the Author

MICHELLE KULP is the #1 best-selling author of *over 20 books and loves helping other authors build a brand and a business with books.*

Check out Michelle's books here: **https://www.amazon.com/Michelle-Kulp/e/B006D4EQIY/**

Learn more about Michelle's Bestseller Programs at: **www.bestsellingauthorprogram.com**

Can You Do Me A Favor?

If you enjoyed this book or found it useful, I'd be very grateful if you'd post a short review on Amazon. Your support really does make a difference, and I read all the reviews personally to get your feedback and make this book even better.

Thanks again for your support!

Affiliate Disclosure

This book contains affiliate links. If you buy using my links, I get a small commission (at no additional cost to you) so I can write even more books!

Made in the USA
Middletown, DE
22 September 2021